MONARCH
ILLUSTRATED GUIDE TO
CROCHET

EDITED BY
PAM DAWSON

MONARCH PRESS · NEW YORK

© Marshall Cavendish Limited 1974, 1975, 1976, 1977
This volume first published 1977
Reprinted 1977

Standard Book Number: 0-671-18768-6

Library of Congress Catalog Card Number: 76-29160

Published by
MONARCH PRESS, a Simon & Schuster Division of
Gulf & Western Corporation
Simon & Schuster Building
1230 Avenue of the Americas
New York, N.Y. 10020

Printed in Great Britain

Crochet abbreviations

alt	alternate(ly)	**patt**	pattern
approx	approximate(ly)	**rem**	remain(ing)
beg	begin(ning)	**rep**	repeat
ch	chain(s)	**RS**	right side
cont	continu(e) (ing)	**sc**	single crochet
dec	decrease	**sl st**	slip stitch
dc	double crochet	**sp**	space(s)
dtr	double treble	**st(s)**	stitch(es)
foll	follow(ing)	**tog**	together
gr(s)	group(s)	**tr**	treble
hdc	half double crochet	**tr tr**	triple treble
in	inch(es)	**WS**	wrong side
inc	increase	**yd(s)**	yard(s)
No.	number	**yo**	yarn over
		yrh	yarn round hook

Symbols

An asterisk, *, shown in a pattern row denotes that the stitches shown after this sign must be repeated from that point. Square brackets, [], denote instructions for larger sizes in the pattern. Round brackets, (), denote that this section of the pattern is to be worked for all sizes.

Gauge—this is the most important factor in successful crochet. Unless you obtain the gauge given for each design, you will not obtain satisfactory results.

Picture Credits
Camera Press 8B; 33
100 Idees de Marie Claire Mirand 8T;
Ulster Folk and Transport Museum 3

Photographers: Steve Bicknell, Roger Charity, Richard Dunkley, Jean Paul Froget, John Garrett, Melvin Grey, Graham Henderson, Trevor Lawrence, Chris Lewis, Sandra Lousada, Peter Pugh-Cook, John Ryan, John Swannell, Jerry Tubby, Rupert Watts.

CONTENTS

HISTORY OF CROCHET

Nobody can really pinpoint the day or year when someone picked up a bone or stick and some yarn and started knotting chains of fabric into what is now known as crochet. If you were to ask any number of the millions of people all over the world who practice this simple, yet very creative craft, you would not find many who could tell you much about its history. That, however, is not quite as surprising as it sounds. Its origins are very obscure, although archaeological finds do lead us to believe that Arabia may have been the original area where wool was first worked with just one needle or hook. Ancient crochet specimens have been found in Egypt, and it can be presumed that the craft is of an age parallel with knitting, its sister craft. We know that it does go back at least as far as the days of Solomon (around 950 BC), and some biblical historians credit its use even earlier— 1200 BC—when the Israelites fled Egypt during the Exodus. They were said to have worked with wool in this way during their long trek across the Sinai desert. Actually, the evidence of this early use is quite substantial. The start of modern civilization usually dates from the time (about 5500 BC) when the Sumerians left central Asia and settled in the plains of Babylon—now Iraq. Babylon was the center for wool crafts, just as Egypt was known as the home of fine linen weaving. Babylon's pleasant climate made sheep-rearing a good prospect there, although that was not the only reason for the growth of the wool crafts in that area. Unlike the Egyptians, who appeared to have loved clarity of line in everything, the Babylonians were fond of ornate designs, made of heavy woolen fabric covered with elaborate decoration. It is almost certain that crochet work was used early in time there for this purpose, although later in Babylonian history, there was a revolt against the luxury of over-ornate clothes and the people needed to resort to the simple wool "sack" again, often knitted or worked in crochet.

Also, crochet and other wool crafts had a very profound place in the philosophy of the time. Creating fabric without any artificial aid was seen as a declaration of man's kinship with a god. It was an acknowledgement of the fact that he owed his skill and intellect to some greater being.

Crochet patterns in use in India are very similar to Moslem patterns found in North Africa, this again giving strength to the theory that crochet has been a continuously used craft in the Middle East for thousands of years; and although it never quite died out over the centuries, the art did suffer an almost total eclipse when more mechanical fabric-making methods were developed, and did not begin to flourish again until the time of the Renaissance. Then, ecclesiastical crochet, along with other fabrics of the time, acquired a high standard of technique and beauty. Much crochet work during that period was imitative of the more expensive lace or embroidery, such as needlepoint, Richelieu, Guipure, Honiton and filet.

It is no wonder, however, that the art of crochet earned the nickname of "nuns' work". At that time, wool crafts, such as crochet or knitting, were common occupations in convents. They remained the almost exclusive domain of the clergy (unlike weaving which lay people practised in their own homes) until a later time, when crochet was thought to be suitable for the more comfortable young ladies of the parish to learn. Nuns established it as one of the main crafts to be taught in the "finishing courses" of the day.

The word "crochet" is probably derived from the French word "croc", meaning hook—but has only really been in popular use since the early 1800s, when the production of fine cotton thread in the newly established English mills made it easy to carry out the craft. Paradoxically enough, it took a disaster to make the craft a really widespread and popular pastime. It was the Irish potato famines of the 1840s and '50s which revived an almost forgotten skill and made it into a major cottage industry. Crop failures forced millions of farming families to look for an alternative method of earning much-needed cash. Making crochet collars, ruffles and other adornments was a simple, though time-consuming way, and crochet work was much in demand by the well-to-do ladies of the time. There had been a history of crochet in Ireland since the end of the eighteenth century. The craft had probably been introduced from France by a young Irish woman, Honoria Nagle, who was lucky enough to have been sent to Paris to be educated. There, she became aware of the vast difference between the rich and the poor. The squalor of the poor compared with the ludicrous extravagance of the court made her determined to do something worthwhile in her homeland when she returned. She recruited four other young women who were sympathetic to her cause, and they, too, went to learn the craft from the Carmelite nuns in France. The five determined women passed the basic skills on to any one of the poor of County Cork who were willing to learn. Whoever had a spare hour or two among these hard-working people could be found busy with the crochet hook. And it was not just woman's work.

Irishmen and boys tending sheep or goats on the hills were expected to contribute their share of hours and income.

Irish crochet became a craft in its own right. Its workers incorporated beautiful designs taken from their rural backgrounds. Motifs included farmyard animals, roses, wheels and, of course, the legendary shamrock leaf. The art became a widespread cottage industry and was also included in the syllabus of the educational system in Ireland.

The main crochet centers were Cork and its surrounding district in the south, and Monaghan in the north. County Cork became a principal center of the industry and by the 1870s it is estimated that there were from 12,000 to 20,000 women in the area producing crochet, using continental patterns adapted from original lace designs from France, Italy and Greece.

Many Irish men and women saved the extra money which they earned by creating Irish crochet for their passage to America, taking their skills with them. Eventually there were many immigrants in the prosperous Midwest who could thank the humble crochet hook for their deliverance from the starvation which had killed thousands in their homeland.

In England, Prince Albert's inspired Great Exhibition of 1851 did much to promote the craft by bringing it to the attention of designers and manufacturers all over the world. In fact, the Victorians at that time almost smothered the art with their enthusiasm for it. Ladies became addicted to the crochet hook and made coverings to decorate everything imaginable. Nothing escaped them. Antimacassars, bedspreads, tablecloths, coasters were all produced with an almost feverish addiction. One wonders now whether these objects were made as useful household items or merely to indulge their passion for crochet. Even piano legs were discreetly covered with crochet frills!

Unfortunately, Victorian over-indulgence helped to dampen the enthusiasm of following generations for the craft, and it ceased to be fashionable for several decades. Luckily it did not disappear completely. It has a remarkable survival record and was revived in the 1950s along with a new appreciation of all the well-known handcrafts. Crochet has become widely popular, partly as a reaction to mass-production, and it is probably used more creatively now than at any time in its long history.

Below An exquisite example of Irish crochet

BASIC STITCHES

The crochet hook

There are a variety of hook sizes to choose from and these range from very fine to very thick. Aluminum or plastic hooks are graded from size A up to K. An appropriately sized hook should be selected for working each thickness of yarn. For example, use a size K hook for thick rug yarn, a size H hook for knitting worsted weight yarn, a size F for sport weight yarn and a fine steel hook ranging anywhere from No.1 through No. 14. For cotton thread, the size of the hook depends on the fineness of the cotton. A beginner will find it much easier to work with a fairly large hook such as an H and a knitting worsted weight yarn.

Unlike knitting, all crochet is made up from one working loop on the hook at any time. This first working loop begins as a slip loop. To make a slip loop, hold the cut end of yarn in the left hand and wrap the yarn around the first and second fingers. Place the hook under the first finger and draw yarn through loop on the fingers, removing loop from left hand. Draw the yarn tightly onto the hook to keep it in place. This first slip loop does not count as a stitch, but is merely a starting loop for any pattern, and is the last loop fastened off at the end of the work. The left hand holds the yarn to feed it towards the hook, and there are several ways of holding it to control the flow of yarn important for achieving an even fabric. Try to remember always to keep the thumb and first finger of the left hand as close to the hook as possible and to move up the work as each new stitch is completed.

To work chain stitches

Hold the hook in the right hand between the thumb and first finger, letting the hook rest against the second finger, and place the hook under the yarn between the first and second fingers of the left hand from front to back. Let the hook catch the yarn and draw through a loop on the hook, thus replacing the stitch. One chain has now been completed and the abbreviation for this is "ch". Repeat this action to make the necessary number of chains.

An alternative to this method of making a foundation chain is the double chain. To work this, make 2 chain in the usual way, insert hook into the 2nd chain from hook, * yarn around hook and draw through a loop, yarn around hook and draw through both loops on hook, *, continue to make a length of double chain by inserting the hook into the 2nd or left hand loop of the 2 loops which have just been dropped from the hook and repeat from * to *. This method gives a firm foundation and is easy to work.

Left hand workers should reverse the instructions, reading left for right and right for left. To follow the illustrations, prop up the book in front of a mirror where the reversed image can be clearly seen.

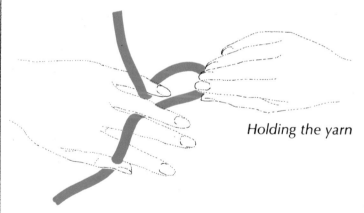

Holding the yarn

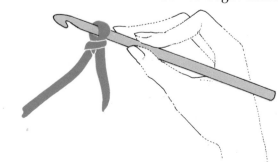

Position of hook to begin chain stitches

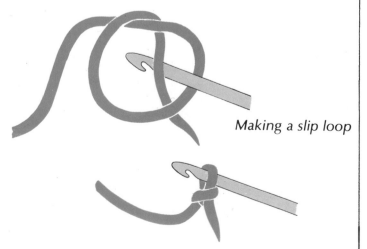

Making a slip loop

Basic stitches

Various stitches can now be worked into the foundation chain to form a crochet fabric. Each stitch gives a different texture and varies in depth, and every row gives a new chain line into which the next row is worked. When stitches are worked back and forth in rows, there is no right or wrong side of the fabric, and the work is turned at the end of each row ready to begin the next row.

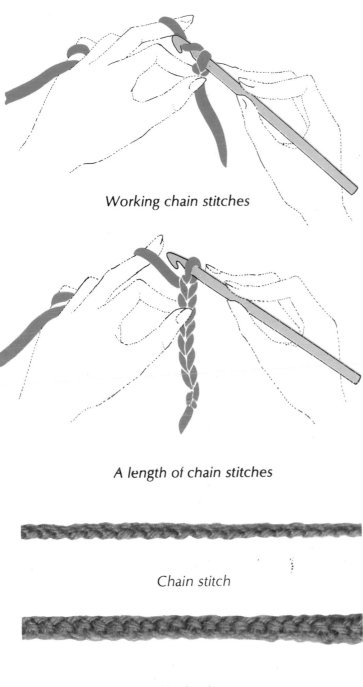

Working chain stitches

A length of chain stitches

Chain stitch

Single chain

Slip stitch The first stitch with the smallest depth is the slip stitch and this is abbreviated as "sl st". To work slip stitch into the foundation chain work the desired length, say 10 chain, and place the hook into the last chain, then place hook under the yarn in the left hand – this is called "yarn around hook" and is abbreviated as "yrh" or "yo" –, and draw yarn through the chain and the loop on the hook. Continue in this manner to the end of the chain.

Single crochet The second stitch, which has a greater depth than slip stitch, is single crochet and this is abbreviated as "sc". To work this stitch make 10 foundation chain, but remember that this stitch is deeper than slip stitch. Therefore, before you work this row, provision must be made to lift the working loop on the hook to the height of the single crochet stitches. For single crochet, work one chain more than the required number of stitches, in this case 11 chain in all, and work the first single crochet into the 2nd chain from the hook. These extra chains are called "turning chains" and the number of chains vary according to the depth of the stitch being worked. To work single crochet, place the hook under both loops of the chain or just under one loop of the chain, place yarn around hook and draw yarn through both loops on hook. One single crochet has now been worked and this is repeated to the end of the row. Check that 10 single crochet have been worked, noting that the turning chain counts as the first single crochet on this row only. Turn the piece, work one chain to count as the first single crochet of the next row, skip the first single crochet of the previous row which has been replaced by a turning chain then work one single crochet into each stitch of the previous row including the first turning chain at the beginning of the previous row.

Fastening off When you have worked the fabric to the necessary length, cut the yarn about 6 inches from the work, thread the end through the one loop on the hook and pull tight. The remaining end can be darned in later.

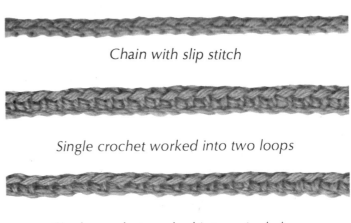

Chain with slip stitch

Single crochet worked into two loops

Single crochet worked into a single loop

Sample worked in single crochet

FABRIC STITCHES

There are numerous crochet stitches and, by experimenting with different types of yarn, you can achieve many effects. Here we give instructions for working some of the basic stitches and several variations that may be formed from them. Work each sample on 10 stitches. Each stitch has a given depth and it is important that provision is made for this depth at the start of each row with "turning chains".

Half double crochet

Work 10ch plus 1ch to be the turning chain. Place yarn around hook – this is abbreviated as "yo" –, insert hook into 3rd ch from hook, yo and draw through a loop (3 loops on hook), yo and draw through all 3 loops. One half double has now been completed and this is abbreviated as "hdc". Continue in this way into each ch to the end of the row. Turn work. Start a new row with 2ch to count as the first hdc and work 1hdc into each stitch to end, including the turning chain at the beginning of the previous row.

Double crochet

Work 10ch plus 2ch to be the turning chain. Yo and insert hook into 4th ch from hook, yo and draw through a loop (3 loops on hook), yo and draw through first 2 loops on hook, yo and draw through remaining 2 loops. One double crochet has now been completed. This is abbreviated as "dc". Work 1dc into each ch to the end of the row. Turn work. Start a new row with 3ch to count as the first dc and work 1dc into each stitch to end, including the 3rd of the turning chain 3 of the previous row.

Treble crochet

Work 10ch plus 3ch to be the turning chain. Yo twice, insert hook into the 5th ch from hook, yo and draw through a loop (4 loops on hook), (yo and draw through first 2 loops on hook) twice, yo and draw through remaining 2 loops. One treble has now been completed and this is abbreviated as "tr". Work 1tr into each ch to the end of the row. Turn work. Start a new row with 4ch to count as first tr and work 1tr into each stitch to the end of the row, including the 4th ch of the turning chain 4 of the previous row.

Double trebles

Work 10ch plus 4ch to be the turning chain. Yo three times, insert hook into 6th ch from hook, yo and draw through a loop (5 loops on hook), (yo and draw through first 2 loops on hook) four times. One double treble has now been completed and this is abbreviated as "dtr". Start new rows with 5ch to count as first dtr and work 1dtr into each stitch to the end of the row, including the 5th ch of the 5 turning chain.

Ridged single crochet

This is produced by working in sc, but the hook is inserted into the back loop only of each stitch of every row. The unworked front loops of the stitches produce a pronounced ridged effect.

Russian stitch

This is another stitch that is formed by working in single crochet, but not turning the work at the end of each row. Instead, the yarn is fastened off and cut when each row has been completed and the cut ends are darned in later. There is a definite right and wrong side to this stitch.

Raised treble crochet

These are worked on the surface of a basic single crochet fabric to give a vertical ridged effect. Make 21ch and work 1sc into 3rd ch from hook, then work 1sc into each ch to the end of the row. Turn work. Start the pattern row with 1ch and 1sc into next sc, *yo twice and insert hook into the horizontal loop of next sc on the third row below, yo and complete the tr in the usual way, 1sc into each of next 3sc, rep from * to the end of the row. Always working 3 rows of single crochet between the pattern rows, work subsequent pattern rows by inserting the hook under the vertical bar of the previous tr and completing the tr in the usual way.

Counterpane stitch

As the name implies, "counterpanes" or bedspreads, were made in this stitch. The fabric produced is soft and elastic. Work 11ch. Yo, insert hook into 3rd ch from hook, yo and draw a loop through this stitch and the first loop on the hook, yo and draw through the remaining 2 loops. Repeat into each stitch throughout, always working 2ch for the first stitch at the beginning of every row.

Double crochet in relief

This is a more decorative stitch with a ridged effect. Make 12ch and work 1dc into 4th ch from hook, then work 1dc into each ch to the end of the row. Turn work. Start a new row with 3ch to count as the first dc and work across the row in dc by placing the hook between the first and second dc of the previous row horizontally, yo and draw through a loop, yo and complete the stitch. At the end of the row work 1dc into the 3rd of the 3 turning chain.

A selection of squares worked in the various stitches learned so far may be made in Knitting Worsted yarn and a size 11 crochet hook. Each will have a different texture and, made in a variety of colors, the squares will look most attractive. They then can be sewn together to make an attractive area rug.

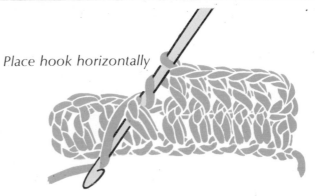

Place hook horizontally

First projects

One of the most convenient ways of trying out new crochet stitches is to combine learning with the making of practical items. These two projects not only afford the beginner the opportunity of trying out her new skills, but also show the versatility of crochet when worked with unusual materials.

Mini pillows

These pillows, about 9inches square, are worked in half double crochet but can be made in either double or single crochet.

Materials

4oz of tubular rayon macramé cord, straw, or very narrow ribbon
One size K crochet hook
9in square pillow pad

Working the crochet

Using size K hook make enough ch to measure 9in, about 22ch, including one extra chain to count as turning ch.
1st row Into third ch from hook work 1hdc, then 1hdc into each ch to end. Turn. If you had 22ch to start with you should now have 21hdc.
2nd row 2ch to count as first hdc, skip first hdc, 1hdc into each hdc to end, working the last hdc under the turning ch of the previous row. Rep second row until work measures 18in from beg. Fasten off.

Finishing

Fold work in half WS tog and join 2 side edges with a sl st. Insert cushion pad and join the remaining edge.

Rag rug

This rug, measuring 8ft 8in by 4ft 4in, is another example of using materials other than crochet wools. If you have a lot of scrap cotton fabric in a rag-bag, you can tear it up into strips about ¾ inch wide. Wind up the strips into balls, separating the colors. Work two or three rows with one color then change

to another to build up an interesting pattern. Because the rug is worked in strips it is easy to handle while you work. If you don't feel like tackling a rug, use slightly thinner strips of fabric – about ½ inch wide – to make country-style table mats.

Materials

Lengths of cotton fabric in 4 colors. (The total amount of material will depend on the length of rug desired and the way in which stripes of colors are arranged: 6yds of 36in wide fabric will work out to about 30in in length.)

One size K crochet hook
Button thread

To work the crochet

1st strip Using size K hook and any color, make enough ch to measure 13 inches in width, about 27ch should be the correct amount and this includes one ch for turning.
1st row Into third ch from hook work 1sc, then 1sc into each ch to end. Turn. If you had 27ch to start with you should now have 26sc.
2nd row 1ch to count as first sc, 1sc into each sc to end, working the last sc under the turning ch of the previous row. Turn. Rep second row for desired length, changing colors as desired and working over the ends each time a new strip is joined in to secure them.
2nd strip Make enough ch (about 19 should be right including 1ch for turning) to measure 9 inches in width.
3rd strip Make enough ch (about 35 should be right including 1ch for turning) to measure 17 inches in width.
4th strip Work as given for first strip to make 13 inches in width.

Finishing

Sew strips together with button thread.

SHAPING
Increasing and decreasing

Crochet patterns can be increased or decreased in two ways – either at the side edges or in the course of a row. More than one stitch may be increased or decreased at a time and is usually worked at the beginning and end of a row. To increase several stitches, extra chains are added, and to decrease several stitches at the beginning of a row, the necessary number to be decreased are worked across in slip stitch and then remain unworked on subsequent rows; and at the end of a row, the required number of stitches are simply left unworked.

In most designs the shaping required either to insure a properly fitting garment or to make provision for essential openings, such as armholes and neckbands, is achieved by increasing or decreasing at a given point in the pattern. Because of the depth of most crochet stitches, unless this shaping is worked neatly and evenly, a noticeable gap will be left in the pattern, and this can spoil the appearance of the finished garment. The methods given here will overcome this problem, and wherever you are instructed to increase or decrease in a pattern without being given specific details, choose the method which will give the best results.

Increasing

To increase one stitch in the course of a row, simply work twice into the same stitch. For example, when working in double crochet continue along the row in the usual way until you reach the position for the increase, put yarn over hook, insert hook into next stitch and draw through yarn (three loops on the hook), yarn over hook and draw through two loops on hook, yarn over hook and draw through last two loops on hook, yarn over hook and insert hook into the same stitch again and draw through yarn (three loops on the hook), yarn over hook and draw through two loops on hook, yarn over hook and draw through last two loops on hook. One loop is now left on the hook and one double crochet has been increased. This method applies to all stitches.

To increase one stitch at each end of row, work twice into the first and last stitch of the previous row. When using thick yarns, however, a smoother edge is formed if the increase is worked into the second stitch at the beginning of the row and into the next to last stitch at the end of the row. This method applies to all stitches.

To increase several stitches at the beginning of a row, make a chain equivalent to one less than the number of extra stitches required plus the required number of turning chains. If six stitches are to be increased when working in double crochet, for example, make five chains plus three turning chains, the next double crochet for the new row being worked into the fourth chain from the hook. The three turning chains count as the first stitch.

To increase several double crochet at the end of a row, the best way is to make provision for these extra stitches at the beginning of the previous row. To do this make three chain to count as the turning chain, then make the exact number of chains required for the increased stitches, say six. Work in slip stitch along these first six chains, then complete the row by working one double crochet into each stitch of the previous row, noting that the three turning chains have already been worked to count as the first stitch.

To increase several stitches at the beginning and end of the same row, combine the two previous methods, noting that the increase row will end by working one double crochet into the turning chain and in each of the six slip stitches of the previous row.

Decreasing

To decrease one stitch in the course of a row when working in single crochet, simply skip one stitch of the previous row at the given point. Because single crochet is a short stitch, this skipped stitch will not leave a noticeable hole.

To decrease one stitch when working in half double crochet, work along the row until the position for the decrease is reached, yarn over hook and insert hook into next stitch, yarn over hook and draw through loop, yarn over hook and insert hook into next stitch, yarn over hook and draw through loop (five loops on hook), yarn over hook and draw through all loops on hook. One half double crochet has now been decreased by making one stitch out of two.

To decrease one stitch when working in double crochet, work along the row until the position for the decrease is reached, yarn over hook and insert hook into next stitch, yarn over hook and draw through loop, yarn over hook and draw through two loops on hook, yarn over hook and insert hook into next stitch, yarn over hook and draw through loop, yarn over hook and draw through two loops on hook, yarn over hook and draw through remaining three loops on hook. One double crochet has now been decreased by making one stitch out of two.

To decrease one stitch when working in treble crochet, work along the row until the position for the decrease is reached, yarn over hook twice and insert hook into next stitch, yarn over hook and draw through loop, yarn over hook and draw through two loops on hook, yarn over hook and draw through two loops on hook (two loops on hook), yarn over hook twice, insert hook into next stitch, yarn over hook and draw through loop, yarn over hook and draw through two loops on hook, yarn over hook and draw through two loops on hook (three loops

on hook), yarn over hook and draw through all loops on hook. One treble crochet has now been decreased by making one stitch out of two.

To decrease one stitch at each end of a row when working in single crochet, make two turning chains at the beginning of the row, skip the first two single crochet of the previous row, noting that the turning chain forms the first stitch, work one single crochet into the next stitch, continue in single crochet along the row until only one single crochet and the turning chain of the previous row remain, skip the last single crochet and work one single crochet into the turning chain.

To decrease one stitch at each end of a row when working in half double crochet, make one turning chain at the beginning of the row instead of two, skip the first half double crochet of the previous row, noting that the turning chain forms this stitch, work in half double crochet across the row until only one half double crochet and the turning chain of the previous row remain, work the last half double crochet and the turning chain together to make one stitch. At the end of the next row, work one half double crochet into the last half double crochet and skip the turning chain.

To decrease one stitch at each end of a row when working in double crochet and treble crochet, work as for half double crochet, noting that only two and three turning chains respectively are worked at the beginning of the decrease row.

To decrease several stitches at the beginning of a row, slip stitch over the required number of stitches, make the required number of turning chains for the stitch being used and continue along the row.

To decrease several stitches at the end of a row, continue along the row to within the number of stitches to be decreased and turn the work, noting that the turning chain of the previous row must be counted as one of the stitches.

How to make a belt or pillow

To practice the methods of increasing and decreasing, you can make attractive triangle shapes using odds and ends of Knitting Worsted and a size 1 crochet hook. To make a belt, begin with three chain and work in single crochet, increasing one stitch at the beginning and end of every row until the desired size is reached, then fasten off. Continue making triangles in this way for the desired length of the belt, then sew them together as shown. Finish one end of the belt with a buckle.

To make a pillow you will need eight large triangles, four for each side. Begin with 70 chain for each triangle and work in half double crochet, decreasing one stitch at each end of every row until two stitches remain, then work these two stitches together to form a point. Sew four triangles together for each side, points to center, then sew outside edges together, inserting a zipper in center of the last edge. Insert a pillow pad to complete the project.

A pretty pull-on hat

Size
To fit an average head

Gauge
24 sts and 16 rows to 4in in patt worked with size E crochet hook

Materials
2 × 2oz balls sport yarn
One size E crochet hook
1yd narrow ribbon

Hat
Using size E hook make 5ch. Join with a sl st to first ch to form a ring.

1st round 3ch to count as first hdc and 1ch sp, (work 1hdc into ring, 1ch) 7 times. Join with a sl st to 2nd of first 3ch. 8 sps.

2nd round 3ch to count as first hdc and 1ch sp, work 1hdc into first ch sp, 1ch, *work 1hdc, 1ch, 1hdc all into next ch sp – called inc 1 –, 1ch, rep from * to end. Join with a sl st to 2nd of first 3ch. 16 sps.

3rd round 3ch, work 1hdc into first ch sp, 1ch, work 1hdc into sp between hdc groups, 1ch, *inc 1 into next inc 1, 1ch, 1hdc into sp between hdc groups, 1ch, rep from * to end. Join with a sl st to 2nd of first 3ch. 24 sps.

4th round 3ch, skip first 1ch sp, *work 1hdc into next 1ch sp, 1ch, rep from * to end. Join with a sl st to 2nd of first 3ch. The 4th round forms the patt and is rep throughout.

5th round 3ch, work 1hdc into first ch sp, 1ch, (1hdc into next 1ch sp, 1ch) twice, *inc 1, 1ch, (1hdc into next 1ch sp, 1ch) twice, rep from * to end. Join with a sl st to 2nd of first 3ch. 32 sps.

6th round As 4th.

7th round 3ch, work 1hdc into first ch sp, 1ch, (1hdc into next 1ch sp, 1ch) 3 times, *inc 1, 1ch, (1hdc into next 1ch sp, 1ch) 3 times, rep from * to end. Join with a sl st to 2nd of first 3ch. 40 sps.

8th round As 4th.

Cont inc 8 sps in this way on next and every alt round until there are 64 sps. Mark end of last round with colored thread to show beg of rounds. Work 4th patt round 16 times more, without inc and without joining rounds.

Shape brim
Next round *Patt 7 sps, inc 1, rep from * to end.

Next round *Patt 8 sps, inc 1, rep from * to end.

Rep 4th patt round 4 times more, without inc and without joining rounds. Fasten off.

Finishing
Do not block. Thread ribbon through lower edge of crown to tie at back.

DECORATIVE FABRIC STITCHES

This chapter is about decorative fabric stitches, telling you how to work them and how they might be used. They are all variations of the basic stitches already described. Included with them are examples of cluster and bobble stitches, which look very effective when used with basic stitches such as double crochet and single crochet, since they form a raised surface and add texture to the work.

Aligned stitch

Using size H hook and Knitting Worsted, make 22ch.
1st row (Yo and insert hook into 4th ch from hook, yo and draw through a loop, yo and draw through first 2 loops on hook) twice, yo and draw through remaining 3 loops – one aligned st has now been formed –, rep into every ch to the end of the row. Turn.
2nd row 3ch to count as first st, skip first aligned st, * yo and insert hook into next aligned st, (yo and draw through a loop, yo and draw through first 2 loops on hook), yo and rep this step once more into the same st, yo and draw through 3 remaining loops on hook, rep from * to the end of the row, working last aligned st into 3rd of the 3ch. Turn.
The last row is repeated throughout to form the pattern.

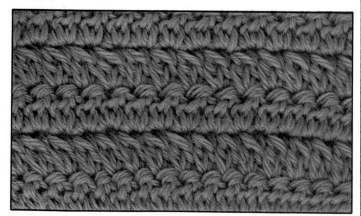

Crossed half double crochet

Using size H hook and Knitting Worsted, make 21ch.
1st row Yo and insert hook into 3rd ch from hook, yo and draw through a loop, yo and insert hook into next ch, yo and draw through a loop, yo and draw through all 5 loops on hook, 1ch, * yo and insert hook into next ch, yo and draw through a loop, yo and insert hook into next ch, yo and draw through a loop, yo and draw through all 5 loops on hook, 1ch, rep from * to last ch, 1hdc into last ch. Turn.

2nd row 3ch, yo and insert hook into first 1ch space, yo and draw through a loop, yo and insert hook into next 1ch space, yo and draw through a loop, yo and draw through all 5 loops on hook, 1ch, * yo and insert hook into same 1ch space, yo and draw through a loop, yo and insert hook into next 1ch space, yo and draw through a loop, yo and draw through all 5 loops on hook, 1ch, rep from * to end, 1hdc into 2nd of the 3ch. Turn.
The last row is repeated throughout to form the pattern.

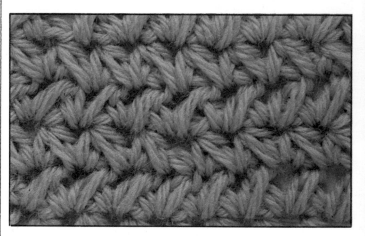

Granite stitch

Using size H hook and Knitting Worsted, make 22ch.
1st row Into 3rd ch from hook work (1sc, 1ch and 1sc), skip next ch, * (1sc, 1ch and 1sc) into next ch, skip next ch, rep from * to last ch, 1sc into last ch. Turn.
2nd row 1ch, * (1sc, 1ch and 1sc) into 1ch space of next group, rep from * end, 1sc into the turning ch. Turn.
The last row is repeated throughout to form the pattern.

Palm leaves

Using size H hook and Knitting Worsted, make 22ch.

1st row Into 4th ch from hook work 1sc, * 2ch, skip next 2ch, 1sc into next ch, rep from * to end. Turn.

2nd row 3ch to count as first dc, 1dc into first sc, * 3dc into next sc, rep from * to end, working 2dc into first of the 3ch. Turn.

3rd row 3ch, 1sc into 2nd dc of the first 3dc group, * 2ch, 1sc into 2nd dc of next 3dc group, rep from * to end, working last sc into 3rd of the 3ch. Turn.

Repeat the 2nd and 3rd rows throughout to form the pattern.

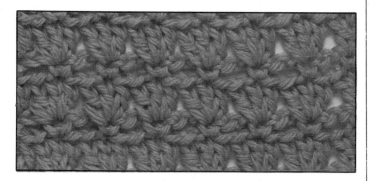

Cock's head doubles

Using size H hook and Knitting Worsted, make 22ch.

1st row Into 4th ch from hook work 1dc, * (yo and insert hook into next ch, yo and draw through a loop, yo and draw through first 2 loops on hook) twice, yo and draw through all 3 loops, 1ch, rep from * to end, omitting the 1ch at the end of the last rep.

2nd row 4ch, yo and insert hook into first st, yo and draw through a loop, yo and draw through first 2 loops, skip next st, yo and insert hook into next st, yo and draw through a loop, yo and draw through first 2 loops, yo and draw through all 3 loops, * 1ch, yo and insert hook into same st that last st was worked into, yo and draw through a loop, yo and draw through first 2 loops, skip next st, yo and insert hook into next st, yo and draw through a loop, yo and draw through first 2 loops, yo and draw through all 3 loops, rep from * to end, 1ch, 1dc into 3rd of the 3ch. Turn.

3rd row As 2nd, but note that the last st is worked into the 3rd of the 4ch. Turn.

The last row is repeated throughout to form the pattern.

Forget-me-not stitch

Using size H hook and Knitting Worsted, make 25ch.

1st row Into 4th ch from hook work (1dc, 2ch and 1sc), * skip next 2ch, (2dc, 2ch and 1sc) into next ch, rep from * to end. Turn.

2nd row 3ch, (1dc, 2ch and 1sc) into first 2ch space, * (2dc, 2ch and 1sc) into next 2ch space, rep from * to end. Turn.

The last row is repeated throughout to form the pattern. This stitch looks very attractive when two colors are used on alternate rows.

To design a dirndl skirt

Any one of these attractive stitches that you have just learned, together with a knowledge of checking gauge are all you will need to design a lovely dirndl skirt.

For example, if you are a 36 inch hip size, you will need one inch ease. This means that each piece of your skirt will measure $18\frac{1}{2}$ inches across. If your gauge is 4 sts to one inch, then you will require $18\frac{1}{2} \times 4 = 74$ stitches for the basic pattern.

No shaping is required. You just work to the desired length and gather the waist with rows of shirring elastic.

Wall hanging

Another use for the various stitches learned thus far is to make them into a wall hanging. This will look particularly attractive if you choose one color and work each stitch in a different shade of this color. A very good finishing touch to this would be to mount the hanging on a brass pole.

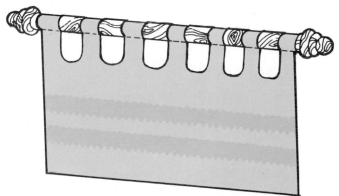

CLUSTER AND BOBBLE STITCHES

Cluster and bobble stitches

Edgings using either the bobble or cluster stitch make ideal trimmings for the neckline or hemline of a dress and also edgings for jackets, vests and household linens. The same stitches can also be used to make square or circular motifs for a bedspread or evening stole, and they can replace stitches on a basic design, adding a great deal of interest to a simple fabric.

Here three examples of the many variations of cluster stitch are illustrated and explained in detail. For these samples a size G crochet hook and Knitting Worsted were used, although the hook size and type of yarn will vary depending on the purpose of the work.

Cluster or pine stitch

Make 26ch.

1st row Into 3rd ch from hook work 1sc, 1sc into each ch to end. Turn.

2nd row 1ch to count as first sc, skip first sc, 1sc into each sc, ending with 1sc into the turning chain. Turn.

3rd row (cluster row) 4ch, skip first 2sc, ** yo and insert hook into next sc, yo and draw through a loop extending it for $\frac{3}{8}$ inch, * yo and insert hook into same sc, yo and draw through a loop, extending it for $\frac{3}{8}$ inch, rep from * 3 times, yo and draw through all 11 loops on hook – called 1cl –, 1ch, skip next sc, rep from ** ending with 1dc into the turning chain. Turn.

4th and 5th rows Work in sc. Fasten off.

Using the cluster stitch, practice making square motifs. Worked in one color and a cotton yarn, they are ideal for making quilts or tablecloths, or worked in fine, multi-colored yarns they are lovely for attractive evening stoles.

In the instructions for the square motif given here we

used 4 colors which are referred to as A, B, C and D.

Square motif

With A, make 5ch. Join into ring with a slip stitch.

1st round 1ch to count as first sc, 15sc into ring, ending with a sl st into first ch. 16sc. Fasten off A and join in B.

2nd round 4 ch to count as first dc and linking ch, * 1dc into next sc, 1ch, rep from * ending with a sl st into 3rd of the 4 starting ch. Fasten off B and join in C.

3rd round Sl st into next 1ch space, * 3ch, 1cl into same 1ch space, rep from * ending with 3ch, sl st into top of first cl. Fasten off C and join in D.

4th round Sl st into next 3ch space, 1ch, 2sc into same space, 3sc into each of next 2 spaces, * (1hdc, 1dc, 2ch, 1dc, 1hdc) into next space for corner, 3sc into each of the next 3 spaces, rep from * twice more, 1 corner into next space, sl st into first ch. Fasten off.

Raised clusters

By using the method of raising clusters on a basic fabric, many designs such as diagonals and zigzags may be incorporated.

The instructions given below are for raised clusters on a single crochet background.

Make 25ch.

1st to 3rd rows Work in sc as for the basic cluster sample.

4th row 1ch to count as first sc, skip first sc, 1sc into each of next 3sc, * insert hook into next sc, yo and draw through a loop, (yo and insert hook into space on the 3rd row directly below this stitch, yo and draw through a loop, yo and draw through first 2 loops on hook) 5 times, yo and draw through all 6 loops on hook – called 1 raised cl – , 1sc into each of next 4sc, rep from * to end.

5th to 7th rows Work in sc.

8th row Repeat the raised cluster on every 5th stitch depending on the effect that you want to create.

You will see that diagonals or alternating clusters have been formed in our illustrations. Repeat rows 1 through 8 to achieve this effect.

Two more raised stitches are the bobble and the

Bobble stitch

popcorn stitch. The instructions given here are for an allover bobble design and a popcorn stitch that is worked into a braid.

Bobble stitch

Make 26ch.

1st row Into 3rd ch from hook work 1sc, 1sc into each ch to end. Turn.

2nd row 1ch to count as first sc, * 4ch, skip 2sc, leaving the last loop of each st on hook work 6dtr into next sc, yo and draw through all 7 loops on hook – called B1 – , 4ch, skip next 2sc, 1sc into next sc, rep from * ending with 1sc into turning chain. Turn.

3rd row 5ch to count as first dc and linking ch, 1sc into first B1, * 5ch, 1sc into next B1, rep from * ending with 2ch, 1dc into the turning chain. Turn.

4th row 5ch to count as first dc and linking ch, 1sc into next sc, * 4ch, B1 into next 5ch space, 4ch, 1sc into next sc, rep from * ending with 2ch, 1dc into 3rd of the turning chain. Turn.

5th row 1ch to count as first sc, * 5ch, 1sc into next B1, rep from * ending with 5ch, 1sc into 3rd of the turning chain. Turn.

6th row 1ch to count as first sc, * 4ch, B1 into next 5ch space, 4ch, 1sc into next sc, rep from * ending with 1sc into the turning chain. Turn.

The 3rd through 6th rows are repeated throughout to form the pattern.

Popcorn stitch

Make 25ch.

1st row Into 4th ch from hook work 1dc, 1dc into each ch to end. Turn.

2nd row 3ch to count as first dc, skip first dc, 1dc into each dc, ending with 1dc into the turning chain.

3rd row 3ch to count as first dc, skip first dc, 1dc into next dc, * 1ch, 5dc into next dc, slip working st off the hook and pick up the ch st worked before the 5dc, pick up working loop and draw through the ch st – 1 popcorn st has now been worked – , 1dc into each of next 2dc, rep from * ending with 1dc into the turning chain. Turn.

4th and 5th rows Work in dc. Fasten off.

BLOCKING AND FINISHING

In the previous chapters, many stitches and some ways of working them have been explained, using a variety of materials. This chapter is designed to give you some useful hints on the blocking and finishing of your work and on how to apply these and various other interesting techniques to the making of many useful decorative things such as the bags we show here.

Gauge

Before starting a piece of work that has a definite size requirement, for example, a sweater to fit a 34 inch bust, it is important to make sure that the garment will measure the correct size when it is completed. A gauge sample must be worked before you start. Follow the gauge guide at the beginning of the pattern and, using the suggested yarn and hook, make a small square approximately 4in in width and depth. Place a ruler on the work and count how many stitches and rows there are to the inch. If there are too many stitches, then your gauge is too tight and you must practice with a larger hook until you gain the correct gauge. Too few stitches mean that you are working too loosely and need to use a smaller hook.

Blocking

Part of the pleasing appearance of crochet is its textured surface. Many people prefer not to block the work as they fear the effect of a warm iron and damp cloth will spoil this texture. Also, with so many new and different kinds of yarn on the market, blocking could quite well be unnecessary. Always read the manufacturer's instructions on the yarn label to check if this final finish is recommended and also the way in which it should be done.

As a general rule, most yarns containing a high percentage of natural fibers such as wool and cotton can be blocked under a damp cloth with a warm iron. Man-made yarns such as nylon and acrylics need a cool iron and dry cloth.

Most crochet, especially when it is very open in texture, does need blocking out on completion. When you are blocking the individual pieces before finishing use a clean, flat covered surface onto which you pin the pieces out to the correct measurements with rustless dressmaking pins.

When done cover the work with a damp cloth and leave until the cloth is absolutely dry.

Cotton crochet items such as delicate edgings or table cloths and place mats often look better for a light starching.

For this use a starch solution (about two teaspoonfuls to a pint of hot water), or a gum arabic solution. Dab the solution over the article while it is being blocked out.

Joining in new yarn

In crochet, it is better to avoid tying knots when joining in new yarn. Work until about 3 inches of the yarn is left, lay this across the top of the previous row to the left, lay the beginning of the new yarn with it and work over both ends with the second ball of yarn.

If the join comes when chain is being worked, lay the new thread alongside the first one, the ends pointing

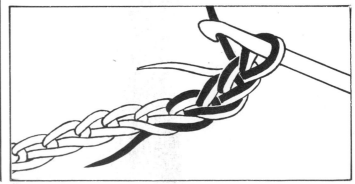

in opposite directions, and work with the double thickness until the first thread runs out.

Joining two pieces of crochet work

There are two methods of doing this – either by sewing the pieces together or by using crochet stitches to make a seam.

Sewing Place the two pieces of work with right sides together and pin firmly. Overcast the edge using a matching yarn. When the seam is completed it may be necessary to block it.

When joining stripes or patterns take care to see that the seams match exactly to insure a professional finish.

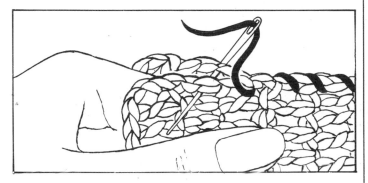

Crochet Joining work with crochet stitches can form part of the design and look very attractive. In the illustration you will see a section of a bag where the gusset has been joined to the main part with single crochet.

Methods of making a handbag

Generally there are two types of handbags, one with a gusset and one without. The gusset is a narrow piece of fabric between the two main sections used to give the bag a three-dimensional effect.

Commercial handles for bags may be purchased from the needlework counters of most large stores. The traditional wooden frames illustrated do not require a

gusset. Simply work two pieces of crochet to the required size and join together either by sewing or crocheting, leaving an opening in the top edge of the handles to be inserted and hemmed into place.

If you have used crochet stitches to join your bag, then you could insert tassels through the joining stitches along the lower edge at whatever spacing you like. Our sample illustration has been worked in different colors to clarify the various stages of finishing and the method of adding the tassels is shown clearly.

Other types of commercial handles available are the bamboo rings and various metal frames which have a screw-in bar and clasp fastening.

A firm handle may not be required and a gusset strip can be made to fit around the bag with an extension which is left free for a handle as shown in our illustration.

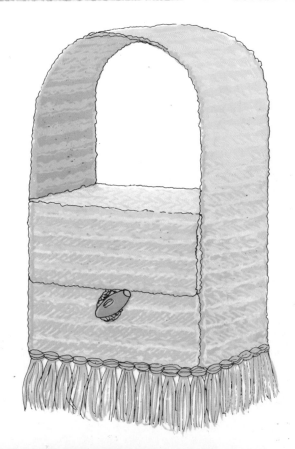

FIRST SIMPLE GARMENTS
Smart dress set

A simple dress to crochet with a cardigan and beret to match.

Sizes
Directions are to fit 32in bust. Changes for 34 : 36 : 38 and 40in bust are in brackets [ ].
34[36:38:40:42]in hips
Dress length to shoulder, 39[39:39¼:39¼:39½]in
Jacket length to shoulder, 23½[23½:23½:24:24]in
Sleeve seam 17½in

Gauge
Dress and beret 19 sts and 24 rows to 4in in patt worked with size F crochet hook
Jacket 21 sts and 13 rows to 4in in patt worked with size F crochet hook

Materials
Dress 9[10:11:12:13] × 2oz balls Brunswick Pomfret Sport yarn
One size F crochet hook
One 20 in zipper

Jacket 7[7:8:8:9] × 2oz balls Brunswick Pomfret Sport yarn
One size F crochet hook
3 buttons

Beret 2 × 2oz balls Brunswick Pomfret Sport yarn
One size F crochet hook

Dress front
**Using size F hook make 111[115:121:125:131]ch.
Base row (WS) Into 2nd ch from hook work 1sc, 1sc into each ch to end. Turn. 110[114:120:124:130] sts.
Start patt.
1st row 1ch, 1sc into each st to end. Turn.
This row forms patt. Work 7 more rows in patt.
Shape sides
Cont in patt, dec one st at each end of next and every foll 8th row until 88[92:98:102:108] sts rem. Work 7 rows without shaping. **
Shape waist darts
1st row Dec one st, 1sc into each of next 21[22:25:26:28] sts, dec one st, 1sc into each of next 38[40:40:42:44] sts, dec one st, 1sc into each st to last 2 sts, dec one st. Turn.
Work 7 rows without shaping.
9th row Dec one st by working 2sc tog, 1sc into each of next 20[21:24:25:27] sts, dec one st, 1sc into each of next 36[38:38:40:42] sts, dec one st, 1sc into each st to last 2 sts, dec one st. Turn.
Work 7 rows without shaping. Cont dec

in this way on next and every foll 8th row until 68[72:78:82:88] sts rem. Cont without shaping until work measures 24½in from beg, ending with a WS row.
Shape bust darts
1st row 1ch, 1sc into same st, 1sc into each of next 17[18:21:22:24] sts, 2sc into next st, 1sc into each of next 30[32:32:34:36] sts, 2sc into next st, 1sc into each st to last st, 2sc into last st. Turn.
Work 7 rows without shaping.
9th row 1ch, 1sc into same st, 1sc into each of next 18[19:22:23:25] sts, 2sc into next st, 1sc into each of next 32[34:34:36:38] sts, 2sc into next st, 1sc into each st to last st, 2sc into last st. Turn.
Work 7 rows without shaping. Cont inc in this way on next row and foll 8th rows. 84[88:94:98:104] sts. Cont without shaping until front measures 31½[31½:31½:32½:32½]in from beg, ending with a WS row.
Shape armholes
1st row Sl st over first 5[5:6:7:8] sts, 1ch, patt to last 5[5:6:7:8] sts, turn.
Dec one st at each end of next and every foll alt row until 62[66:70:70:74] sts rem. Cont without shaping until armholes measure 5¾[5¾:6:6:6¼]in from beg, ending with a WS row.
Shape neck
Next row Patt 25[27:28:28:30] sts, turn. Complete this side first. Keeping armhole edge straight, dec one st at neck edge on each of next 7 rows, ending at armhole edge.
Shape shoulder
1st row Sl st across first 3[4:5:5:4] sts, 1ch, patt to end. Turn.
2nd row Patt to last 4[4:4:4:5] sts, turn.
3rd row Sl st over first 4[4:4:4:5] sts, 1ch, patt to end. Turn.
4th row Patt 3[4:4:4:4] sts. Fasten off.
With RS of work facing, skip first 12[12:14:14:14] sts for center front neck, rejoin yarn to next st, 1ch, 1sc into each st to end. Turn.
Dec one st at neck edge on each of next 7 rows, ending at neck edge.
Shape shoulder
1st row Patt to last 3[4:5:5:4] sts, turn.
2nd row Sl st over first 4[4:4:4:5] sts, 1ch, patt to end. Turn.
3rd row Patt 7[8:8:8:9] sts. Turn.
4th row Sl st across first 4[4:4:4:5] sts, 1ch, patt to end. Fasten off.

Dress back
Work as given for front from ** to **
Shape waist darts
1st row Dec one st, 1sc into each of next 21[22:25:26:28] sts, dec one st, 1sc into each of next 38[40:40:42:44] sts, dec

one st, 1sc into each st to last 2 sts, dec one st. Turn.
Work 3 rows without shaping.
5th row 1ch, 1sc into each of next 21[22:25:26:28] sts, dec one st, 1sc into each of next 36[38:38:40:42] sts, dec one st, 1sc into each st to end. Turn.
Work 3 rows without shaping.
9th row Dec one st, 1sc into each of next 20[21:24:25:27] sts, dec one st, 1sc into each of next 34[36:36:38:40] sts, dec one st, 1sc into each st to last 2 sts, dec one st. Turn.
Work 3 rows without shaping.
13th row 1ch, 1sc into each of next 20[21:24:25:27] sts, dec one st, 1sc into each of next 32[34:34:36:38] sts, dec one st, 1sc into each st to end. Turn. 76[80:86:90:96] sts.
Work one row without shaping.
Divide for back opening
Next row 1ch, 1sc into each of next 37[39:42:44:47] sts, turn.
Complete this side first.
1st row 1ch, 1sc into each st to end. Turn.
2nd row Dec one st, 1sc into each of next 19[20:23:24:26] sts, dec one st, 1sc into each st to end. Turn.
Work 3 rows without shaping.
6th row 1ch, 1sc into each of first 19[20:23:24:26] sts, dec one st, 1sc into each st to end. Turn.
Work 3 rows without shaping.
10th row Dec one st, 1sc into each of next 18[19:22:23:25] sts, dec one st, 1sc into each st to end. Turn.
Work 3 rows without shaping.
14th row 1ch, 1sc into each of first 18[19:22:23:25] sts, dec one st, 1sc into each st to end. Turn.
Work 3 rows without shaping.
18th row Dec one st, 1sc into each of next 17[18:21:22:24] sts, dec one st, 1sc into each st to end. Turn.
Work 3 rows without shaping.
22nd row 1ch, 1sc into each of first 17[18:21:22:24] sts, dec one st, 1sc into each st to end. Turn 29[31:34:36:39] sts.
Cont without shaping until back measures 24½in from beg, ending with a WS row.
Shape side edge and dart
1st row 1ch, 1sc into same st, 1sc into each of next 17[18:21:22:24] sts, 2sc into next st, 1sc into each st to end. Turn.
Work 3 rows without shaping.
5th row 1ch, 1sc into each of next 18[19:22:23:25] sts, 2sc into next st, 1sc into each st to end. Turn.
Work 3 rows without shaping.
9th row 1ch, 1sc into same st, 1sc into each of next 18[19:22:23:25] sts, 2sc into next st, 1sc into each st to end. Turn
Cont inc at side edge in this way on every foll 8th row and for dart on every

4th row until there are 41[43:46:48:51] sts. Cont without shaping until back measures same as front to underarm, ending at side edge.

Shape armhole

1st row Sl st over first 5[5:6:7:8] sts, 1ch, patt to end. Turn.
Dec one st at armhole edge on next and every alt row until 31[33:35:35:37] sts rem. Cont without shaping until armhole measures same as front to shoulder, ending at armhole edge.

Shape shoulder

1st row Sl st across first 3[4:5:5:4] sts, 1ch, patt to end. Turn.

2nd row Patt to last 4[4:4:4:5] sts, turn.

3rd row Sl st across first 4[4:4:4:5] sts, 1ch, patt 7[8:8:8:9] sts, turn.

4th row Work in patt 3[4:4:4:4] sts. Fasten off. With RS of work facing, rejoin yarn to rem sts at back opening and complete to correspond to first side, reversing shaping.

Finishing

Block each piece lightly under a damp cloth with a warm iron.
Join shoulder and side seams.

Neck and back opening edging Using size F hook and with RS of work facing, rejoin yarn to left back neck edge at opening edge. Work one row sc round neck, down right back opening and up left back opening. Do not turn, but work one row in sc from left to right instead of from right to left.

Armhole edging Using size F hook and with RS of work facing, work as given for neck and back edging.
Block seams lightly. Sew zipper into back opening.

Jacket right front

****Using size F hook make 44[47:50:53:56] ch.

Base row (WS) Into 2nd ch from hook work 1sc, *2ch, skip 2ch, 1sc into next ch, rep from * to end. Turn. 43[46:49:52:55] sts.
Start patt.

1st row 2ch, 1dc into first sc, *skip 2ch, 3dc into next sc, rep from * ending with skip 2ch, 2dc into last sc. Turn.

2nd row 1ch, 1sc into first dc, *2ch, skip 2dc, 1sc into next dc, rep from * to end. Turn.
The last 2 rows form patt. Work 7 more rows in patt, ending with a RS row.

Shape side edge

Maintaining patt, dec one st at beg of next row and at same edge on every foll 3rd row until 37[40:43:46:49] sts rem. Cont without shaping until front measures 10in from beg, ending with a RS row. **

Shape side and front edges

1st row Inc in first st, patt to last 2 sts, dec one st. Turn.

2nd and 3rd rows Patt to end. Turn.

4th row Dec one st, patt to end. Turn.

5th and 6th rows Patt to end. Turn.
Rep last 6 rows twice more. 34[37:40:43:46] sts.

Shape armhole

Next row Sl st over first 4[5:5:6:6] sts, 1ch, patt to last 2 sts, dec one st. Turn.
Cont dec at front edge as before, *at the*

same time dec one st at armhole edge on next 4[5:7:7:8] rows. Keeping armhole edge straight, cont dec at front edge on every 3rd row until 19[20:21:23:25] sts rem. Cont without shaping until armhole measures 7[7:7:7½:7½]in from beg, ending at armhole edge.

Shape shoulder

1st row Sl st over first 4[5:5:5:7] sts, 1ch, patt to end. Turn.

2nd row Patt to last 5[5:5:6:6] sts, turn.

3rd row Sl st over first 5[5:5:6:6] sts, 1ch,

patt to end. Fasten off.

Left front
Work as given for right front from ** to **, reversing shaping.
Shape front and side edges
1st row Dec one st, patt to last st, inc in last st. Turn.
2nd and 3rd rows Patt to end. Turn.
4th row Patt to last 2 sts, dec one st. Turn.
5th and 6th rows Patt to end. Turn.

Rep last 6 rows twice more. Turn.
Shape armhole
Next row Dec one st, patt to last 4[5:5:6:6] sts, turn.
Complete armhole and front edge shaping as given for right front, reversing shaping. Cont without shaping until armhole measures 7[7:7:7½:7½]in from beg, ending at neck edge. Turn.
Shape shoulder
1st row Patt to last 4[5:5:5:7] sts, turn.
2nd row Sl st over first 5[5:5:6:6] sts, 2ch, patt to end. Turn.
3rd row Patt 5[5:6:6:6] sts.
Fasten off.

Back
Using size F hook make 92[98:104:110:116] ch. Work base row as given for right front. 91[97:103:109:115] sts. Work 9 rows patt as given for right front.
Shape sides
Dec one st at each end of next and every foll 3rd row until 79[85:91:97:103] sts rem. Cont without shaping until piece measures 10in from beg, ending with a RS row. Inc one st at each end of next and every foll 6th row 3 times in all. 85[91:97:103:109] sts.
Work 5 rows without shaping.
Shape armholes
Next row Sl st over first 4[5:5:6:6] sts, 1ch, patt to last 4[5:5:6:6] sts, turn.
Dec one st at each end of next 4[5:7:7:8] rows. 69[71:73:77:81] sts.
Cont working in patt without shaping until armholes measure same as front to shoulder, ending with a RS row.
Shape shoulders
1st row Sl st over first 4[5:5:5:7] sts, 1ch, patt to last 4[5:5:5:7] sts, turn.
2nd row Sl st over first 5[5:5:6:6] sts, 2ch, patt to last 5[5:5:6:6] sts, turn.
3rd row Sl st over first 5[5:5:6:6] sts, 1ch, patt over next 5[5:6:6:6] sts, sl st over next 31 sts, patt over next 5[5:6:6:6] sts.
Fasten off.

Sleeves
Using size F hook make 41[44:44:47:47] ch. Work base row as given for right front. 40[43:43:46:46] sts. Work 3 rows patt as given for right front.
Maintaining patt, inc one st at each end of next and every foll 3rd row until there are 50[53:55:62:64] sts, then inc one st at each end of every foll 4th row until there are 64[67:69:72:74] sts. Cont without shaping until sleeve measures 17½in from beg, ending with a RS row.
Shape top
Next row Sl st over first 4[5:5:6:6] sts, 1ch, patt to last 4[5:5:6:6] sts, turn.
Dec one st at each end of every row until

34[35:37:34:36] sts rem. Dec 2 sts at each end of next 4 rows. 18[19:21:18:20] sts. Fasten off.

Finishing
Block each piece under a damp cloth with a warm iron. Join shoulder seams. Set in sleeves. Join side and sleeve seams.
Border Using size F hook and with RS of work facing, rejoin yarn to right front at lower edge. Work one row sc up right front edge, working 3sc into each 2 row ends, cont across back neck, working into each st, then work down left front as given for right front. Turn.
Next row 1ch 1sc into each st to end. Turn. Rep last row once more. Mark position for 3 buttonholes on right front, the first ½in below first row of front edge shaping and the last to come 2½in from lower edge with the third spaced evenly between.
Next row (buttonhole row) Work in sc to end, making 3 buttonholes when markers are reached by working 3ch and skipping 3 sts. Work 3 rows sc, working 3sc into 3ch buttonhole loop on first row. Fasten off. Block seams and border lightly. Sew on buttons.

Beret
Using size F hook make 6ch. Join with a sl st to first ch to form a ring.
1st round 1ch, work 11sc into a ring. Join with a sl st to first ch. 12 sts.
2nd round 1ch, 1sc into same st, 1sc into next st, *2sc into next st, 1sc into next st, rep from * to end. Join with a sl st to first 1ch. 18 sts.
3rd round 1ch, 1sc into same st, 1sc into each of next 2 sts, *2sc into next st, 1sc into each of next 2 sts, rep from * to end. Join with a sl st to first 1ch. 24 sts.
4th round 1ch, 1sc into same st, 1sc into each of next 3 sts, * 2sc into next st, 1sc into each of next 3 sts, rep from * to end. Join with a sl st to first 1ch. 30 sts.
Cont inc in this way on every round until there are 132 sts. Work 10 rounds without shaping.
Shape headband
Next round *Dec one st, 1sc into each of next 20 sts, rep from * to end. Join with a sl st to first st.
Next round *Dec one st, 1sc into each of next 19 sts, rep from * to end. Join with a sl st to first st.
Cont dec in this way on every round until 84 sts rem. Turn.
Next round 1ch, 1sc into each sc to end. Join with a sl st to first 1ch. Turn.
Rep last round 3 times more. Fasten off.

Finishing
Block lightly as for dress.

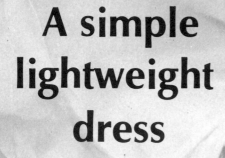

A simple lightweight dress

Short and simple, here's a lightweight dress that will look good day or evening.

Size
Directions are to fit 34in bust, changes for 36, 38 and 40in bust sizes are in brackets [ ].
Length to shoulder, $36[36\frac{1}{4}:36\frac{1}{2}:36\frac{3}{4}]$in
Sleeve seam, 5in

Gauge
20 sts and 9 rows to 4in in dc worked with size E crochet hook;
22 sts and 20 rows to 4in in sc worked with size E crochet hook

Materials
17[20:23:25] 125yd balls Lily Sugar 'n Cream Yarn in main color, A
1 ball each of contrast colors, B and C
One size E crochet hook
20in zipper

Skirt
Using size E hook and A, make 111ch

and start at waist, working from top to lower edge.

1st row (RS) Into 3rd ch from hook work 1sc, 1sc into each of next 18ch, 1hdc into each of next 20ch, 1dc into each of next 70ch. Turn. 110 sts.

2nd row 3ch to count as first dc, 1dc into front loop only of next 69dc, 1hdc into front loop only of next 20hdc, 1sc into front loop only of next 19sc, 1sc into turning ch. Turn.

3rd row 1ch to count as first sc, 1sc into front loop only of next 19sc, 1hdc into front loop only of next 20hdc, 1dc into front loop only of next dc, 1dc into turning ch. Turn.

The 2nd and 3rd rows form the patt and are rep throughout. Cont in patt until work measures 25[27:29:31]in from beg, measured across the waist edge. Fasten off.

Hem

Using size E hook, B and with RS of work facing, rejoin yarn to lower edge of skirt.

Next row 2ch to count as first sc, (1dc, 1ch, 1dc, 1sc) into first row end, *1ch, 1sc into next row end, 1ch, (1sc, 1dc, 1ch, 1dc, 1sc) into next row end, rep from * to end. Break off B. Join in C. Do not turn.

Next row Rejoin yarn at beg of row, 2ch, (1dc, 1ch, 1dc, 1sc) into first ch sp between dc's, *1ch, 1sc into next sc, 3ch, 1sc into same sc, 1ch (1sc, 1dc, 1ch, 1dc, 1sc) into next 1ch sp between dc's, rep from * to end. Fasten off.

Bodice

Using size E hook, A and with RS of work facing, rejoin yarn and work 150 [162:174:186]sc across waist edge. Work 3 rows sc, working into front loop only of each sc throughout.

Shape darts

Next row 1ch, work 1sc into each of next 40[43:46:49]sc, (2sc into next sc) twice, 1sc into each of next 19[22:25:28] sc, (2sc into next sc) twice, 1sc into each of next 22sc, (2sc into next sc) twice, 1sc into each of next 19[22:25:28] sc, (2sc into next sc) twice, 1sc into each of next 41[44:47:50]sc. Turn. 158[170:182:194]sc.

Work 3 rows without shaping.

Next row 1ch, work 1sc into each of next 41[44:47:50]sc, (2sc into next sc) twice, 1sc into each of next 21[24:27:30]sc, (2sc into next sc) twice, 1sc into each of next 24sc, (2sc into next sc) twice, 1sc into each of next 21[24:27:30]sc, (2sc into next sc) twice, 1sc into each of next 42[45:48:51]sc. Turn. 166[178:190:202]sc.

Work 3 rows without shaping. Cont inc 8 sts in this way on next and every foll 4th row until there are 198[210:230:242]sts. Cont without shaping until work measures 8in from waist, or desired length to underarm, ending with a WS row.

Divide for armholes

Next row Patt across 45[48:52:55] sts, turn.

Complete left back first. Dec one st at beg of next and at same edge on every row until 35[38:42:45] sts rem. Cont without shaping until armhole measures 5½[5¾:6:6¼]in from beg, ending at armhole edge.

Shape neck

Next row Patt across 20[22:24:26] sts, turn.

Dec one st at beg of next and at same edge on every row until 16[18:20:22] sts rem. Cont without shaping until armhole measures 7[7¼:7½:7¾]in from beg, ending at neck edge.

Shape shoulder

Next row Patt across 8[9:10:11] sts, turn and fasten off.

With RS of work facing, skip first 8[8:10:10] sts for underarm, rejoin yarn to next st and patt across 92[98:106:112] sts for front, turn.

Dec one st at each end of next 10 rows 72[78:86:92] sts. Cont without shaping until armholes measure 3½[3¾:4:4¼]in from beg, ending with a WS row.

Shape neck

Next row Patt across 26[28:30:32] sts, turn.

Complete this side first. Dec one st at beg of next and at same edge on every row until 16[18:20:22] sts rem. Cont without shaping until armhole measures same as back to shoulder, ending at neck edge.

Shape shoulder

Next row Patt across 8[9:10:11] sts, turn and fasten off.

With RS of work facing, skip first 20[22:26:28] sts for center neck, rejoin yarn to rem sts and patt to end. Complete to match first side, reversing shaping.

With RS of work facing, skip first 8[8:10:10] sts for underarm, rejoin yarn to rem sts and patt to end. Complete right back to correspond to left back, reversing shaping.

Sleeves

Using size E hook and A, make 22ch and work from side edge to side edge.

1st row (RS) Into 4th ch from hook work 1dc, 1dc into each ch to end. Turn. 20dc.

2nd row 3ch to count as first dc, *1dc into front loop only of next dc, rep from * ending with 1dc into turning ch. Turn.

Shape top

Next row 3ch, 1hdc, into 3rd of these 3 ch, *1dc into front loop only of next dc, rep from * ending with 1dc into turning ch. Turn. 22 sts.

Next row 3ch to count as first dc, 1dc into front loop only of next 19dc, 1hdc into front loop only of next hdc, 1hdc into turning ch. Turn.

Next row 3ch, 1hdc into 3rd of these 3 ch, 1hdc into front loop only of next 2hdc, 1dc into front loop only of each dc to end. Turn. 24 sts.

Next row 3ch to count as first dc, 1dc into front loop only of next 19dc, 1hdc into front loop only of next 3hdc, 1hdc into turning ch. Turn.

Cont inc in this way, rep last 2 rows 4[5:6:7] times more. 32 [34:36:38] sts.

Next row 5ch, 1sc into 3rd of these 5ch, 1sc into each of next 2ch, 1hdc into front loop only of each of next 14[16:18:20] hdc, 1dc into front loop only of each dc to end. Turn. 36[38:40:42] sts.

Next row 3ch, 1dc into front loop only of next 19dc, 1hdc into front loop only of next 14[16:18:20] hdc, 1sc into front loop only of next 3sc, 1sc into turning ch. Turn.

Rep last 2 rows 2[3:4:5] times more 44 [50:56:62] sts. Work 12 rows patt as now set without shaping, ending at top edge.

Next row Sl st across first 4sc and into next sc, 1ch to count as first sc, patt to end. Turn. 40[46:52:58] sts.

Next row Patt to end. Turn.

Rep last 2 rows 2[3:4:5] times more. 32[34:36:38] sts.

Next row Sl st across first 2hdc and into next hdc, 2ch to count as first hdc, patt to end. Turn. 30[32:34:36] sts

Next row Patt to end. Turn.

Rep last 2 rows until 20dc rem. Work 1 row dc. Fasten off.

Cuff

Using size E hook, B and with RS of work facing, work along lower edge of sleeve as given for hem. Fasten off.

Neckband

Join shoulder seams. Using size E hook, B and with RS of work facing, work evenly round neck edge as given for hem. Fasten off.

Finishing

Block each piece under a damp cloth with a warm iron. Join sleeve seams. Set in sleeves, easing in fullness at top. Join center back seam leaving an opening for zipper to reach to top of neckband. Sew in zipper. Press seams.

Using rem yarn make a twisted cord or braided belt.

CROCHET IN ROUNDS
CIRCULAR MOTIFS

Crochet may very easily and effectively be worked into circles or squares instead of back and forth in rows. Each piece is worked from the same side. This means that there is a definite right and wrong side to the work.

Circular shapes are an important technique in crochet. Sun hats, berets, bags and doilys are among the many articles worked in this way.

Attractive shapes may be joined together to give a patchwork fabric that works well for shawls, rugs, vests, boleros and evening skirts.

Again, try experimenting in various yarns to see the many effects that may be achieved.

To work a circle in crochet

Using size H hook and Knitting Worsted make 6ch. Join together to form a ring with a sl st into the first ch.

1st round 3ch to count as the first dc, then work 15dc into the ring. Join with a sl st to the 3rd of the first 3ch. 16dc.

2nd round 3ch, 2dc into each dc of the previous round, 1dc into the base of the turning ch. Join with a sl st to the 3rd of the first 3 ch. 32dc.

3rd round 3ch, (1dc into next stitch, 2dc into next stitch) 15 times, 1dc into next stitch, 1dc into base of the turning ch. Join with a sl st to the 3rd of the first 3ch. 48dc.

4th round 3ch, (1dc into each of next 2 stitches, 2dc into next stitch) 15 times, 1dc into each of next 2 stitches, 1dc into base of the turning ch. Join with a sl st to the 3rd of the first 3ch. 64dc.

Continue in this way, working 1 extra dc on each round until the circle is the desired size. To practice this method of making a circle and produce a useful item for the home at the same time, make two circles to any desired size and use them to cover a pillow pad or, using three thicknesses of Speed-Cro-Sheen Cotton and a size K hook, make a bath mat. A fringed edging would add the final touch to either of these items.

Another way to make a circular motif

Make 6ch. Join with a sl st to first ch to form a ring.

1st round 2ch to count as first sc, work 7sc into ring. Do not join, but cont working rounds, working next 2sc into second of first 2 ch.

2nd round Work 2sc into each sc to end. 16sc.

3rd round Work 1sc into each sc to end.

4th round Work 2sc into each sc to end. 32sc.

5th round Work 1sc into each sc to end.

6th round 2sc into first sc, 1sc into next sc,*2sc into next sc, 1sc into next sc, rep from * to end. 48sc.

7th round Work 1 round without shaping.

8th round 2sc into first sc, 1sc into each of next 2sc, *2sc into next sc, 1sc into each of next 2sc, rep from * to end. 64sc.

Cont inc 1sc on every other round until the motif is the desired size.

To do this, the space between each 2sc into 1sc increases by one stitch every increasing round so that on round 10, work 2sc into next sc, 1sc into next 3sc; and on round 12, work 2sc into next sc, 1sc into next 4sc. Cont increasing 16sc on every alternate round in this way until the circle is desired size. Sl st into first st of previous round and fasten off.

String place mat (page 24)
Size
12in in diameter

Materials
1 ball of garden twine

One size H crochet hook

Place mat
Work as given for circular motif until 14 rounds have been completed and total 112sc. Do not fasten off.

To make a scallop edging
Next round 3ch to count as first sc and 1ch sp, skip first 2sc, 1sc into each of the next 3sc, *1ch, skip 1sc, 1sc into each of next 3sc, rep from * to last 2sc, 1sc into each of last 2sc. Join with sl st to second of first 3ch.
Next round Into each 1ch sp work (1sc, 3dc, 1sc). Join with sl st to first sc. Fasten off.

Using circles to make a clown
This toy is made up of circles in various sizes. Odds and ends of Knitting Worsted in red, yellow, orange and black and size G crochet hook are used. For the main part, make a total of 95 circles by working the first and second rounds of the circle motif. The black cuffs and ankle ruffles have the third round added, while the neck ruffle has the fourth round worked and the skirt has an additional fifth round. Make 2 small black circles for each hand and foot, joining each pair of circles and stuffing them with cotton batting. For the head work 3 rounds of the circle motif and include a circle of stiff cardboard with the stuffing.
Thread elastic through the center of each circle and join them together in this way: each arm consists of 17 small circles and a cuff which is inserted 1 circle before the hand; the body has 11 circles plus the skirt, and the legs have 25 circles each plus a ruffle which again is inserted 1 circle before the foot.

Straw belt
Size
To fit 23[25:27]in waist
(Each motif measures 2¼in in diameter)
Figures in [ ] refer to 25 and 27in sizes respectively

Materials
3[3:4] hanks of straw in 1 color or in odds and ends of different colors
1 size F crochet hook

Belt
With size F hook and any color work first 3 rounds as for the circular motif.
Join next color and work 2 more rounds as for the circular motif. Fasten off.
Make 9[10:11] more motifs in the same way.

Finishing
Join motifs tog where edges touch to form one row. Make 3 separate ch, each to measure 48[50:52]in long. Working on wrong side, stitch one ch across the back of top

WORKING WITH SQUARES

To work a square in crochet

Either make this square entirely in one color or use a different color for each round.

Using size H crochet hook and Knitting Worsted, make 6ch. Join to form a ring with a sl st into the first ch.

1st round 6ch, work (1dc and 3ch) 7 times into the ring. Join with a sl st to the 3rd of the first 6ch.

2nd round Sl st into the first 2ch space, so that the next group of dc will be worked into a space and not into a stitch, work 3ch to count as the first dc, 3dc into this same space, (2ch and 4dc into the next space) 7 times, 2ch. Join with a sl st to the 3rd of the first 3ch.

3rd round Sl st into each of next 4 stitches to insure that the next group of dc's will be worked into a 2ch space, 3ch, 5dc into this same space, 1ch, (6dc and 3ch into next space, 6dc and 1ch into next space) 3 times, 6dc into next space, 3ch. Join with a sl st to the 3rd of the first 3ch.

4th round Sl st into each of next 6 stitches to insure that the hook is over the next 1ch space, 4ch, (1sc into space between the 3rd and 4th dc of next 6dc group, 3ch, 2dc, 3ch, 2dc all into next space, 3ch, 1sc into space between 3rd and 4th dc of next 6dc group, 3ch, 1sc into next 1ch space, 3ch) 3 times, 1sc into space between 3rd and 4th dc of next 6dc group, 3ch, 2dc, 3ch, 2dc all into next 3ch space, 3ch, 1sc into space

between 3rd and 4th dc of next 6dc group, 3ch. Join with a sl st to 2nd of the first 4ch. Fasten off.

Granny squares using 2 or more colors

(Breaking off yarn at end of each round.) Make starting ch and work first round as for motif in one color. Break off yarn and fasten off.

2nd round Join next color to any 2ch sp with a sl st, 3ch to count as first dc, work 2dc into same ch sp, *1ch, work (3dc, 2ch, 3dc) into next 2ch sp to form corner, rep from * twice more, 1ch, 3dc into same 2ch sp, as at beginning of round, 2ch. Join with a sl st to third of first 3ch. Break off yarn and fasten off.

3rd round Join next color to any 2ch sp with a sl st, 3ch to count as first dc, work 2dc into same ch sp, *1ch, 3dc into 1ch sp, 1ch, work (3dc, 2ch, 3dc) into 2ch sp, rep from * twice more, 1ch, 3dc into 1ch sp, 1ch, 3dc into same 2ch sp as at beginning of round, 2ch. Join with a sl st to third of first 3ch. Break off yarn and fasten off.

4th round Join next color to any 2ch sp with a sl st, 3ch to count as first dc, work 2dc into same ch sp, *(1ch, 3dc into next 1ch sp) twice, 1ch, work (3dc, 2ch, 3dc) into 2ch sp, rep from * twice more, (1ch, 3dc into next 1ch sp) twice, 1ch, 3dc into same 2ch sp as at beginning of round, 2ch. Join with a sl st to third of first 3ch. Break off yarn and fasten off. Darn in ends of yarn where colors were joined.

To make a half-square

Using one or more colors Each row must be started with a fresh strand of yarn at the same side at which the row was first started.

Make 5ch. Join with sl st to first ch to form a ring.

1st row Using same color, 4ch to count as first dc and 1ch sp, work (3dc, 2ch, 3dc) into a ring, 1ch, 1dc into a ring. Fasten off.

2nd row Join next color to third of first 4ch with sl st, 4ch, 3dc into first 1ch sp, 1ch, work (3dc, 2ch, 3dc) into 2ch sp, 1ch, 3dc into last 1ch sp, 1ch, 1dc into top of last dc on previous row. Fasten off.

3rd row Join next color to third of first 4ch with sl st, 4ch, 3dc into first 1ch sp, 1ch, 3dc into next 1ch sp, 1ch, work (3dc, 2ch, 3dc) into 2ch sp, (1ch, 3dc into next 1ch sp) twice, 1ch, 1dc into top of last dc on previous row. Fasten off.

4th row Join next color to third of first 4ch with sl st, 4ch, 3dc into first 1ch sp, 1ch, (3dc into next 1ch sp, 1ch) twice, work (3dc, 2ch, 3dc) into 2ch sp, (1ch, 3dc into next 1ch sp) 3 times, 1ch, 1dc into last dc. Fasten off.

Square pillow

A pillow 16in square

Materials

8¾oz of Knitting Worsted in one color; 1¾oz in each of 7 contrasting colors, A, B, C, D, E, F and G.
One size H crochet hook
Pillow pad 16in square
8in zipper

Large square

Using size H crochet hook and any color, work first 4 rounds as for square motif, changing color on each round.

5th round Join in any color with sl st to corner 2ch sp, 3ch to count as first dc, 2dc into same sp, *(1ch, 3dc into next 1ch sp) 3 times, 1ch, (3dc, 2ch, 3dc) into corner 2ch sp, rep from * twice more, (1ch, 3dc into next 1ch sp) 3 times, 1ch, 3dc into same sp as beg of round, 2ch. Join with sl st to third of first 3ch. Fasten off.

Cont in this way, changing the color as shown, and working one more group of 3dc and 1ch on each side of every round until work measures 16in across. Fasten off. Darn in all ends. Make another square in the same manner

Finishing

With RS of squares tog, join 3 edges.

Turn RS out. Insert pillow pad. Join rem seam, leaving sp to insert zipper in center.

Edging Using size H hook and any color, rejoin yarn with sl st to any corner sp through both thicknesses. Into each ch sp round all edges work (1 sl st, 4dc, 1 sl st) working through both thicknesses, except across the zipper opening, where you work through only one thickness. Join with sl st to first sl st. Fasten off. Sew in zipper.

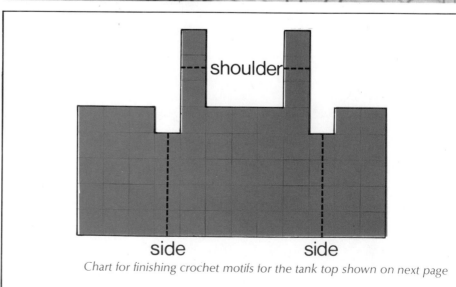

Chart for finishing crochet motifs for the tank top shown on next page

Tank top

Sizes

34[36/38 :39/40]in bust
Length to shoulder 19½[21:22½]in
The figures in brackets [ ] refer to 36/38 and 39/40in bust respectively.

Gauge

One square motif for first size measures 3in × 3in worked with size C hook; for second size measures 3¼in × 3¼in worked with size D hook; for third size measures 3½ × 3½in worked with size E hook.

Materials

Brunswick Fore'n Aft Sport Yarn
3[4:4] × 2oz balls in main color, A
3[4:4] balls of contrast color, B
One size C[D:E] crochet hook 8in zipper

1st square motif (make 10)
Using size C[D:E] hook and B, make 4ch. Join with a sl st into first ch to form a ring.
1st round 3ch to count as first dc, 2dc into ring, *1ch, 3dc into ring, rep from * twice more, 1ch. Join with a sl st into 3rd of 3ch.
2nd round Sl st into next ch sp, 3ch to count as first dc, 2dc into same sp, 1ch, 3dc into same sp, *1ch, into next ch sp work 3dc, 1ch and 3dc, rep from * twice more, 1ch. Join with a sl st into 3rd of 3ch. Break off B.
3rd round Join in A. Sl st into next ch sp, 3ch to count as first dc, 3dc into same sp, 1ch, 4dc into same sp, 1sc into next ch sp, *into next ch sp work 4dc, 1ch and 4dc, 1sc into next ch sp, rep from * twice more. Join with a sl st into 3rd of 3ch.
4th round Sl st into next ch sp, 3ch to count as first dc, 2dc into same sp, 1ch, 3dc into same sp, into next ch sp 2 rounds below work 3tr, 1ch and 3tr, *into next ch sp of previous round work 3dc, 1ch 3dc, into next ch sp 2 rounds below work 3tr, 1ch and 3tr, rep from * twice more. Join with a sl st to 3rd of 3ch. Fasten off.

2nd square motif (make 10)
As 1st square motif in color sequence of 2 rounds A and 2 rounds B.

3rd square motif (make 11)
As 1st square motif in color sequence of 1 round B, 2 rounds A and 1 round B.

4th square motif (make 10)
As 1st square motif in color sequence of 1 round B, 1 round A, 1 round B and 1 round A.

5th square motif (make 11)
As 1st square motif in color sequence of 1 round A, 2 rounds B and 1 round A.

6th square motif (make 12)
As 1st square motif in color sequence of 1 round A, 1 round B, 1 round A and 1 round B.
There are now 64 square motifs in all.

Finishing

Block each square under a damp cloth with a warm iron. Using A, join squares as shown opposite, making a patchwork with the different color combinations.
Edging Using size C[D:E] hook and A, work 1 row sc around each armhole, neck and around shoulder edges and lower edge. Block seams.

A bright bag made of Granny squares

Chart for finishing bag

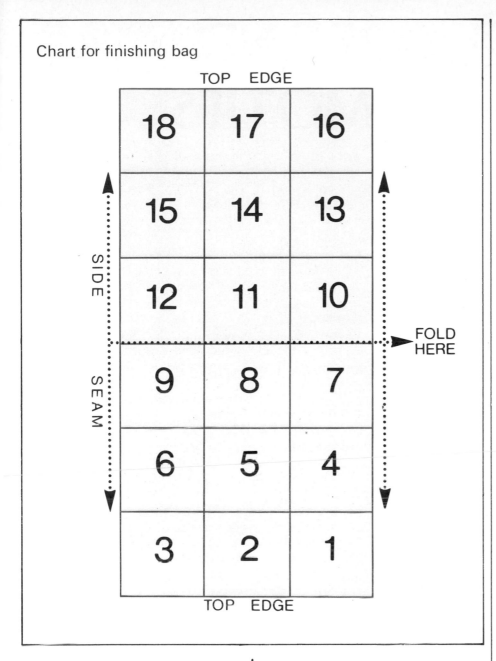

TOP EDGE

18	17	16
15	14	13
12	11	10
9	8	7
6	5	4
3	2	1

SIDE SEAM

FOLD HERE

TOP EDGE

5th round Using C, 1ch, *4ch, . sp work (3dc, 3ch, 3dc) to form c. 4ch, 1sc into hdc, 1sc into 3ch sp, 1sc into hdc, rep from * twice more, 4ch, work corner, 4ch, 1sc into hdc, 1sc into 3ch sp. Join with a sl st to first ch. Break off C. Join in D.

6th round Using D, 1ch, *5ch, 1dc into each of next 3dc, 5ch, insert hook into 3rd ch from hook and work 1dc to form a picot – called 5ch picot –, 2ch, 1dc into each of next 3dc, 5ch, sl st into next sc, 4ch, insert hook into 3rd ch from hook and work 1sc to form picot – called 4ch picot –, 1ch, skip 1sc, sl st into next sc, rep from * twice more, 5ch, 1dc into each of next 3dc, 5ch picot, 2ch, 1dc into each of next 3dc, 5ch sl st into next sc, 4ch picot, 1ch. Join with a sl st to first ch. Fasten off.

Second motif
Using colors as desired, work as given for 1st motif until 5th round has been completed.

6th round (joining) Using any color, 1ch, *5ch, 1dc into each of next 3dc, 2ch, with RS of 1st motif facing RS of 2nd motif, work 1sc into 5ch picot at corner of 1st motif, 2ch, 1dc into each of next 3dc of 2nd motif, sl st into first of 5ch after last dc on 1st motif, 4ch, sl st into next sc of 2nd motif, 1ch, 1sc into 4ch picot of 1st motif, 1ch, skip 1sc on 2nd motif, sl st into next sc on 2nd motif, 4ch, sl st into last ch before next 3dc on 1st motif, 1dc into each of next 3dc on 2nd motif, 2ch, 1sc into 5ch picot at corner of 1st motif, 2ch, then complete round as given for 1st motif.
Work 16 more motifs in same way, using colors as desired and joining each motif where edges touch, as shown on chart.

Finishing
Darn in all ends. Press on WS under a dry cloth with a cool iron.

Top edges Using size I hook, A and with RS of work facing, rejoin yarn to corner picot at end of motif, 3ch to count as first dc, work 14 more dc evenly across first motif, work (15dc across next motif) twice. Turn. 45dc. Work 2 more rows dc. Fasten off. Work along other end in same way.
With RS facing fold motifs in half and join side seams as shown on chart. Seam lining in same way. Turn bag RS out and insert loose lining. Fold top edge over handle to WS and sew in place. Work other handle in same way. Sew top of lining to WS of top edge, easing in fullness. Sew lining to side edges of opening.

Size
18in wide by 18in deep

Gauge
Each motif measures 6in × 6in worked with size I crochet hook

Materials
6 ounces Knitting Worsted in main color, A
1 ounce each of 5 contrast colors, B, C, D, E and F
One size I crochet hook
2 round wooden handles
Lining material 18in wide × 36in long

First motif
Using size I hook and A, make 6ch. Join with a sl st to first ch to form a ring.
1st round Using A, 2ch to count as first sc, work 15sc into ring. Join with a sl st to 2nd of first 2ch.
2nd round Using A, 5ch to count as first hdc and 3ch, *skip 1sc, 1hdc into next sc, 3ch, rep from * 6 times more. Join with a sl st to 2nd of first 5ch. Break off A. Join in B.
3rd round Using B, work (1sc, 1hdc, 1dc, 1hdc, 1sc, 1ch) into each ch sp to end. Join with a sl st to first sc. 8 petals. Break off B. Join in C.
4th round Using C, 2ch to count as first hdc, *3ch, 1sc into dc of next petal, 4ch, 1sc into dc of next petal, 3ch, 1hdc into 1ch sp before next petal, 3ch, 1hdc into same ch sp, rep from * twice more, 3ch, 1sc in dc of next petal, 4ch, 1sc in dc of next petal, 3ch, 1hdc into last 1ch sp after last petal, 3ch. Join with a sl st to 2nd of first 2ch.

SQUARE AND WHEEL MOTIFS

The simple stitches you have learned can be used for all kinds of motifs, including these two completely different lacy ones. The motifs can be worked in fine or thick yarns, depending on the project in work or on personal choice.

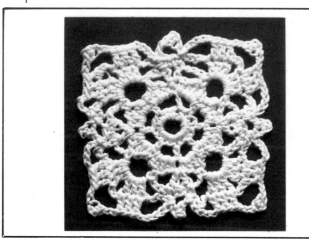

Square lace motif

Make 6ch. Join with sl st to first ch to form a ring.

1st round 2ch to count as first sc, work 15sc into ring. Join with sl st to second of first 2ch.

2nd round 4ch to count as first hdc and 2ch, *skip 1sc, 1hdc into next sc, 2ch, rep from * 6 times more. Join with sl st to second of first 4ch.

3rd round Work (1sc, 1hdc, 1dc, 1hdc, 1ch) into each ch sp to end. Join with sl st to first sc. 8 petals.

4th round 2ch to count as first hdc, *3sc, 1sc into dc of next petal, 4ch, 1sc into dc of next petal, 3ch, 1hdc into 1ch sp before next petal, 2ch, 1hdc into same ch sp, rep from * twice more, 3ch, 1sc into dc of next petal, 4ch, 1sc into dc of next petal, 3ch, 1hdc into last 1ch sp after last petal, 2ch. Join with sl st to second of first 2ch.

5th round 1ch, *4ch, into 4ch sp, work (3dc, 3ch, 3dc) to form corner, 4ch, 1sc into hdc, 1sc into 2ch sp, 1sc into hdc, rep from * twice more, 4ch, into 4ch sp work (3dc, 3ch, 3dc), 4ch, 1sc into hdc, 1sc into 2ch sp. Join with sl st to first ch.

6th round 1c, *5ch, 1dc into each of next 3dc, 5ch, insert hook into third ch from hook to form a loop (see diagram) and work 1sc to form picot – called 5ch picot – 2ch, 1dc into each of next 3dc, 5ch, sl st into next sc, 4ch, insert hook into third ch from hook and work 1sc to form picot – called 4ch picot – 1ch, skip 1sc, sl st into next sc, rep from * twice more, 5ch, 1dc into each of next 3dc, 5ch picot, 2ch, 1dc into each of next 3dc, 5ch, sl st into next sc, 4ch picot, 1ch. Join in with sl st to first ch. Fasten off.

Catherine wheel motif

Make 8ch. Join with sl st to first ch to form a ring.

1st round 1ch to count as first sc, work 15sc into a ring. Join with sl st to first ch. 16 sts. Do not break off yarn.

First spoke

1st row Make 14ch, work 1sc into third ch from hook, 1sc into next ch, work 10sc around the chain, 1sc into each of last 3ch, sl st into next sc along the ring, turn.

2nd row Work 1sc into each of first 3sc, (4ch, skip 1sc, 1sc into next sc) 5 times, 1sc into each of next 2sc, 1sc into second of first 2ch. Turn.

3rd row 1ch to count as first sc, 1sc into each of next 3sc, (4sc into 4ch loop, 1sc into next sc) 5 times, 1sc into each of last 2sc, sl st into next sc. Turn.

Second spoke

1st row Make 13ch, sl st into center st of third loop along first spoke, turn, work 1sc into each of next 3ch, work 10sc along the ch, 1sc into each of last 3ch, sl st into next sc, turn and complete as for first spoke, but on next row end with 1sc into each of last 3sc instead of last 2sc and turning ch.

Work 6 more spokes in the same way and when working the last one, join the center of the 3rd loop to the tip of the first spoke. Fasten off. 8 spokes.

Last round Rejoin yarn with sl st to top of any spoke. 1ch to count as first sc, work 1sc into each st around outside edge of motif. Join with sl st to first ch. Fasten off.

Forming a picot loop

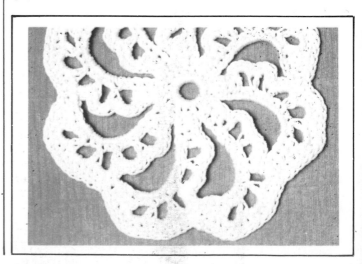

Cafe curtains
Size
55in wide × 55in long, excluding tabs.
Each motif measures 5in in diameter

Materials
9 × 100yd balls of Speed-Cro-Sheen in
main color, A, 10 balls of contrast color,
B, 9 balls of contrast color, C and 7 balls
each of contrast colors, D and E
1 ball makes 2 motifs

One steel crochet hook No.0
Length of wooden curtain rod

Curtain
Make 22 Catherine wheel motifs in A, 20
in B, 18 in C, 14 in D and 13 in E.

Finishing
Join motifs tog as shown in illustration
on opposite page.
Tabs Using size 0 hook, over color and

with RS of first top motif facing, rejoin
yarn with sl st to fifth sc along edge,
3ch to count as first dc, work 1dc into
each of next 5sc, turn. 6 sts. Cont
working rows of dc across these 6 sts
until tab is long enough to fit over top
of curtain rod and down to top of motif.
Fasten off.
Work 10 more tabs in same way. Sew
tabs in place to back of each motif, as
shown in illustration on opposite page.

Place mat and coaster
Size
Place mat 11¼in wide × 9in long and coaster 4½in square.
Each motif measures 2¼in square

Materials
300yd ball of No.20 mercerized cotton (1 ball makes approximately 36 motifs)
One steel crochet hook No.7.

Place mat
Work as given for square lace motif, joining 5 motifs to form one row and 4 rows in all, a total of 20 motifs.

Coaster
Work as given for square lace motif, joining 2 motifs to form one row and, 2 rows in all, a total of 4 motifs.

Below: Crochet place mat and coaster

To join square lace motifs
Work first 5 rounds as given on previous page.

6th round (joining round) 1ch, *5ch, 1dc into each of next 3dc, 2ch. With RS of completed motif A facing RS of motif B which is to be joined, work 1sc into 5ch picot at corner of motif A, 2ch, 1dc, into each of next 3dc of motif B, sl st into first of 5ch after last dc on motif A, 4ch, sl st into next sc of motif B, 1ch, 1sc into 4ch picot of motif A, 1ch, skip 1sc on motif B, sl st into next sc on motif B, 4ch, sl st into last ch before next 3dc on motif B, 2ch, 1sc into 4ch picot at corner of motif A, 2ch. One side has been joined. Complete around motif B as for square lace motif A. Fasten off.
Work in the same way where the squares have to be joined on two sides.

Above: Diagram to show how Catherine wheel motifs are joined for a café curtain

Catherine wheel motifs used in a circular tablecloth

USING COLOR
PATCHWORK EFFECTS

This chapter explains how to work crochet with various colors to form a patchwork effect. Several samples are shown and explained in detail to help you follow the methods involved in this technique. As with patchwork crochet using separate shapes (see later) it is best to use the same weight of yarn throughout the work to make sure that your fabric will have an even tension. Multicolored fabrics can be worked in straight lines, or in circles and other shapes in the same manner as solid colored crochet. The most popular stitch to give a good fabric is single crochet.

Sample 1

Two colors of Knitting Worsted, A and B, have been used to work this basic patchwork design which is formed from checked squares. The techniques covered in this sample show how to join in a new color and how to carry the color not in use along with the work.

To help you make this first sample, we are giving both written instructions and a chart.

Using size G hook and A, make a length of chain with multiples of 5 + 1 stitches.

Note: Practice the method of joining in a new color, given in the 1st row, since it is important that the new color is joined right into the stitch preceding the stitches to be worked with that new color. Further

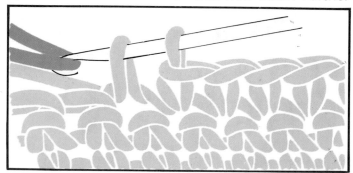

Joining in a new color in the middle of a row

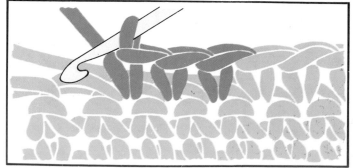

Working over the color which is not in use

instructions for joining in new colors will not be given in detail, and this method should be used throughout. The color not in use is held along the row of work and kept in place by the crochet stitch being worked over the yarn in order to avoid unnecessary or unattractive loops appearing on the work. It also insures that the work is completely reversible.

1st row Using color A, into 3rd ch from hook work 1sc, 1sc into each of next 2ch, insert hook into next ch, yo and draw through a loop, yo with color B and draw through both loops on hook, then using color B, work 1sc into each of next 5ch, using color A, work 1sc into each of next 5ch, cont in this way working 5 sts alternately in A and B to end of row. Turn.

2nd row Using same color as last 5sc of previous row and working new color over color not used on that row, work 1ch to count as first sc, 1sc into each of next 4sc, change color, 1sc into each of next 5sc, cont in this way to end of row, working last sc into turning ch. Turn.

3rd to 5th rows As 2nd.

6th to 10th rows As 2nd, working a square of color A over color B and a square of color B over color A. The 1st through 10th rows form the color sequence for this sample. When you have completed this piece you will see how your work compares with the photograph above and you will then be able to make up your own designs with this technique.

Sample 2

Here we have used the same techniques as explained in sample 1, but a much more varied effect has been achieved with the use of three colors and random shapes. As there is no definite pattern of colors, odd pieces of yarn can quite easily be used. A further technique is employed here, where the yarn not in use is left on the wrong side of the work, ready for taking into the work again on the next row. This method is used when a colored yarn is being used on one block only. Remember that if a color of yarn which is already in use is needed further along the row, then this yarn must be carried along the row until needed. Using size G hook and 3 colors of Knitting Worsted make 24ch. Work in single crochet and follow the chart to make our sample.

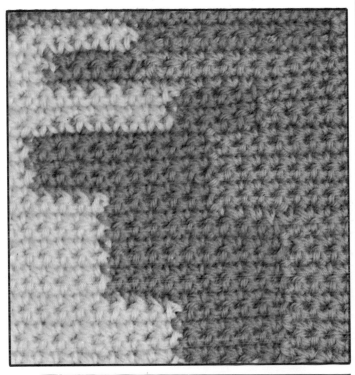

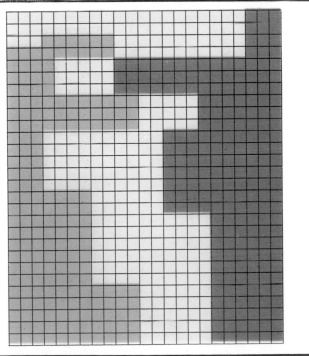

Sample 3

This is a lovely patchwork fabric made up of traditional church window shapes worked in many different colors. The effect of these colors and shapes is very interesting when they are made into such garments as long skirts, jackets or tank tops. Household items such as pillow covers and afghans also look very attractive when they are worked in this way.

As so many colors are used it is a good idea to work a single church window shape to estimate how much yarn is required for each individual shape. Then, when you are deciding on your colors, wind each one into a ball of the correct length.

Using size G hook and Knitting Worsted, make a chain with multiples of 8 + 1 stitches and follow our diagram, changing color for each shape. There is no need to work over the color not in use. This should be left behind the work until the next row where it is needed. When a shape in one color is finished, leave the end of yarn hanging free and darn in all ends on the wrong side of the work for a neat finish when the work is completed.

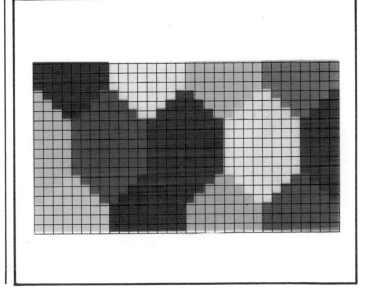

COLOR DESIGNS

Here we continue with our chapters on the use of different colored yarns within a single piece of crochet work, showing how rows of color can be incorporated into a design. This type of design would be ideal for border patterns on a plain piece of work such as a scarf, skirt or bedspread. In some of the samples shown here the lines of color are raised from the background by applying a technique known as blistering, which is described in detail.

Sample 1

This is a double sided fabric, worked in two colors of Knitting Worsted, A and B. Using size G hook and A, make 21ch.

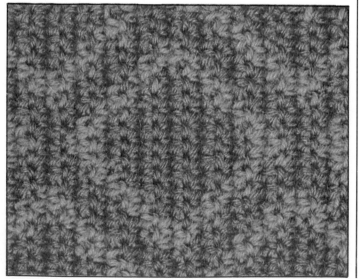

1st row Into 3rd ch from hook work 1sc, 1sc into next ch, join in B as shown in previous chapter, using B and working over A, also see previous chapter, work 1sc into each of next 2ch, using A and working over B work 1sc into each of next 10ch, using B and working over A work 1sc into each of next 2ch, using A and working over B work 1sc into each of next 3ch. Turn. Continue in this way, working in pattern from the chart.

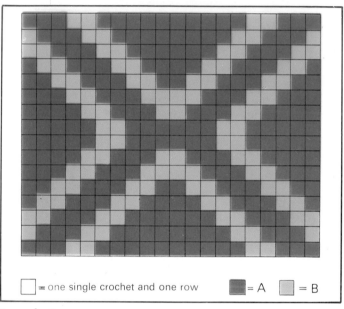

☐ = one single crochet and one row   ■ = A   ☐ = B

Sample 2

Here two colors of Knitting Worsted A and B, have been used to give a raised, or blistered, effect to the work. When working individual narrow rows of color which follow through a design, it is not always necessary to carry the yarn not in use in with the work. Just leave this yarn behind the work ready to be worked into the crochet on the next row. There is a definite right and wrong side to the work when this technique is used. Using size E hook and A, make 21ch.

1st row Into 3rd ch from hook work 1sc, 1sc into each of next 5ch, join in B as shown in previous chapter, leaving A free on WS of work. Using B work 1sc into each of next 6ch joining in A on the last st, pull A taut to form a blister. Using A work 1sc into each of next 7ch. Turn.

2nd row Using A work 1ch to count as first sc, skip first st, 1sc into each of next 6sc joining in B on the last st and keeping A towards you while you work, work 1sc into each of next 6sc using B and joining in A on the last st worked. Leave B on WS of work (towards you) and pull A taut to form a blister. Using A work 1sc into each of next 7sc. Turn.

3rd row Using A work 1ch to count as first sc, skip

first st, 1sc into each of next 6sc joining in B on the last st. Leave A on WS of work (away from you), work 1sc into each of next 6sc using B and joining in A on the last st. Leave B on WS of work and pull A taut to form a blister. Using A work 1sc into each of next 7sc. Turn.

The 2nd and 3rd rows are repeated throughout.

Sample 3

In this sample both the techniques of working over the yarn not in use or leaving it free at the back of the work are used. The background color, A, is carried throughout, while the other colors in the design, B, C and D, are left free at the back of the work when not in use. Using size E hook and A, make 17ch.

1st row Join in color B as shown in previous chapter. Using B work 1sc into 3rd ch from hook, 1sc into each of next 2ch working over A, using A work 1sc into each of next 2ch, using C work 1sc into each of next

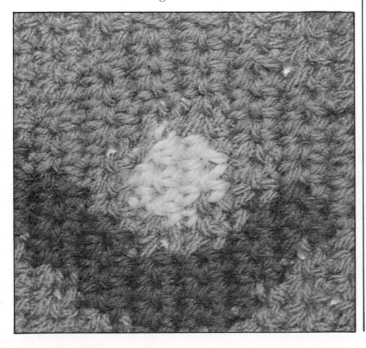

2ch, using A work 1sc into each of next 2ch, using D work 1sc into each of next 4ch, using A work 1sc into next ch. Turn.

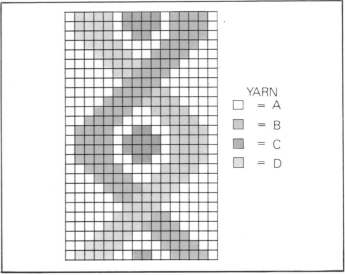

YARN

☐ = A

▨ = B

▩ = C

▨ = D

2nd row Using A, work 1ch to count as first sc, skip first st, 1sc into next sc, using D work 1sc into each of next 4sc, using A work 1sc into each of next 4sc, using B work 1sc into each of next 4sc, using A work 1sc into each of next 2sc. Turn.

Continue working in this way following the chart, noting that yarn C covers only a small area of color so that the yarn may be cut after each motif is finished to avoid unnecessary strands hanging behind the work.

Sample 4

Our belt has been worked in 3 colors of Knitting Worsted, using a size E hook. Follow the chart given for sample 3, omitting color C, and form a blistered or raised effect on the crossover lines by applying the technique used in sample 2, and keeping A taut while it is not in use. A large bead has been added as trim in the center of each diamond.

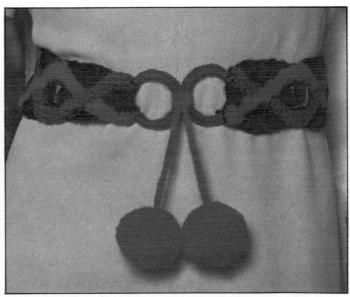

A hat of many colors

Size
To fit an average head

Gauge
12 hdc and 9 rows to 2in in patt worked with size E crochet hook

Materials
1 × one oz ball 3-ply fingering yarn in each of 5 colors, A, B, C, D and E
One size E crochet hook

Note
When using two different colored yarns in the same round, always work over the color not in use and, when changing color, draw the new color through all the loops on the hook of the last st in the old color.

Hat
Using size E hook and A, make 6ch. Join with a sl st to first ch to form a ring.

1st round Using A, 2ch to count as first hdc, 7hdc into ring. Join with a sl st into 2nd of 2ch. 8hdc. Break off A.

2nd round Using B, 2ch to count as first hdc, 1hdc into st at base of ch, *2hdc into next hdc, rep from * to end. Join with a sl st into 2nd of 2ch. 16hdc.

3rd round Working 4 sts each of B and C around, work 2ch to count as first hdc, 2hdc into next hdc, *1hdc into next hdc, 2hdc into next hdc, rep from * to end. Join with a sl st into 2nd of 2ch. 24hdc. Break off B and C.

4th round Using D, 2ch, 1hdc into next hdc, 2hdc into next hdc, *1hdc into each of next 2hdc, 2hdc into next hdc, rep from * to end. Join with a sl st into 2nd of 2ch. 32hdc.

5th round Using 5 sts each of D and E around, work 2ch, 1hdc into each of next 2hdc, 2hdc into next hdc, *1hdc into each of next 3hdc, 2hdc into next hdc, rep from * to end. Join with a sl st into 2nd of 2ch. 40hdc. Break off E.

6th round Using D, 2ch, 1hdc into each of next 3hdc, 2hdc into next hdc, *1hdc into each of next 4hdc, 2hdc into next hdc, rep

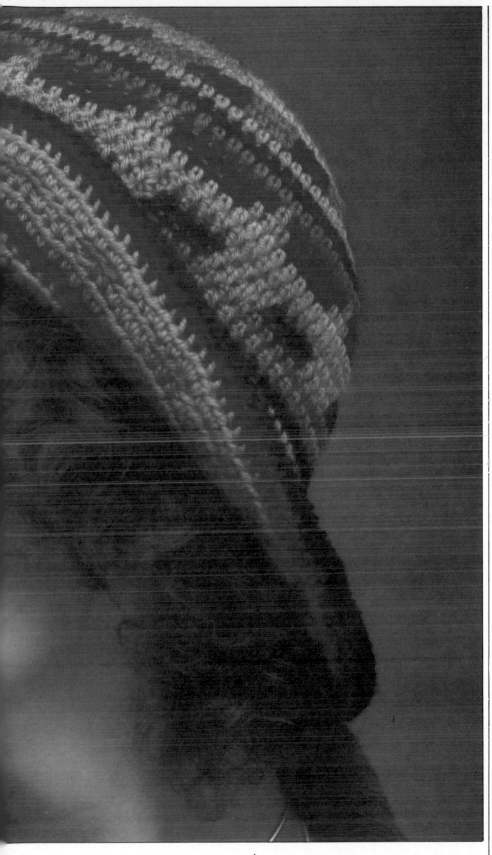

into each of next 7 hdc, 2hdc into next hdc, rep from * to end. Join with a sl st into 2nd of 2ch. 72hdc. Break off A.

10th round Using E, 2ch, 1hdc into each of next 7 hdc, 2hdc into next hdc, *1hdc into each of next 8 hdc, 2hdc into next hdc, rep from * to end. Join with a sl st into 2nd of 2ch. 80hdc. Break off E.

11th round Using 4 sts each of B and D all around, 2ch, 1hdc into each of next 8 hdc, 2hdc into next hdc, *1hdc into each of next 9 hdc, 2hdc into next hdc, rep from * to end. Join with a sl st into 2nd of 2ch. 88hdc.

12th round Using 4 sts each of B and D and working into same colors as on previous round, 2ch, 1hdc into each hdc to end. Join with a sl st into 2nd of 2ch. Break off B and D.

13th round Using E, as 12th. Break off E.

14th round Using C, as 12th. Break off C.

15th round Using B, as 12th. Break off B.

16th round Using one st of A and 7 sts of D all around, as 12th.

17th round Using 3 sts of A and 5 sts of D all round, as 12th. Break off A and D.

18th round Using E, as 12th. Break off E.

19th round Using A, as 12th.

20th round Using 4 sts of A and 4 sts of C all round, as 12th.

21st round As 20th. Break off A and C.

22nd round Using B, as 12th. Break off B.

23rd round Using A, as 12th.

24th round Using C, as 12th.

25th round Using 3 sts of B and 5 sts of F all around, as 12th. Break off B and E.

26th round Using D, as 12th.

27th round As 26th.

Shape brim

28th round Using E, 2ch, 2hdc into next hdc, *1hdc into next hdc, 2hdc into next hdc, rep from * to end. Join with a sl st into 2nd of 2ch. 132hdc. Break off E.

29th round Using B, as 12th. Break off B.

30th round Using C, as 12th. Break off C.

31st round Using 8 sts of A and 4 sts of E all round, as 12th. Break off A and E.

32nd round Using D, 2ch, 1hdc into each of next 4 hdc, 2hdc into next hdc, *1hdc into each of next 5 hdc, 2hdc into next hdc, rep from * to end. Join with a sl st into 2nd of 2ch. 154hdc. Break off D.

33rd round Using A, as 12th.

34th round Using 4 sts of A and 3 sts of B all around, as 12th. Break off A and B.

35th round Using E, 2ch, 1hdc into each of next 5 hdc, 2hdc into next hdc, *1hdc into each of next 6 hdc, 2hdc into next hdc, rep from * to end. Join with a sl st into 2nd of 2ch. 176hdc. Break off E.

36th round Using D, as 12th. Break off D.

37th round Using C and working from left to right (in a backwards direction), work 1sc into each hdc to end. Join with a sl st into first sc. Fasten off.

from * to end. Join with a sl st into 2ch. 48hdc. Break off D.

7th round Using C, 2ch, 1hdc into each of next 4 hdc, 2hdc into next hdc, *1hdc into each of next 5 hdc, 2hdc into next hdc, rep from * to end. Join with a sl st into 2nd of 2ch. 56hdc. Break off C.

8th round Using A, 2ch, 1hdc into each of next 5 hdc, 2hdc into next hdc, *1hdc into each of next 6 hdc, 2hdc into next hdc, rep from * to end. Join with a sl st into 2nd of 2ch. 64hdc.

9th round Using A, 2ch, 1hdc into each of next 6 hdc, 2hdc into next hdc, *1hdc

PATCHWORK CROCHET

Patchwork crochet

Traditionally we think of patchwork as a means of using odds and ends of fabric to make a quilt or piece of clothing. Today there is a great revival of interest in the art, and fabrics are carefully selected and co-ordinated to create colorful and exciting designs.

The same designs may be worked in crochet too, again working with odd pieces of yarn to use up scraps, or choosing a selection of colors to produce a desired effect. A pleasing choice of colors is an important part of patchwork, for this really makes a design. Closely related colors are usually a satisfactory choice, so that if you choose red, you can use all the various shades of red from deep ruby to oranges and yellows. Our samples have been worked in blues and greens to illustrate a variation of the same grading of colors. Patchwork crochet can be used in many ways for both fashion items and household accessories such as quilts, pillow covers, afghans, wall hangings and room dividers. The most suitable fashion items are ones which require little or no shaping, such as straight skirts, jerkins and belts.

In order to achieve a high standard of work, it is necessary to use the same weight of yarn throughout, although to add interest they may be of different textures. As the yarn should be of one weight, then the same size crochet hook should also be used for each. Firm, even stitches, such as single crochet or half doubles, should be used. These will help to give body to the shape.

The shapes described in this chapter are all geometric and include the square, rectangle, diamond, triangle and hexagon. They are all worked in a Knitting Worsted using a size G crochet hook.

To join the separate shapes, place the right sides together and sew them with a firm overcast stitch in the same yarn. The seam should be blocked on the wrong side under a damp cloth with a warm iron as part of the finishing. Where there is more than one color used in the same shape, such as samples 5 and 6, these are fitted into the work as desired.

Sample 1

To work the diamond shape Make 3ch.

1st row Into 3rd ch from hook work 1sc. Turn. 2 sts.

2nd row 1ch to count as first st, 1sc into st at base of ch, 1sc into turning ch. Turn. One st increased.

3rd row 1ch to count as first st, 1sc into st at base of ch, 1sc into next st, 1sc into turning ch. Turn. One st increased.

Cont in this way, inc one st at beg of every row, until there are 20 sts.

Next row 1ch to count as first st, skip next st, 1sc into next st, 1sc into each st to end, ending with 1sc into turning ch. Turn. One st decreased.

Cont in this way, dec one st at beg of every row, until 2 sts rem. Fasten off.

Sample 2

To work the church window shape Work as for sample 1, but when the required size or width is reached (20 sts, for example), work 14 rows without shaping. Then work the decrease shaping as before.

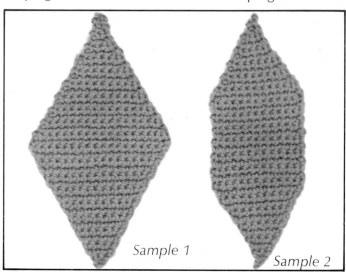

Sample 1   *Sample 2*

Sample 3

To work the triangle Make 3ch.

1st row Into 3rd ch from hook work 1hdc. Turn. 2 sts.

2nd row 2ch to count as first hdc, 1hdc into st at base of ch, 2hdc into 2nd of 2ch. Turn. 2 sts increased.

3rd row 2ch to count as first hdc, 1hdc into st at base of ch, 1hdc into each of next 2 sts, 2hdc into 2nd of 2ch. Turn. 2 sts increased.

Cont in this way, inc one st at each end of every row, until there are 24 sts or the triangle is the desired size. Fasten off.

Sample 4

To work the hexagon Make 5ch. Join with a sl st into first ch to form a ring.

1st round 4ch, *1dc into ring, 1ch, rep from * 10 times more. Join with a sl st into 3rd of 4ch.

2nd round 3ch to count as first dc, 2dc into next 1ch sp, 1dc into next dc, 1ch, *1dc into next dc, 2dc into next 1ch sp, 1dc into next dc, 1ch, rep from * 4 times more. Join with a sl st into 3rd of 3ch.

3rd round 3ch to count as first dc, 1dc into st at base of ch, 1dc into each of next 2dc, 2dc into next dc, 2ch,

*2dc into next dc, 1dc into each of next 2dc, 2dc into next dc, 2ch, rep from * 4 times more. Join with a sl st into 3rd of 3ch. Fasten off.
This completes the sample illustrated, but a smaller or larger shape can be made by working in the same way, inc one st at each end of every block of dc and one ch between blocks on every round, until the shape is the desired size.

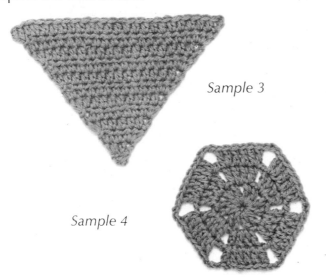

Sample 3

Sample 4

Sample 5

Four colors, A, B, C and D, are used for this sample square. Note the effect of the colors when four squares are joined together. Using A, make 17ch.
1st row Into 3rd ch from hook work 1sc, 1sc into each ch to end. Turn. 16 sts.
2nd row 1ch to count as first sc, 1sc into each sc to end, ending with 1sc into turning ch. Turn.
Rep last row twice more. Break off A. Join in B.

Note: Care should be taken when joining in a new color. It is better to work 2 turning chains instead of 1 and then pull up the old color tightly. Work 4 rows in sc with each of B, C and D. Fasten off. Sew or weave in the cut ends. Place squares to give the desired pattern and sew together.

Sample 6

Here four triangular shapes, as in sample 3, have been worked with four colors shown in each, and then joined together.
Work 2 triangles with 4 rows each in A, B, C and D, and then 2 more triangles using the color sequence of D, C, B and A. Arrange with alternate colors meeting and then sew them together. Finish the cut ends by weaving them back into the work on the wrong side.

Sample 7

This sample is made up of brick shapes. There are 16 in all, 4 in each color.
To work the brick shape Make 11ch.
1st row Into 3rd ch from hook work 1sc, 1sc into each ch to end. Turn. 10 sts.
2nd row 1ch to count as first sc, 1sc into each sc to end, ending with 1sc into turning ch. Turn.
Rep last row 3 times more. Fasten off.
Work the desired number of bricks in each color and place them carefully in rows of one color before sewing into place. When finished, sew or weave in all the cut ends on the wrong side of the work.

A patchwork jacket

Sizes

Directions are to fit 34in bust. Changes for 36, 38 and 40in bust are in brackets [ ].
Length to shoulder, 27[27:30:30]in
Sleeve seam, 18[18:20:20]in

Gauge

18 sts and 9 rows to 4in in dc worked with size E crochet hook

Materials

5[5:6:6] × 4oz balls Bucilla Knitting Worsted in main color, A 1[1:1:1] ball each of contrast colors, B, C and D 1[1:1:2] balls of contrast color, E
One size E crochet hook
26[26:28:28]in open ended zipper

Back

Using size E hook and A, make 82 [88:94:86]ch.
1st row Into 4th ch from hook work 1dc, 1dc into each ch to end. Turn. 80[86:92: 94]dc.
2nd row 3ch to count as first dc, skip first dc, 1dc into each dc to end.
Turn. Rep 2nd row 40[40:49:49] times more.
Shape raglan armholes
Next row Sl st across first 6[6:7:7]dc, 1dc into each dc to last 6[6:7:7]dc, turn.
Next row 3ch to count as first dc, yo insert hook into next dc, yo and draw through loop, yo and draw through 2 loops on hook, yo and insert hook into next dc, yo and draw through loop, yo and draw through 2 loops on hook, yo and draw through 3 loops on hook – called dec 1 –, 1dc into each dc to last 3dc, dec 1, 1dc into last dc.
Turn. Rep last row 19[19:21:21] times more.
Fasten off.

Sleeves

Using size E hook and A, make 40 [40:49:49]ch. Work 1st row as given for back. 38[38:47:47]dc.
1st and 2nd sizes only
Work 2 rows dc.
4th row 3ch, 2dc into next dc – called inc 1 –, 1dc into each dc to last 2dc, inc 1, 1dc into last dc.
Turn.
Work 2 rows dc without shaping. Cont inc in this way on next and every foll 3rd row until 34 rows have been worked from beg, then inc in same way on every foll 2nd row 5 times in all. 70[70]dc.
3rd and 4th sizes only
Work 4 rows dc. Inc as given for 1st and 2nd sizes on next and every foll 4th row until 21 rows have been worked, then inc in same way on every foll 3rd row

until there are 77[77]dc.
All sizes
Shape raglans
Next row Sl st across first 6[6:7:7]dc, 3ch, 1dc into each dc to last 6[6:7:7]dc, 3ch, 1dc into each dc to last 6[6:7:7]dc, turn.
Dec one st at each end of every row until 30[30:31:31]dc rem.
Next row 3ch, dec 1, 1dc into each of next 9dc, dec 1, 1dc into each of next 2[2:3:3]dc, dec 1, 1dc into each of next 9dc, dec 1, dc into last dc. Turn.
Next row 3ch, dec 1, 1dc into each of next 7dc, dec 1, 1dc into each of next 2[2:3:3]dc, dec 1, 1dc into each of next 7dc, dec 1, 1dc into last dc. Turn.
Cont dec in this way on next 4 rows. 6[6:7:7]dc.
Fasten off.

Left and right fronts

Work motifs for fronts, noting that colors may be varied as desired and should be twisted at back of work when being changed.
1st motif
Using A, make 16[16:18:18]ch.
1st row Into 4th ch from hook work 1dc, 1dc into each ch to end. Turn. 14[14:16:16] dc.
2nd row 3ch to count as first dc, skip 1dc, 1dc into each dc to end. Turn.
Rep 2nd row 5[5:6:6] more times.
Fasten off and sew or weave in ends.
Work 1 more motif in same way using A, then 2 motifs each in B, C, D and E. 10 motifs, 5 for each front.
2nd motif
Using A, work first 2 rows as given for 1st motif. Break off A. Join in E. Complete as given for 1st motif. Work 1 more motif in same way, then 2 more using D and C and 2 more using E and B. 6 motifs, 3 for each front.
3rd motif
Using B, make 7[7:8:8] ch, join in D and make 9[9:10:10] ch.
1st row Using D, into 4th ch from hook work 1dc, 1dc into each of next 5[5:6:6] ch working last 2 loops of last dc with B – called 1dcNc –, using B, work 1dc into each ch to end. Turn. 7[7:8:8]dc each in D and B.
2nd row Using B, 3ch to count as first dc, 1dc into each of next 6[6:7:7]dc, keeping B to front of work and D to back under hook to work 1dcNc with D in last dc, using D, work 1dc into each dc to end. Turn.
3rd row Using D, 3ch, work 1dc into each of next 6[6:7:7]dc, keeping yarn at back of work and working 1dcNc with B in last dc, using B, work 1dc into each dc to end. Turn.
Rep 2nd and 3rd rows twice more, then

2nd row 0[0:1:1] times more. Fasten off and sew or weave in ends. Work 1 more motif in same way, then 2 motifs using A and D and 2 using C and E. 6 motifs, 3 for each front.

4th motif

Using B and C, work first 3 rows as given for 3rd motif.

4th row Using B, 3ch, 1dc into each dc to end. Turn.

5th row Using B, 3ch, 1dc into each of next 6[6:7:7]dc, keeping yarn at back of work, join in C and work 1dcNc on last dc, 1dc into each dc to end. Turn.

6th row Using C, 3ch, 1dc into each of next 6[6:7:7]dc, keeping C to front of work and B back under hook, work 1dc Nc with B in last dc, 1dc into each dc to end. Turn.

7th row As 5th

Rep 6th row 0[0:1:1] times more. Fasten off and sew or weave in ends. Work 1 more motif.

5th motif

Using B, work first 3 rows as for 1st motif, joining in E and working 1dcNc in last dc. Break off B.

4th row Using E, 3ch, work 1dc into each of next 6[6:7:7]dc, join in C and work 1dcNc in last dc, 1dc into each dc to end. Turn.

5th row Using C, 3ch, work 1dc into each of next 6[6:7:7]dc, 1dcNc with C in last dc using E, 1dc into each dc to end. Turn. Rep 4th and 5th rows once more, then 4th row 0[0:1:1] times more. Fasten off and sew or weave in ends. Work 1 more motif in same way, then 2 more using C, E and D and 2 more using A, B and E. 6 motifs, 3 for each front.

6th motif

Using E, make 7[7:8:8] ch, join in D and make 9[9:10:10] ch.

1st row Using D, into 4th ch from hook work 1dc, 1dc into each of next 4[4:5:5] ch, keeping yarn at back of work join in C and work 1dcNc in last dc, using C, 1dc into each of next 2ch. Keeping yarn at back of work join in E and work 1dcNc in last dc, 1dc into each of next 6[6:7:7] ch. Turn.

2nd row Using E, 3ch, 1dc into each of next 4[4:5:5]dc, keeping E to front of work and C to back under hook and working 1dcNc with C in last dc, using C, 1dc into each of next 4dc, keeping C to front of work and D to back under hook and working 1dcNc with D on last dc, using D, 1dc into each dc to end. Turn.

3rd row Changing colors as for 1st row, using D, 3ch, 1dc into each of next 3[3:4:4]dc, using C, 1dc into each of next 6dc, using E, 1dc into each dc to end. Turn.

4th row Changing colors as for 2nd row,

using E, 3ch, 1dc into each of next 2[2:3:3]dc, using C, 1dc into each of next 8dc, using D, 1dc into each dc to end. Turn.

5th row Changing colors as for 1st row, using D, 3ch, 1dc into next dc, using C, 1dc into each of next 10dc, using E, 1dc into each dc to end. Turn.

6th row Changing colors as for 2nd row, using E, 3ch, 1dc into each of next 0[0:1:1]dc, using C, 1dc into each of next 12dc, using D, 1dc into each dc to end. Turn.

7th row Using C, 3ch 1dc into each dc to end. Turn.

Rep 7th row 0[0:1:1] times more. Fasten off and sew or weave in ends. Work 1 more motif in same way, then 2 using B, A and C, 2 using E, C and B, 2 using A, D and B, 2 using B, C and E and 2 using D, A and E. 12 motifs making 6 diamond shapes, 3 for each front.

Quarter raglan motif

Using D, make 10[10:12:12] ch. Work 1st row as given for 1st motif. 8[8:9:9]dc.

2nd row 3ch, dec 1, 1dc into each dc to end. Turn.

3rd row 3ch, 1dc into each dc to last 3dc,

dec 1, 1dc to last dc. Turn.
Rep 2nd and 3rd rows twice more, then 2nd row 0[:1:1] times more. Fasten off. Make another quarter motif in same way.

Three-quarter raglan motif

Using C, make 16[16:18:18] ch. Work 1st row as given for 1st motif. 14[14:16:16]dc.

2nd row 3ch, 1dc into next dc, dec 1, 1dc into each dc to end. Turn.

3rd row 3ch, 1dc into each dc to last 4dc, dec 1, 1dc into each of last 2 dc. Turn.
Rep 2nd and 3rd rows twice more, then 2nd row 0[0:1:1] times more. 8[8:9:9]dc. Fasten off.

Neck motif

Using E, make 16[16:18:18] ch.

1st row Into 4th ch from hook work 1dc, 1dc into each ch to last 4ch, dec 2 working over next 3ch as given for dec 1, 1dc into last ch. Turn.

2nd row 3ch, dec 2, 1dc into each dc to end. Turn.

3rd row 3ch, 1dc into each dc to last 4dc, dec 2, 1dc into last dc. Turn.
Rep 2nd and 3rd rows once more, then 2nd row once more. Fasten off.

Finishing

Block each piece under a damp cloth with a warm iron. Sew motifs tog with bound off edge to cast on edge, with the exception of 6th motif which must be sewn cast on edges tog to form diamond shape. Join 3 motifs, arranging as desired or as shown in diagram, to form one row. Join 5 more rows in same way, then join these 6 rows tog to form one front to underarm. Join 2 motifs working from front edge for 7th row then join quarter raglan motif for armhole edge. Join one motif for front edge with three-quarter raglan motif for armhole edge for 8th row, then join neck motif to raglan edge of armhole, leaving 9dc at neck edge free for 9th row. Join other front in same way, reversing motifs.

Collar Using size E hook, A and with RS of work facing, work 86[86:90:90] sc around neck edge. Work 1 row dc, dec one st at each side of sleeve, (4 dec). Cont dec in same way, work 1 row sc and 1 row dc. Work 2[2:3:3] rows sc without shaping. Fasten off.

Lower edge Using size E hook, A and with RS of front facing, work 2[2:3:3] rows dc along the lower edge for hem. Fasten off. Work other front in same way.

Front edges Using size E hook, A and with RS of work facing, work 3 rows sc along each front edge. Fasten off. Join raglan, side and sleeve seams. Turn up hem at lower edge and sew in place. Turn up 2[2:3:3] rows dc at cuffs and sew in place. Sew in zipper. Block seams.

Joining motifs for left front

FREE SHAPING

This chapter illustrates a creative and individual way of crocheting, this being a breakaway from the accepted traditional methods of working in straight rows back and forth.

Here the method of making free and unusual lines and shapes, which are then worked around to form a flat fabric, is explained. To achieve this type of work, increased and decreased stitches must be introduced at certain points on the piece, so our samples are explained in detail to help you understand the technique and encourage you to try out your own ideas.

You will see that color is very important since the fabric is formed by using different colors of yarn for each new row or part of a design thus creating somewhat of a patchwork effect.

Start by making a square or rectangular shape which

could be used as a pillow cover or enlarged to make a rug. Later fashion garments can be attempted or, possibly before that, a border design on a plain skirt.

Sample 1

The basic shape here consists of two circles. By using the same method of work and varying the number of stitches between increases and decreases, you can use several circles in a row, three to form a triangle or four to form a square. The sample has been worked in five colors of Knitting Worsted, A, B, C, D and E.

To work the basic circles (make 2) Using size F hook and A, make 3ch. Join with a sl st into first ch to form a ring.

1st round 1ch to count as first sc, 7sc into ring. Join with a sl st into first ch.

2nd round 1ch, 1sc into st at base of ch, *2sc into next sc, rep from * to end. Join with a sl st into first ch. 16sc.

3rd round 1ch, 1sc into st at base of ch, 1sc into next sc, *2sc into next sc, 1sc into next sc, rep from * to end. Join with a sl st into first ch. 24sc.

4th round 1ch, 1sc into st at base of ch, 1sc into each of next 2sc, *2sc into next sc, 1sc into each of next 2sc, rep from * to end. Join with a sl st into first ch. 32sc.

5th round 1ch, 1sc into st at base of ch, 1sc into each of next 3sc, *2sc into next sc, 1sc into each of next 3sc, rep from * to end. Join with a sl st into first ch. 40sc. Break off A, and leave working st on a holder.

Join in B to either circle. **Replace working st onto hook, 1ch, 1sc into st at base of ch, 1sc into each of next 4sc, *2sc into next sc, 1sc into each of next 4sc, rep from * to end of round. Join with a sl st into first ch. **. Turn work.

1st row 1ch to count as first sc, skip first sc, 1sc into each of next 5sc. Turn work.

2nd–6th rows As 1st.

Join in 2nd circle Place circle to be joined behind the present work with RS tog and rep from ** to ** as for 1st circle, working through double fabric for first 7 sts. Break off yarn, thread cut end through working st and pull up tightly.

Join in C With RS of work facing, join C to first increased sc of left hand circle (as shown in diagram) and working in a counter-clockwise direction around the circle, 1ch, 1sc into st at base of ch, 1sc into each of next 5 sts, (2sc into next sc, 1sc into each of next 5 sts) 5 times, cont along row ends of straight strip with B by working 2sc tog, 1sc into each of next 4 sts, work 2sc tog, then cont around right hand circle by working (1sc into each of next 5sc, 2sc into next sc) 6 times, 1sc into each of next 5sc and then cont along 2nd side of straight strip and with B work 2sc tog, 1sc into each of next 4 sts, work 2sc tog, 1sc into each of next

5 sts. Join with a sl st into first ch. Break off yarn, thread cut end through working st and pull up tightly.

Join in D With RS of work facing, join in D by inserting hook into first ch of last round and cont in a counter-clockwise direction around entire piece by working 1ch, 1sc into st at base of ch, (1sc into each of next 6 sts, 2sc into next st) 5 times, 1sc into each of next 5 sts, work 2sc tog, 1sc into each of next 3sts, work 2sc tog, 1sc into each of next 5 sts, (2sc into next st, 1sc into each of next 6 sts) 5 times, 2sc into next st, 1sc into each of next 5 sts, work 2sc tog, 1sc into each of next 3 sts, work 2sc tog, 1sc into each of next 5 sts. Join with a sl st into first ch. Break off yarn, thread cut end through working st and pull up tightly.

Join in E With RS of work facing, join in E by inserting hook into first ch of last round and cont around piece by working 1ch, 1sc into st at base of ch, (1sc into each of next 7 sts, 2sc into next st) 5 times, 1sc into each of next 4 sts, work 3 sts tog using dc instead of sc, 1dc into each of next 2 sts, work 3dc tog, 1sc into each of next 4 sts, (2sc into next st, 1sc into each of next 7 sts) 5 times, 2sc into next st, 1sc into each of next 4 sts, work 3dc tog, 1dc into each of next 2 sts, work 3dc tog, 1sc into each of next 4 sts. Join with a sl st into first ch. Break off yarn, thread cut end through working st and pull up tightly.

Join in B With RS of work facing, join in B by inserting hook into first ch of last round and cont around piece by working 1ch, 1sc into st at base of ch, (1sc into each of next 8 sts, 2sc into next st) 5 times, 1sc into each of next 2 sts, work 3dc tog, 1dc into each of next 3 sts, work 3dc tog, 1sc into each of next 2 sts, (2sc into next st, 1sc into each of next 8 sts) 5 times, 2sc into next st, 1sc into each of next 2 sts, work 3dc tog, 1dc into each of next 3 sts, work 3dc tog, 1sc into each of next 2 sts. Join with a sl st into first ch. Break off yarn, thread cut end through working st and pull up tightly.

Join in A Cont as before by working 1ch, 1sc into st at base of ch, (1sc into each of next 9 sts, 2sc into next st) 5 times, work 3dc tog, 1dc into each of next 4 sts, work 3dc tog, 2sc into next st, (1sc into each of next 9 sts, 2sc into next st) 5 times, work 3dc tog, 1dc into each of next 4 sts, work 3dc tog. Join with a sl st into first ch.

Final round Using A, 1ch, 1sc into st at base of ch, (1sc into each of next 10 sts, 2sc into next st) 4 times, 1sc into each of next 29 sts, (2sc into next st, 1sc into each of next 10 sts) 4 times, 1sc into each of next 8 sts. Join with a sl st into first ch. Fasten off.

Sample 2

Five colors of Knitting Worsted A, B, C, D and E have been used for this sample. Using size F hook and A, make a chain with multiples of 6 +1 stitches.

1st row Into 3rd ch from hook work 1sc, 1sc into each ch to end. Turn.

2nd row 1ch to count as first sc, skip first st, 1sc into each of next 5ch, *10ch, into 3rd ch from hook work 1sc, 1sc into each of next 7ch, 1sc into each of next 6sc, rep from * to end. Turn.

3rd row Join in B, 1ch, skip first st, 1sc into each of next 4sc, *work 2sc tog, 1sc into each of next 7sc, 3sc into tip of chain length, 1sc into each of next 7 sts, work 2sc tog, 1sc into each of next 4 sts, rep from * ending with 1sc into turning ch. Turn.

4th row Join in C, 1ch, skip first st, 1sc into each of next 3 sts, *work 2sc tog, 1sc into each of next 7 sts, (2sc into next st) twice, 1sc into each of next 7 sts, work 2sc tog, 1sc into each of next 3 sts, rep from * ending with 1sc into turning ch. Turn.

5th row Join in D, 1ch, skip first st, 1sc into each of next 2sc, *work 2sc tog, 1sc into each of next 7 sts, (2sc into next st) 3 times, 1sc into each of next 7 sts, work 2sc tog, 1sc into each of next 2 sts, rep from * ending with 1sc into turning ch. Turn.

6th row Join in E, 1ch, skip first st, 1sc into next sc, work 2sc tog, 1sc into each of next 7 sts, *(2sc into next st, 1sc into next st) twice, 2sc into next st, 1sc into each of next 7 sts, work 2sc tog, skip next st, work 2sc tog, insert hook into next to last sc just worked, yo and draw a loop through st on hook, (insert hook into next sc on right, yo and draw through a loop, insert hook into next sc on left, yrh and draw through a loop, yrh and draw through all loops on hook) 7 times to join shapes tog, rep from * omitting joining on last rep, working in sc to end. Fasten off.

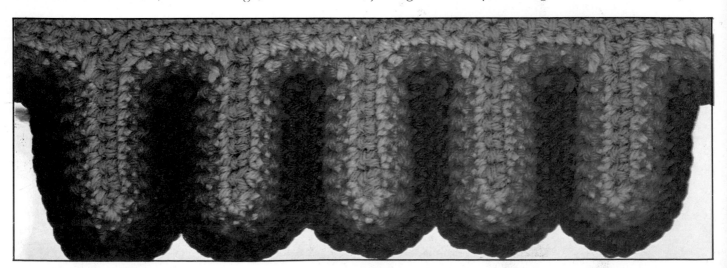

Bedspread in color

Size
To fit average single bed, 36in wide

Gauge
Motifs 1, 2 and 3 measure 8½in square

Materials
Brunswick Fore 'n Aft Sport Yarn
4 × 2oz balls Mint, A
3 balls Turquoise, B
3 balls Pansy, C
4 balls Dark Lime, D
4 balls Dark Green, E
4 balls Black, F
3 balls Purple, G
3 balls Pastel Ombre, H
3 balls Seaspray Ombre, I
One size H crochet hook

Bedspread
The bedspread is made of 8 square motifs using variations of 9 colors which are sewn together. Borders and more motifs are then worked onto the basic design.

Square motif (1)
Using size H hook and A, work 4ch. Join with a sl st into first ch to form a ring.

1st round 3ch, 11dc into circle. Join with a sl st into 3rd of the 3ch.

2nd round Sl st into first sp between dc, 3ch, 1dc in same sp, *2dc into next sp between dc, rep from * around. Join with a sl st into 3rd of the 3ch. Break off A and join in B.

3rd round Sl st into first sp between dc, 3ch, 2dc into same sp, skip next sp, * 3dc into next sp, skip next sp, rep from * around. Join with a sl st into 3rd of the 3ch. Break off B and join in G.

4th round Sl st into first sp between groups of 3dc, (3ch, 2dc, 1ch – to form corner sp, 3dc) into same sp, skip next 2 sp between dc, 1dc into each of next 4 sp, skip next 2 sp, *(3dc, 1ch, 3dc) into next sp, skip next 2 sp, 1dc into each of next 4 sp, skip next 2 sp, rep from * around. Join with a sl st into 3rd of the 3ch. Break off G and join in E.

5th round Sl st into corner sp, (3ch, 2dc, 1ch, 3dc) into same sp, *skip next 2 sp between dc, 1dc into each of next 5 sp, skip next 2 sp, (3dc, 1ch, 3dc) into corner sp, rep from * around. Join with a sl st into 3rd of the 3ch. Break off E and join in A.

6th round Sl st into corner sp, (3ch, 2dc, 1ch, 3dc) into same sp, *skip next 2 sp between dc, 1dc into each of next 6 sp, skip next 2 sp, (3dc, 1ch, 3dc) into corner sp, rep from * around. Join with a sl st into 3rd of the 3ch.
Break off A and join in G.

7th round Sl st into corner sp, (3ch, 2dc, 1ch, 3dc) into same sp, *(skip next 2 sp between dc, 3dc into next sp – thus forming 1sh) 3 times, (3dc, 1ch, 3dc) into corner sp, rep from * around. Join with a sl st into 3rd of the 3ch. Fasten off G and join in C.

8th round Sl st into corner sp, (3ch, 2dc, 1ch, 3dc) into same sp, *(skip next sh, 3dc into sp between next 2 shs) 4 times, skip next sh, (3dc, 1ch, 3dc) into corner sp, rep from * around. Join with a sl st into 3rd of the 3ch. Break off C. Make another motif in the same way.

Square motif (2)
Make 3 motifs in the same way as above, but work in color sequence as follows:

1st and 2nd rounds Work with H.
3rd round Work with A.
4th round Work with D.
5th round Work with E.
6th round Work with B.
7th round Work with H.
8th round Work with C.

Square motif (3)
Make 3 motifs using color sequence as follows:

1st and 2nd rounds Work with B.
3rd round Work with I.
4th round Work with B.
5th round Work with F.
6th round Work with G.
7th round Work with D.
8th round Work with C.

Using C, join these 8 motifs tog as shown in diagram.

Next round Join E to corner sp marked (a) on diagram, (3ch, 2dc, 1ch, 3dc) into corner, *work a 4dc sh into each sp between shs to (b) on diagram, 2dc into (b), (4dc sh into each sp to next corner, (3dc, 1ch, 3dc) into corner) twice, rep from *around motifs. Join with a sl st into 3rd of the 3ch. Break off E and join in D.

Next round Sl st into corner sp, (3ch, 2dc, 1ch, 3dc) into same sp, *4dc sh into each sp between shs to within one sp of point (b), 1dc into next sp, skip 2dc at (b), 1dc into next sp, (4dc sh into each sp to corner, (3dc, 1ch, 3dc) into corner) twice, rep from * around. Join with a sl st into 3rd of the 3ch. Break off D.

Semi-circular motif (4)
Using size H hook and A, work 4ch. Join with a sl st into first ch to form a ring.

1st row 3ch, 6dc into ring. Turn.
2nd row Sl st into first sp, 3ch, 1dc into same sp, 2dc into each sp to end. Turn. Break off A and join in B.
3rd row As 2nd row.
Break off B and join in E.

4th row Sl st into first sp, 3ch, 1dc into same sp, skip next sp, *3dc sh into next sp, skip next sp, rep from * to last sp, 2dc into last sp. Turn. Break off E and join in H.
5th row 3ch, 3dc sh into each sp between shs, 1dc into 3rd of the 3ch. Turn.
6th row Sl st into first sp, 3ch, 1dc into same sp, *4dc sh into next sp between shs, rep from * to last sp, 2dc into last sp. Turn. Break off H and join in E.
7th row 3ch, 4dc sh into first sp between shs, *5dc sh into next sp, rep from * to last sp, 4dc into last sp, 1dc into 3rd of the 3ch. Turn. Break off E.

Make 3 more motifs in the same way and join the main section as shown in the diagram. Cont working a border around the main piece as foll:

1st round With RS of work facing join A to point (*) on diagram and work 4dc shs into each sp between shs to point (b), dec at (b) by working 1dc into sp at either side of previous dec, cont in shs to next corner, 4dc into corner, *3dc sh into 3rd dc of previous 5dc sh, 3dc sh into next sp between shs, rep from * around semicircular motif and cont around piece dec at each point (b), working (3dc, 1ch, 3dc) into each corner and working around motifs as shown above. Break off A and joint in G.

2nd round As 1st round, but work 3dc shs into each sp between shs around motif 4. Break off G and join in F.

3rd round As 2nd round. Break off F and join in G.

4th round Working all around work 1dc into each dc and 1dc into each sp, 1dc into each of 3 sp at point (b), (3dc, 1ch, 3dc) into each corner, skipping 3dc before and after each corner sp. Break off G and join in F.

5th round Working all around work 1dc into each dc, (3dc, 1ch, 3dc) into each corner, and at point (b) dec over 3dc by working 1dc into each of the 3dc and leaving the last lp of each on hook, yo and draw through all 4 lps on hook. Break off F and join in D.

6th round As 4th round, but dec over 5dc at each point (b). Break off D and join in F.

7th round As 5th round, but dec over 5dc at each point (b). Break off F and join in C.

8th round As 7th round, but work 2dc into every 10th dc around motif 4. Break off C and join in D.

9th round As 7th round. Break off D and join in F.

10th round As 7th round, but at each point (b) dec over 2dc, 1tr into next dc, dec over next 2dc. Break off F and join in G.

11th round As 7th round, but dec over

2dc only at each point (b).
Break off G and join in H.
12th round As 7th round, but do not dec at point (b) and work 5dc shs into each corner sp. Break off H and join in B.
13th round As 12th round, but work 5dc into 3rd dc of previous 5dc sh at corners. Break off B and join in E.
14th round As 12th round.

Motif (5)

Work as for semi-circular motif (4) until 2nd row has been completed. Break off A and join in B.
3rd row 3ch, skip first sp, 1dc into next sp, 1dc into each sp to last 2 sp, 1dc into each of last 2 sp. Turn. Break off B and join in E.
4th row 3ch, 1dc into first sp, *skip next sp, 3dc into next sp, skip next sp, 2dc into next sp, rep from * to end. Turn.

Break off E and join in H.
5th row 3ch, *2dc into next sp, 3dc into next sp, rep from * to end, 1dc into 3rd of the 3ch. Turn.
6th row 3ch, 1dc into first sp, *3dc into next sp, 2dc into next sp, rep from * to end. Turn. Break off H and join in E.
7th row 3ch, 3dc into each sp to end, 1dc into 3rd of the 3ch. Turn. Break off E and join in H.
8th row 3ch, 2dc into first sp, *3dc into next sp, rep from * to last sp, 2dc into last sp, 1dc into 3rd of the 3ch. Turn. Break off H and join in E.
9th row 4ch, 1tr between 1st and 2nd dc (4tr into next sp) twice, *4dc into next sp, rep from * to last 2 sp, 4tr into each of next 2 sp, 1tr between last 2dc, 1tr into 4th of the 4ch. Turn.
10th row 4ch, 2tr into first sp, 5tr into next sp, *5dc into next sp, rep from * to

last 2 sp, 5tr into next sp, 2tr into last sp, 1tr into 4th of the 4ch. Turn. Break off E and join in H.
11th row 4ch, 5tr into first sp, *5dc into next sp, rep from * to last sp, 5tr into last sp, 1tr into 4th of the 4ch. Break off H.

Make one more motif in the same way and join to the main part as shown in the diagram. Cont with the border as foll:
15th round Join in A and work 1dc into each dc around and (3dc, 1ch, 3dc) into 3rd dc of every·5dc sh. Break off A and join in D.
16th round *3dc sh into next sp, skip next 2 sp, rep from * around, but work (3dc, 1ch, 3dc) into each corner. Break off D and join in A.
17 round Work 3dc shs into each sp and over motif (5), 4dc shs over the curves and (3dc, 1ch, 3dc) into each corner. Break off A and join in F.
18th round As 17th round. Break off F and join in C.
19th round As 17th round. Break off C and join in I.
20th round As 17th round. Break off I. Complete the piece by working the following extensions:
1st row Join I to point marked (c) on diagram, 3ch and 3dc into same sp, 4dc sh into each sp between shs to point marked (d) on diagram. Turn. Break off I and join in B.
2nd row Sl st into first sp between shs, 3ch and 3dc into same sp, 4dc sh into each sp to end. Turn. Break off B and join in E.
3rd row As 2nd row. Break off E and join in H.
4th row As 2nd row. Break off H and join in D.
5th row As 2nd row. Break off D and join in A.
6th row As 2nd row. Break off A.
Work a similar extension at the opposite end of the cover, then work around the cover as follows:
Join E to any sp between shs, 3ch and 3dc into same sp, 4dc sh into each sp between shs around, sl st into 3rd of the 3ch. Break off E. Finish off all ends.

Finishing
Tassels (make 6)
Cut 20in lengths of each color. Using 40 strands tog, tie them in the middle, fold in half and tie again 2in from the top Attach the tassels as shown.

Fringe
Cut lengths of each color as for tassels. Using 8 strands tog, draw center of threads through each sp between shs around outer edge and knot into place.

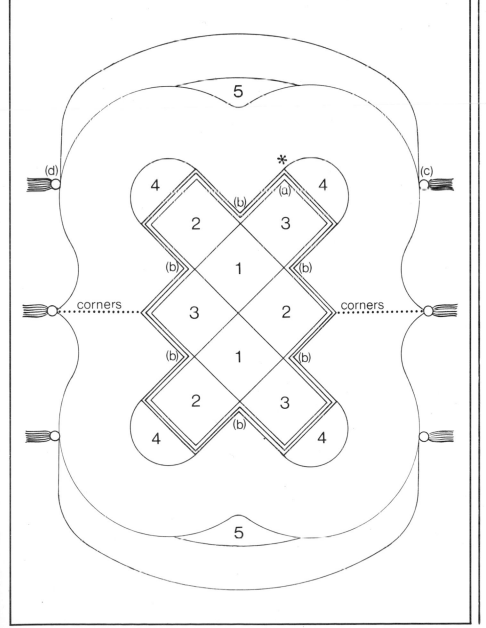

LACE CROCHET
FILET CROCHET

Filet is the French name for "net" and you will recognize this type of crochet by its simple lacy quality. It is made up of two simple stitches, already learned, the chain and the double crochet. The doubles are worked in groups to form a solid block and the space between each block is covered with a length of chain which corresponds in number to the group of doubles over which it is worked.

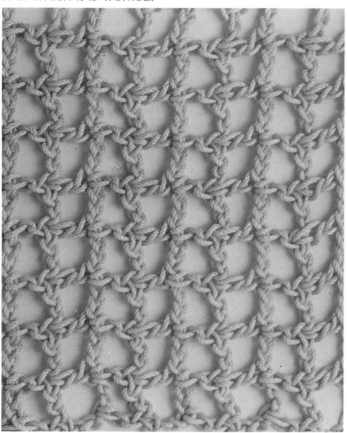

The composition of filet crochet forms the basis of the work and this is usually made up of single doubles with two chain separating them. However, when, for the purpose of design, various spaces are filled in with doubles, a block is formed and from the basic net many different patterns can be made.

An easy way of designing your own pattern is to use squared graph paper. Presuming that each square across represents a stitch and each square up equals a row, then block in squares accordingly to create your own individual design.

Instructions are given for working the basic net and for one of the many variations on this theme. Most yarns are suitable for filet crochet, although cotton or finer yarns are more popular since they add to the lightness and airiness of the work.

Basic filet crochet
Using size B hook and a cotton yarn, make 32ch.
1st row Into 8th ch from hook work 1dc, *2ch, skip next 2ch, 1dc into next ch, rep from * to end. Turn.
2nd row 5ch to count as first dc plus linking ch, skip first 2ch space, 1dc into next dc, *2ch, skip next 2ch space, 1dc into next dc, ending with 1dc into 3rd of the turning chain. Turn.
The last row is repeated throughout.

Filet crochet using blocks and spaces
Using size B hook and a cotton yarn, make 32ch.
1st row Work as given for 1st row of basic filet crochet.
2nd row 5ch to count as first dc plus linking ch, skip first 2ch space, 1dc into next dc, *2ch, skip next 2ch space, (1dc into next dc, 2dc into next 2ch space) twice, 1dc into next dc, rep from * once more, 2ch, skip next 2ch space, 1dc into next dc, 2ch, 1dc into 3rd of the turning chain. Turn.
3rd row 5ch, skip first 2ch space, 1dc into next dc, *2ch, skip next 2ch space, 1dc into each of next 7dc, rep from * once more, 2ch, skip next 2ch space, 1dc into next dc, 2ch, 1dc into 3rd of the turning chain. Turn.
4th row 5ch, skip first space, 1dc into next dc, 2ch,

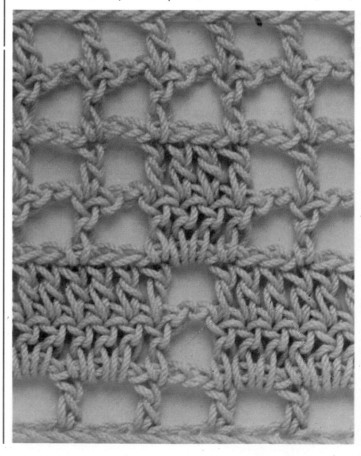

skip next space, 1dc into next dc, (2ch, skip next 2dc, 1dc into next dc) twice, 2dc into next space, (1dc into next dc, 2ch, skip next 2dc) twice, 1dc into next dc, 2ch, skip next space, 1dc into next dc, 2ch, 1dc into 3rd of the turning chain. Turn.

5th row 5ch, skip first space, 1dc into next dc, (2ch, skip next space, 1dc into next dc) twice, 2ch, skip next space, 1dc into each of next 4dc, (2ch, skip next space, 1dc into next dc) 3 times, 2ch, 1dc into 3rd of the turning chain. Turn.

6th row 3ch, (2dc into next space, 1dc into next dc) twice, (2ch, skip next space, 1dc into next dc) 5 times, 2dc into next space, 1dc into next dc, 2dc into last space, 1dc into 3rd of the turning chain. Turn.

7th row 3ch, skip first dc, 1dc into each of next 6dc, (2ch, skip next space, 1dc into next dc) 5 times, 1dc into each of next 5dc, 1dc into 3rd of the turning chain. Fasten off.

If you have managed to work this sample successfully, then you are ready to make up a design of your own using the method described above.

Very fine cotton used for this work produces a beautiful filet crochet lace. Worked into strips the piece you make can be used for a lace insertion or edging or you can make the strips a bit wider and cover the cuffs of a favorite blouse. The instructions below are for making two simple lace edgings.

Lace edging 1

Make a chain the length that you desire, using a multiple of 3 stitches plus 2.

1st row Into 4th ch from hook work 1dc, 1dc into each ch to end. Turn.

2nd row 5ch to count as first dc plus 2 linking ch, skip first 3dc, 1dc into next dc, *2ch, skip 2dc, 1dc into next dc, rep from * ending with 1dc into 3rd of the turning chain. Turn.

3rd row 3ch, *2dc into next space, 1dc into next dc, rep from * to end. Fasten off.

Lace edging 2

Make a chain the length that you desire, using a multiple of 6 stitches plus 5.

1st row Into 8th ch from hook work 1dc, 1dc into each of next 3ch, * 2ch, skip next 2ch, 1dc into each of next 4ch, rep from * to end. Turn.

2nd row 5ch, skip first 3dc, *1dc into next dc, 2dc into next space, 1dc into next dc, 2ch, skip 2dc, rep from * ending with last dc into 3rd of the turning chain. Turn.

3rd row As 2nd. Fasten off.

Using the same technique, and still working with very

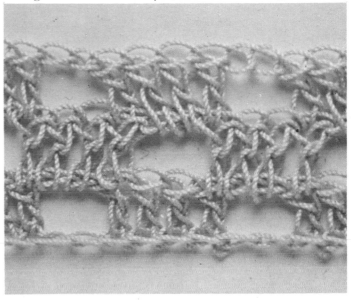

fine yarns, you can make other lovely things for your home, such as pillow covers, tablecloths, placemats and even wall hangings.

Similar strips to those described above, if worked in thicker yarn, can make attractive braids and belts. Plastic strips threaded between the double crochets of the middle row would add interest and firmness to a belt.

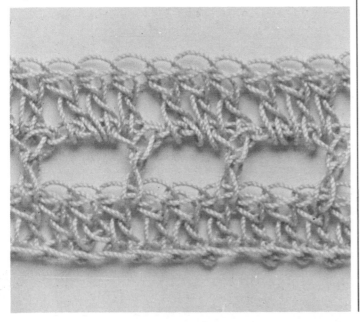

Belt with plastic strip threaded between double crochets

FILET LACE TRIMMINGS

This chapter continues our previous work on filet lace crochet, which is made up of blocks and spaces, and offers different and more advanced techniques. Here we deal particularly with finer yarns used for a more traditional type of work. Filet lace, or crochet lace as it is sometimes called, is in its finest form a popular trimming for underclothes and for many types of household linen. Today it is also fashionable for decorating window shades, Tiffany lampshades and tablecloths—although probably for these latter you will want to use a slightly thicker yarn.

There are fine cotton yarns available in a wide range of colors and thicknesses, varying from No.3 which is the thickest to No.100, the finest. The average range of steel crochet hooks to use with fine cotton varies in size from No.00 hook to No.14.

Traditionally, filet lace crochet is produced in white or ecru, although more contemporary designs sometimes call for colored yarns. It is particularly important, however, if you are trimming underclothes that you have the right color lace. If it should not be available, you can dye the yarn you have with a water dye, first rewinding the ball of cotton into a skein and then, following the dye manufacturer's instructions. Contrast colors can also be used very effectively.

When the lace trimming has been completed, it should be washed and blocked before it is applied to a garment. This will prevent any shrinkage later on. Sew the lace on to the garment with hemming or embroidery stitches.

There are two methods of working the lace trimming – in narrow strips, beginning with the number of stitches required for the depth of the lace and working until the desired length has been completed, or working the number of stitches to give the required length of work and then working in rows to give the correct depth.

Our photograph shows a sample of filet lace crochet where blocks and spaces have been increased and decreased. You will also see a chart of this design. Earlier we showed you a simple way of charting a design, but now we would like to teach you the professional way of doing it.

In our chart here, one space across represents either a block of double crochets or a space and each space up represents a row. To help you follow the chart, the techniques of increasing and decreasing are explained in detail below, and then there are instructions of how to work our sample.

To increase a block at the beginning of a row. Work 5 ch. Into 4th ch from hook work 1dc, 1dc into next ch,

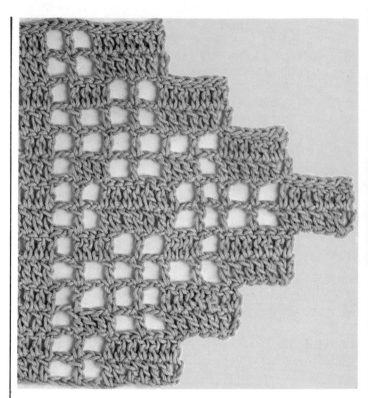

Use this chart to work the sample

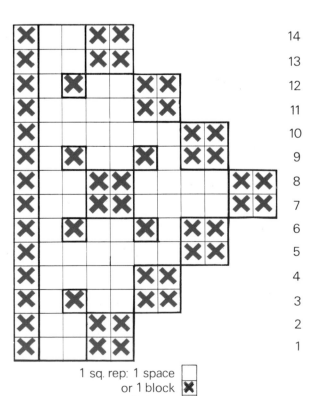

1 sq. rep: 1 space
or 1 block ☒
& 1 row

1dc into next st (i.e. the last st of the previous row), continue across the row in pattern. To increase two blocks as in our chart, work 8ch. Into 4th ch from hook work 1dc, 1dc into each of next 4ch, 1dc into next st.

To increase a space at the beginning of a row Work 7ch which will represent a 2ch space at the end of the last row, 3ch to count as the first dc of the new row and another 2ch between the first dc and the next st, then work 1dc into last st of the previous row.

To decrease a block or space at the beginning of a row Skip the first st, sl st loosely into each of the next 3 sts, then work 3ch to count as the first dc and continue in pattern.

To increase a block at the end of a row Provision has to be made for this increase by working 7ch at the beginning of the previous row, skip the first ch, sl st into each of next 3ch, leaving 3ch which count as the first dc of the new row. Complete the row in pattern. At the end of the following row work 1dc into each of the 3 sl st, thus increasing one block.

To increase a space at the end of a row Work as for increasing a block at the end of a row, but when the increasing is reached, work 2ch, skip next 2 sts, 1dc into the last st.

To decrease a block or space at the end of a row Work to within the last block or space, then turn the work and proceed in pattern.

To work the sample
Make 18ch.

1st row Into 4th ch from hook work 1dc, 1dc into each of next 5 sts, (2ch, skip next 2ch, 1dc into next ch) twice, 1dc into each of next 3ch. Turn.

2nd row 3ch to count as first dc, 1dc into each of next 3dc, (2ch, 1dc into next dc) twice, 1dc into each of next 5dc, 1dc into 3rd of the 3ch. Turn.

3rd row Increase 2 blocks by working 8ch, 1dc into 4th ch from hook, 1dc into each of next 5 sts, (2ch, skip next 2 sts, 1dc into next st) twice, 1dc into each of next 3 sts, 2ch, skip next 2 sts, 1dc into each of next 3 sts, 1dc into 3rd of the 3ch. Turn.

Continue working in pattern from the chart, increasing 2 blocks at the beginning of the 5th and 7th rows and decreasing 2 blocks at the beginning of the 9th, 11th and 13th rows. The 13 rows worked may be repeated to whatever length you desire.

Following here are the instructions and chart for a simple edging which would make an ideal tasselled trimming for a window shade. You will notice that this sample is worked in the width and until the piece is the desired length.

Trimming with tassels
Make 17ch.

1st row Into 8th ch from hook work 1dc, 1dc into each of next 3ch, (2ch, skip 2ch, 1dc into next ch) twice. Turn.

2nd row 5ch, 1dc into 2nd dc, 1dc into each of next 3 sts, 2ch, skip next 2 sts, 1dc into next st. Turn. One

space has been decreased.

3rd row 7ch (thus increasing one space), 1dc into first dc, 1dc into each of next 3 sts, 2ch, skip next 2 sts, 1dc into next dc, 2ch, 1dc into 3rd of the 5ch. Turn.

The 2nd and 3rd rows are repeated throughout. When finished thread two tassels through each increased space.

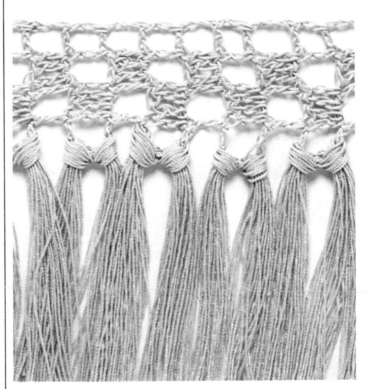

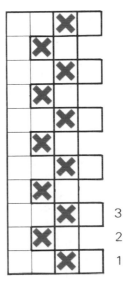

		✕	
	✕		
		✕	
	✕		
		✕	
	✕		
		✕	
	✕		
		✕		3
	✕			2
		✕		1

1 sq. rep: 1 space ☐
or 1 block ✕
& 1 row ☐

DESIGNING AND WORKING CORNERS

The technique of designing and working corners in filet crochet may present problems, but here we shall explain these two procedures in detail. If you follow our charts and instructions, you should not have any difficulty in producing a beautiful mitered corner suitable for use on a fitted couch cover, or details such as a square neckline on clothing.

In the last chapter you were taught how to create your own designs in filet crochet by using squared graph paper; each square across represents either a block or a space and each square up represents a row. Our basic filet chart in the samples here is formed by working single double crochets with two chains between each. You can, however, make the design of the chart to your specifications.

When designing a corner, first draw a diagram and then a line through the corner at an angle of 45 degrees from the outer edge of the design. On one side of the corner sketch in your pattern as you would like it to appear, stopping at the corner line, then mirror your design exactly over this line.

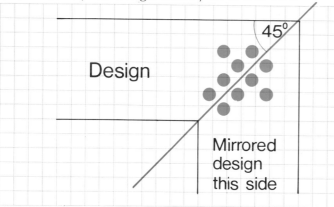

To work sample 1

In our photograph of a mitered corner two colors have been used to clarify the working process. There

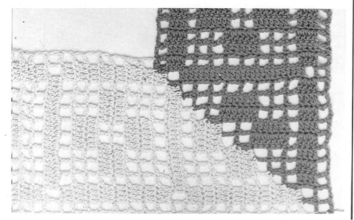

is also a chart of the design which you can follow. Make 41ch.

1st row Into 8th ch from hook work 1dc, 2ch, skip next 2ch, 1dc into each of next 25ch – thus forming 8 blocks –, (2ch, skip next 2ch, 1dc into next ch) twice. Turn.

2nd through 9th row Work in patt from the chart.

10th row Dec one square by skipping first st, sl st into each of next 3 sts, 5ch, skip 2dc, 1dc into each of next 25 sts, 2ch, skip 2dc, 1dc into next dc, 2ch, 1dc into 3rd of the 5ch. Turn.

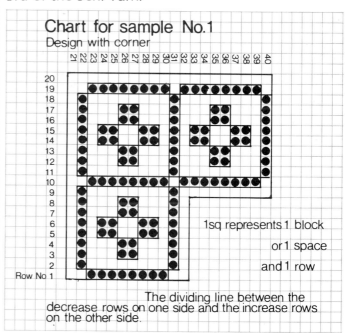

Chart for sample No.1
Design with corner

1sq represents 1 block
or 1 space
and 1 row

Row No 1

The dividing line between the decrease rows on one side and the increase rows on the other side.

11th row 5ch, skip 2ch, 1dc into each of next 4 sts, (2ch, skip 2dc, 1dc into next dc) 8 times, turn. One square has been decreased.

12th row Dec one square by skipping first st, sl st into each of next 3 sts, 5ch, skip 2ch, 1dc into next dc, 2ch, skip 2dc, 1dc into each of next 7 sts, (2ch, skip 2dc, 1dc into next dc) 3 times, 1dc into each of next 3dc, 2ch, 1dc into 3rd of the 5ch. Turn.

13th row 5ch, skip 2ch, 1dc into each of next 4dc, (2ch, skip 2dc, 1dc into next dc) 3 times, 1dc into each of next 6dc, 2ch, skip 2dc, 1dc into next dc, turn. One square has been decreased.

14th row Dec one square by skipping first st, sl st into each of next 3 sts, 5ch, skip 2dc, 1dc into next dc, 2ch, skip 2dc, 1dc into each of next 7 sts, 2ch, skip 2ch, 1dc into each of next 4dc, 2ch, 1dc into 3rd of the 5ch. Turn.

15th row 5ch, skip 2ch, 1dc into each of next 4dc, 2ch, skip 2ch, 1dc into each of next 7dc, 2ch, skip 2ch, 1dc into next dc, turn. One space has been decreased.

16th row Dec one square by skipping first st, sl st into each of next 3 sts, 5ch, skip 2dc, 1dc into next dc, 2ch, skip 2dc, 1dc into next dc, 2ch, skip 2ch, 1dc into each of next 4dc, 2ch, 1dc into 3rd of the 5ch. Turn.

17th row 5ch, skip 2ch, 1dc into each of next 4dc, (2ch, skip 2ch, 1dc into next dc) twice, turn. One space has been decreased.

18th row Dec one square by skipping first st, sl st into each of next 3 sts, 5ch, skip 2ch, 1dc into each of next 4dc, 2ch, 1dc into 3rd of the 5ch. Turn.

19th row 5ch, skip 2ch, 1dc into next dc, 2ch, skip 2dc, 1dc into next dc, turn. One space has been decreased.

20th row Decrease one space by skipping first st, sl st into each of next 3 sts, 5ch, 1dc into 3rd of the 5ch of previous row. Turn the work and sl st into each of the sts across the top of last space worked.

21st row 5ch, sl st into corner of last space on left of the previous row. Do not turn.

22nd row 3ch, 1dc into each of next 2ch, (i.e. down side of space), sl st into corner of last space on left of the previous row, turn, skip first st, sl st into each of next 3 sts, 2ch, skip 2ch, 1dc into 3rd of the 5ch. Turn.

23rd row 5ch, skip 2ch, 1dc into each of next 4dc, 2ch, sl st into corner of last space of the row on the left. Do not turn.

24th row 5ch, sl st into corner of last space of the row on the left, turn, skip first st, sl st in to each of next 3 sts, 2ch, skip 2ch, 1dc into each of next 4dc, 2ch, 1dc into 3rd of the 5ch. Turn.

25th row 5ch, skip 2ch, 1dc into each of next 4dc, skip 2ch, 1dc into each of next 6 sts, sl st into corner of last space of the row on the left. Do not turn.

26th row 5ch, sl st into corner of last space of the row on the left, turn, skip first st, sl st into each of next 3 sts, 1dc into each of next 6dc, 2ch, skip 2ch, 1dc into each of next 4dc, 2ch, 1dc into 3rd of the 5ch. Turn.

27th row 5ch, skip 2ch, 1dc into each of next 4dc, 2ch, skip 2ch, 1dc into next dc, (2ch, skip 2dc, 1dc into next dc) twice, 1dc into each of next 5 sts, sl st into corner of last space of the row on the left. Do not turn.

28th row 5ch, sl st into corner of last space of the row on the left, turn, skip first st, sl st into each of next 3 sts, 1dc into each of next 6dc, (2ch, skip 2ch, 1dc into next dc) 3 times, 1dc into each of next 3dc, 2ch, 1dc into 3rd of the 5ch. Turn.

29th row 5ch, skip 2ch, 1dc into each of next 4dc, (2ch, skip 2 sts, 1dc into next st) 6 times, 2ch, sl st into corner of the last space of the row on the left. Do not turn.

30th row 2ch, 1dc into each of next 2 sts, sl st into corner of last space of the row on the left, turn, skip first st, sl st into each of next 3 sts, 1dc into each of next 21 sts, 2ch, skip 2dc, 1dc into next dc, 2ch, 1dc into 3rd of the 5ch. Turn.

31st row 5ch, skip 2ch, 1dc into each of next 4 sts, (2ch, skip 2dc, 1dc into next dc) 8 times, 1dc into each of next 2 sts, sl st into corner of last space of the row on the left. Do not turn.

32nd row 5ch, skip 2 sts (i.e. the side of last space on 10th row), 1dc into next st, turn, skip first st, sl st into

each of next 3 sts, 1dc into each of next 4dc, (2ch, skip 2ch, 1dc into next dc) 3 times, 1dc into each of next 6 sts, (2ch, skip 2ch, 1dc into next dc) 3 times, 1dc into each of next 3dc, 2ch, 1dc into 3rd of the 5ch. Turn.

33rd through 39th row Work in patt from the chart.

To work sample 2

Above we gave details on how to work sample 1, but actually it is possible to work entirely from a chart without written directions. Practice working sample 2 from the chart. This illustrates the same technique, but it should be worked in a very fine yarn and it is shown in one color only to show the actual working of the technique.

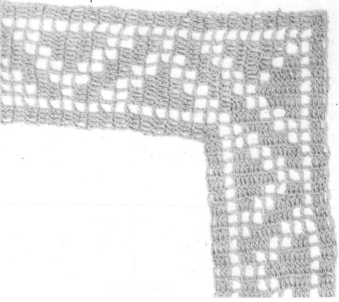

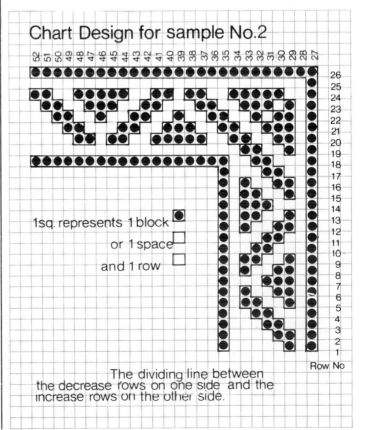

Chart Design for sample No.2

1sq. represents 1 block ⬤
or 1 space ☐
and 1 row ☐

Row No

The dividing line between the decrease rows on one side and the increase rows on the other side.

A butterfly top

Sizes
Directions are to fit 32in bust. Changes for 34 and 36in bust are in brackets [ ]. Side seam, 14[14 :14½]in

Gauge
8 sps and 12 rows to 4in in patt worked with size C crochet hook

Materials
3 × 20grm balls Reynolds Feu d'Artifice
One size C crochet hook
3 snaps
2 glass beads for trim

Back
Using size C hook make 83[89:95]ch.
Base row Into 8th ch from hook work 1dc, *2ch, skip 2ch, 1dc into next ch, rep from * to end. Turn.
1st row 5ch to count as first dc and 2ch, 1dc into next dc, * 2ch, 1dc into next dc, rep from * to end, working last dc into 3rd of 7ch. Turn. 26[28:30] sp. Rep last row 4[4:6] times more, noting that on subsequent rows the last dc will be worked into 3rd of 5 turning ch.
Shape sides
1st row 3ch to count as first dc, 1dc into first dc, patt to end, working 2dc into 3rd of 5ch. Turn.
2nd row 3ch, 1dc into first dc, 1dc into next dc, patt to end, working 2dc into 3rd of 3ch. Turn.
3rd row 3ch, 1dc into first dc, 1dc into each of next 2dc, patt to last 2dc, 1dc into each of next 2dc, 2dc into 3rd of 3ch. Turn.
4th row 5ch, skip 2dc, 1dc into next dc, patt to last 3dc, 2ch, skip 2dc, 1dc into 3rd of 3ch. Turn. 2 sp inc.
Rep last 4 rows twice more. 32[34:36] sp.
Cont without shaping until 31[31:33] rows in all have been worked.
Next row 3ch, *2dc into next sp, 1dc into next dc, rep from * to end. Fasten off.

Front
Work as for back until 2[2:4] rows have been completed. Start butterfly patt.
1st row Patt 7[8:9] sp, 1ch, 1dc into next

sp, 1dc into next dc, patt 10 sp, 1dc into next sp, 1ch, 1dc into next dc, patt to end. Turn.
2nd row Patt 7[8:9] sp, 1dc into next 1ch sp, 1dc into each of next 2dc (1 block of 4dc has been worked), patt 4 sp, 1ch, 1dc into next sp, 1dc into next dc, 1dc into next sp, 1ch, 1dc into next dc, patt 4 sp, 1dc into next dc, 1dc into next 1ch sp, 1dc into next dc, patt to end. Turn.
3rd row Patt 6[7:8] sp, 2dc into next sp, 1dc into each of next 4dc, patt 4 sp, 1dc into next 1ch sp, 1dc into each of next 3dc, 1dc into next 1ch sp, 1dc into next dc, patt 4sp, 1dc into each of next 3dc, 2dc into sp, 1dc into next dc, patt to end. Turn.
Cont working butterfly in this way from chart, *at the same time* shaping sides as for back, until 28 rows of patt have been completed.

Note The chart represents a filet crochet of blocks, spaces, half blocks and half spaces. Spaces are formed by working single doubles with 2ch between them and blocks are spaces which have been filled in by working 2dc into the appropriate 2ch sp. Here spaces have been subdivided into half block/half space by working 1dc and 1ch into a 2ch sp. Patt one more row in sp. Work last row

as for back.
Fasten off.

Straps (make 2).
Using size C hook make 8ch.
1st row Into 4th ch from hook work 1dc, 1dc into each ch to end. Turn. 6dc.
2nd row 3ch to count as first dc, 1dc into each dc to end. Turn.
Rep 2nd row until strap measures 14in from beg, or desired length. Fasten off.

Finishing
Do not block. Join right side seam. Join left side seam to within 3in of lower edge.

Edging Using size C hook and with WS of work facing, rejoin yarn to first ch at lower edge, 3ch, *2dc into first sp, 1dc into next dc, rep from * around lower edge, Turn.
Next row 3ch, *1dc into next dc, rep from * to end.
Cont working in dc up side of opening, working 1dc into each dc and 2dc into each sp, turn and work down other side in same way. Fasten off.
Turn edging to WS on front edge of side opening and sew into place to form overlap. Sew snaps along opening.
Sew straps in position. Sew on beads for butterfly eyes.

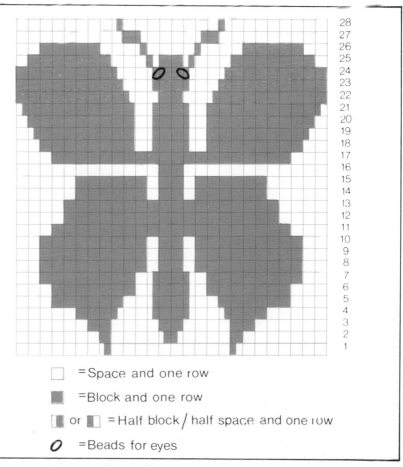

 = Space and one row

 = Block and one row

 or = Half block / half space and one row

O = Beads for eyes

Filet crochet smock

Sizes

Directions are to fit 32in bust. Changes for 34 and 36in bust sizes are in brackets [ ].
↓Length to shoulder, 28[28½:29]in
Sleeve seam, 19in

Gauge

24 sts and 12 rows to 4in in dc worked with size D crochet hook

Materials

15[16:17] × 1oz balls Bucilla Fingering yarn
One size B crochet hook
One size D crochet hook
11 small buttons

Back

Using size B hook make 200[212:224]ch for lower edge.
1st row (WS) Into 3rd ch from hook work 1sc, 1sc into each ch to end. Turn. 199[211:223] sts.
Change to size D hook. Start patt.
2nd row 5ch to count as first dc and 2ch, skip first 3 sts, 1dc into next st, *2ch, skip 2 sts, 1dc into next st, rep from * to end. Turn.
3rd row 5ch, skip first dc, 1dc into next dc, *2ch, 1dc into next dc, rep from * ending with last dc into 3rd of 5ch. Turn.
The last row forms the main patt. Cont in patt until work measures 2in from beg, ending with a WS row. Cont in patt, placing rose motifs as foll:
Next row 5ch, skip first dc, (1dc into next dc, 2ch) 1[2:3] times, work across next 85 sts as given for 1st row of rose motif from chart, (2ch, 1dc into next dc) 5[7:9] times, 2ch, work across next 85 sts as for 1st row of rose motif from chart, (2ch, 1dc into next dc) 1[2:3] times 2ch, 1dc into 3rd of 5ch. Turn.
Next row 5ch, skip first dc, (1dc into next dc, 2ch) 1[2:3] times, work across next 85 sts as given for 2nd row of rose motif from chart, (2ch, 1dc into next dc) 5[7:9] times, 2ch, work across next 85 sts as for 2nd row of rose motif from chart, (2ch, 1dc into next dc) 1[2:3] times, 2ch, 1dc into 3rd of 5ch. Turn.
Cont working in this way until 30 rows of rose motif from chart have been completed. Cont in patt as before until work measures 20in from beg, ending with a RS row.

Shape yoke

Next row 3ch, (1dc into next 2ch sp, 1dc into each of next 2dc) 13[14:15] times, 1dc into next 2ch sp, 1dc into next dc, 1dc into next 2ch sp, 1dc into each of next 3dc, 1dc into each of next three 2ch sp, 1dc into each of next 3dc, 1dc into next 2ch sp, 1dc into each of next 3dc, 1dc into next 2ch sp, (1dc into next 2ch

sp, 1dc into each of next 2dc) 13[14:15] times, 1dc into last ch sp, 1dc into 3rd of 5ch. Turn. 98[104:110] sts.
Next row 3ch, skip first st, 1dc into each st, ending with last dc into 3rd of 3ch. Turn.
Rep last row once more. **

Shape armholes

1st row Sl st across first 3 sts then 3ch, (yo, insert hook into next st, yo and draw through a loop, yo and draw through first 2 loops on hook) 3 times, yo and draw through all 4 loops on hook – called dec 2 –, 1dc into each st to last 7 sts, dec 2, 1dc into next st, turn. 88[94:100] sts.
2nd row 3ch, skip first st, dec 2, 1dc into each st to last 4 sts, dec 2, 1dc into 3rd of 3ch. Turn.
3rd row 3ch, skip first st, (yo, insert hook into next st, yo and draw through a loop, yo and draw through first 2 loops on hook) twice, yo and draw through all 3 loops on hook – called dec 1 –, 1dc into each st to last 3 sts, dec 1, 1dc into 3rd of 3ch. Turn.
Rep last row 5[6:7] times more. 72[76:80] sts. Cont in dc without shaping until armholes measure 7[7½:8]in from beg, ending with a WS row.

Shape shoulders

Next row Sl st across first 4[5:5] sts, 1sc into each of next 5 sts, 1hdc into each of next 5 sts, 1dc into each st to last 14[15:15] sts, 1hdc into each of next 5sts, 1sc into each of next 5 sts. Fasten off.

Front

Work as given for back to **.

Shape armholes and divide for opening

1st row Sl st across first 3 sts and 3ch, dec 2 into next st, 1dc into each of next 40[43:46] sts, turn. Cont on these 42[45:48] sts for first side as foll:
2nd row 3ch, skip first st, 1dc into each st to last 4 sts, dec 2, 1dc into 3rd of 3ch. Turn.
3rd row 3ch, skip first st, dec 1, 1dc into each st to end. Turn.
4th row 3ch, skip first st, 1dc into each st to last 3 sts, dec 1, 1dc into 3rd of 3ch. Turn.
Rep 3rd and 4th rows 2[2:3] times more. 34[37:38] sts.
2nd size only
Rep 3rd row once more. 36 sts.
All sizes
Cont in dc without shaping until armhole measures 4½[5:5½]in from beg, ending at armhole edge.

Shape neck

1st row 3ch, skip first st, 1dc into each st to last 9[10:11] sts, dec 2, 1dc into next st, turn.

2nd row 3ch, skip first st, dec 2, 1dc into each st to end. Turn.
3rd row 3ch, skip first st, 1dc into each st to last 4 sts, dec 2, 1dc into 3rd of 3ch. Turn.
Rep 2nd and 3rd rows once more. 19[20:21] sts. Cont without shaping until front measures same as back to shoulder, ending at armhole edge.

Shape shoulder

Next row Sl st across first 4[5:5] sts, 1sc into each of next 5 sts, 1hdc into each of next 5 sts, 1dc into each of next 5[5:6] sts. Fasten off.
With RS of work facing, return to start of neck shaping and leaving center 4sts unworked, rejoin yarn to next st, 3ch, 1dc into each st to last 7 sts, dec 2, 1dc into next st, turn. Complete to correspond to first side reversing shaping.

Left sleeve

1st piece Using size B hook make 23[25:27]ch.
1st row (WS) Into 3rd ch from hook work 1sc, 1sc into each ch to end. 22[24:26] sts.
2nd row 1ch to count as first sc, skip first st, 1sc into each st to end. Turn.
Rep last row until cuff measures 2in from beg, ending with a WS row. Change to size D hook.
Next row 5ch, skip first st, 1dc into next st, *2ch, 1dc into next st, rep from * to end. 64[70:76] sts.
Cont in main patt as given for back until 1st piece measures 4in from beg, ending with a WS row. Fasten off.
2nd piece Using size B hook make 14ch.
1st row (WS) Into 3rd ch from hook work 1sc, 1sc into each ch to end. 13sts.
2nd row 1ch to count as first sc, skip first st, 1sc into each st to end. Turn.
Rep last row until cuff measures 2in, ending with a WS row. Change to size D hook.
Next row 5ch, skip first st, 1dc into next st, *2ch, 1dc into next st. Rep from * to end. Turn. 37 sts. Cont in patt as for back until 2nd piece measures same as 1st piece, ending with a WS row.
Next row Work in patt across 37 sts of 2nd piece, 2ch, then with RS of work facing, patt across 64[70:76] sts of 1st piece. 103[109:115] sts. Turn.
** Cont in patt until sleeve measures 18in from beg, measured at center, ending with a RS row.
Next row 3ch, (1dc into next 2ch sp, 1dc into next dc) 16[17:18] times, 1dc into each of next two 2ch sp, (1dc into next dc, 1dc into next 2ch sp) 16[17:18] times, 1dc into 3rd of 5ch. Turn. 68[72:76] sts.
Work 2 rows in dc.

Chart for rose motif

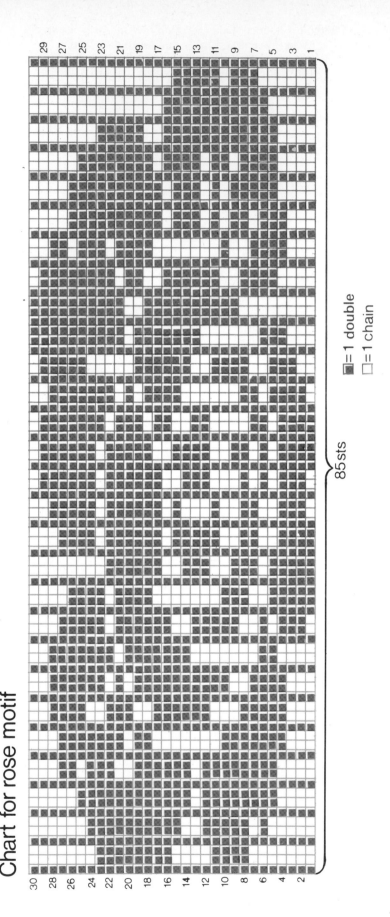

29 27 25 23 21 19 17 15 13 11 9 7 5 3 1

85 sts

■ = 1 double
□ = 1 chain

30 28 26 24 22 20 18 16 14 12 10 8 6 4 2

Shape top

1st row Sl st over first 3 sts and into next st, 3ch, dec 1, 1dc into each st to last 6 sts, dec 1, 1dc into next st, turn.

2nd row 3ch, skip first st, dec 1, 1dc into each st to last 3 sts, dec 1, 1dc into 3rd of 3ch. Turn.

Rep last row 9[9:11] times more. 40[44:44] sts.

Next row 3ch, skip first st, dec 2, 1dc into each st to last 4 sts, dec 2, 1dc into 3rd of 3ch. Turn.

Rep last row 4[5:5] times more. 20 sts. Fasten off.

Right sleeve

1st piece Work as given for 2nd piece of left sleeve and fasten off.

2nd piece Work as given for 1st piece of left sleeve, but do not fasten off.

Next row Work in patt across 64[70:76] sts of 2nd piece, 2ch, then with RS of work facing, patt across 37 sts of 1st piece. Turn. 103[109:115] sts.

Complete as given for left sleeve from ** to end.

Finishing

Block lightly under a damp cloth with a warm iron. Join shoulder seams. Set in sleeves. Join side and sleeve seams.

Neck edging Using size B hook and with RS of work facing, rejoin yarn to top of right front neck and work 3 rows sc around neck edge. Fasten off.

Left front border Using size B hook and with RS of work facing, work 5 rows sc down left side of opening.

Mark position for 5 buttonholes on this border, the first ½in from base of opening, the last 2 sts below top of neck and the others evenly spaced between.

Right front border Work as for left front border, making buttonholes on 3rd row to correspond with markers by working 2ch and skipping 2sc.

Tack down ends of borders to base of opening, the right border over the left one.

Sleeve opening border Using size B hook and with RS of work facing, work 2 rows sc around opening, working 3 button loops evenly spaced along cuff part of larger piece on 2nd row by making 3ch and skipping 2sc.

Lower edging Using size B hook and with RS of work facing, work 1sc into each of first 3 sts, *(sl st, 5ch, sl st, 5ch, sl st, 5ch, sl st) all into next st, 1sc into each of next 5sts, *, rep from * to * 32[34:36] times more, 1sc into next st, rep from * to * 32[34:36] times more, (sl st, 5ch, sl st, 5ch, sl st, 5ch, sl st) all into next st, 1sc into each of last 3 sts. Join with a sl st into first st. Fasten off. Press seams. Sew on buttons.

OPEN LACE DESIGNS

Open lace designs

Open lace is quick and easy to work in crochet since it is formed with large spaces between the stitches, consequently the pattern grows rapidly. Any type of yarn may be used and should be determined by the nature of the work.

There are many uses for the kind of crochet in which an open effect is desired. It can be used for entire garments, which naturally will need to be lined. More commonly, strips of open lace work are used as inserts, especially on evening clothes where the laciness of the crochet looks most effective.

Openwork designs do however serve many more functions as well. String bags, onion bags or simple cotton lace curtains for the windows in your home are examples of a few of the things that you can make once you have practiced some of the samples of open lace work that are given below.

String stitch used as an insert on a bodice

Solomon stitch

Using size C crochet hook and a fine yarn make 35ch loosely.

1st row Extend loop on hook for $\frac{3}{4}$ inch, placing thumb of left hand on loop to keep it extended, yo and draw through a loop, place hook from front to back under left hand vertical loop of stitch just worked, yo and draw through a loop, yo and draw through both loops on hook – called one Solomon st –, sl st into 10th ch from last Solomon st, * 1ch, work 2 Solomon sts, sl st into 5th ch from last Solomon st, rep from * to end. Turn.

2nd row 6ch, work 1 Solomon st, sl st into st between first pair of Solomon sts on previous row, 1ch, * work 2 Solomon sts, sl st into st between next pair of Solomon sts, rep from * ending with last sl st into last of the turning ch of the previous row. Turn.

The last row is repeated throughout to create a very attractive lacy stitch with a 3-dimensional effect.

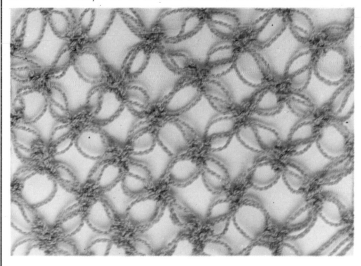

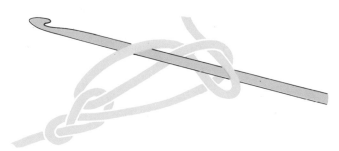

Working a Solomon stitch

Chain lace

Using size C crochet hook and a fine yarn make 44ch.

1st row Into 12th ch from hook work 1sc, *8ch, skip next 3ch, 1sc into next ch, rep from * to end. Turn.

2nd row 8ch, 1sc into first 8ch loop, *8ch, 1sc into next loop, rep from * to end. Turn.
The last row is repeated throughout to form a very simple diamond shaped mesh.
This stitch is ideal for an evening snood or a string bag like the one in our illustration.

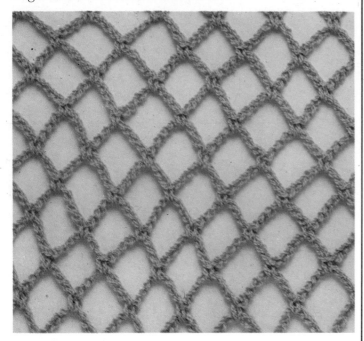

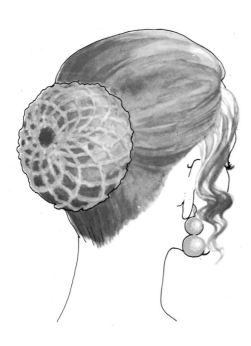

Chain lace used for a snood

To make a string bag

You will need one ball of household string, a brass curtain ring 1¼ inch in diameter and a size F crochet hook.
1st round Form a slip loop on the hook, 1sc into brass ring, *9ch, 1sc into ring, rep from * 21 times more, sl st into first sc.

Next and all following rounds Sl st into first 4ch of next 9ch loop, 1sc into this loop, *9ch, 1sc into next loop, rep from * around ending with 9ch, sl st into first sc of the round. Turn.
When the bag is the desired depth, fasten off and slot drawstrings through the spaces.

String stitch

Using No.0 crochet hook and a fine yarn, make 43ch.
1st row Sl st into 5th ch from hook, skip next ch, 1sc into next ch, *5ch, skip next 5ch, 1sc into next ch, 5ch, sl st into last sc worked, 1sc into same ch as last sc, rep from * to end. Turn.
2nd row Sl st to top of first 5ch loop, 6ch, sl st into 5th ch from hook, 1sc into first loop, *5ch, 1sc into next 5ch loop, 5ch, sl st into last sc worked, 1sc into same loop, rep from * to end. Turn.
The last row is repeated throughout to form the pattern.

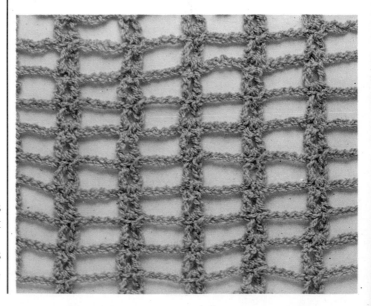

Mohair muffler

Size
12in wide by 96in long

Materials
5 × 40grm balls variegated mohair
One size H crochet hook

The muffler
Using the crochet hook make 20
Solomon's knots, drawing each loop up
to a height of 1 inch.
Continue working in pattern until the
work measures 96in from the beginning.
Fasten off.

Solomon's knot worked in mohair

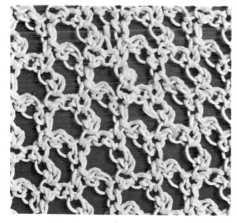

Solomon's knot worked in fine string

Shopping bag

Size
A bag about 14in wide by 16in deep

Materials
2 balls of fine household string
One size E crochet hook

Bag
Using the crochet hook make 40
Solomon's knots, drawing each loop up
to a height of ½in.
Continue in pattern until the work
measures 32in from the beginning.
Fasten off.

Finishing
Make up the bag by folding in half
lengthwise. Join the side seams by
overcasting them, from the lower edge
to within 6in of the top edge.

Handle
Cut 12 lengths of string, each 36in long
for the handle.
Divide the string into 3 groups with 4
lengths in each and braid them together,

knotting each end.
Thread each braid through the last row at the top of the bag from the outer edge to the center and tie the ends together to form a handle.
Complete the other handle in the same way.

Wool shawl

Size

A shawl measuring about 66in across the top edge, excluding the fringe

Materials

3½oz of Fingering Yarn plus 1oz extra for fringe
One size D crochet hook

Shawl

Using the crochet hook make 140 Solomon's knots, drawing each loop to a height of ½in, then shape the sides by working as follows:

Next row Skip knot on hook and next 4 knots, insert hook into center of next knot and work 1sc, *make 2 knots, skip 1 knot along 1st row, 1sc into center of next knot on 1st row, rep from * to end, working last sc into first ch.

Next row Make 3 knots, skip first knot, next unjoined knot and joined knot of last row, 1sc into center of next unjoined knot of last row, *make 2 knots, skip next joined knot of last row, 1sc into center of next unjoined knot of last row, rep from * to end.

Repeat the last row until 2 knots remain. Fasten off.

Cut lengths of yarn, each 16in long. Take 6 strands together at a time and knot into each space along side edges only.

Work 2 rows of fringing (see chapters on Trimmings and Braids later), each row 1in below previous knots. Trim the fringe.

Solomon's knot worked in fingering yarn

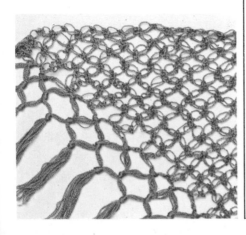

Solomon's knot stitch worked in fingering yarn makes a gossamer shawl.

FUR FABRICS AND LOOP STITCHES

Recently it has become very popular to simulate fur fashions with "fun fur" fabrics. In crochet this is done with the use of loop stitches. Here we tell you how to work three basic loop stitches and in the next chapter we will continue with more advanced techniques. Loop stitches produce an attractive raised effect and form a solid, virtually windproof fabric which is ideal for cooler days. It is important in this work not to underestimate the amount of yarn you will need for any particular garment worked in this stitch, since it does consume a considerable amount.

Vests, jackets and hats made entirely in loop stitch in bright paintbox colors are perfect for children's wear. Or, using the same stitches, create a "fur" trimming effect. Besides using this stitch for clothes, you can also make very attractive bathroom sets and area rugs, particularly if you are using a machine-washable, quick-drying yarn.

Loop stitch

This is loop stitch in its most common form, worked right into the fabric as you proceed in rows.

Using size H crochet hook and Knitting Worsted make 22ch.

1st row 1sc into 3rd ch from hook, work 1sc into every ch to end. Turn.

2nd row 1ch to count as first sc, skip first st of previous row, work a loop by inserting hook into next stitch, place yarn over 1st and 2nd fingers and draw it up

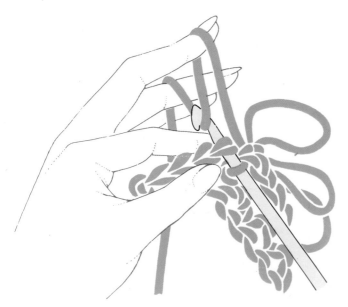

by lifting 2nd finger. Draw through a loop as shown in illustration, then draw loop through st, yo and draw

through both loops on hook, remove 2nd finger from loop and continue making loops in this manner into every st to the end of the row. 1sc into the turning chain. Turn.

Repeat the 2nd and 3rd rows throughout to form the pattern.

Note You will see, as you are working, that the loops are on the back of the fabric. This occurs since you are making the loops on the wrong side of the work. The density of the loops can be changed by working them across the rows in alternate stitches or into the stitches between loops on every other row.

Chain fur stitches

Again these chain loops are formed as part of the fabric, which has a close, curly fur effect, resembling the look of many popular furs.

Using size H crochet hook and a Knitting Worsted make 25ch.

1st row 1dc into 4th ch from hook, work 1dc into every ch to end. Turn.

2nd row 1ch to count as first sc, skip first st of previous row, * 1sc into back loop only of next st, 10ch, rep from * to end of row, working last sc into the turning chain. Turn.

3rd row 3ch to count as first dc, skipping the first st, work 1dc into each st of the last row worked in dc, inserting the hook into the loop skipped in the previous row of sc, 1dc into the turning chain. Turn. Repeat the 2nd and 3rd rows throughout to form the pattern.

Cut fur stitch

Here the loops are added after the basic background – a mesh – has been worked.

Using size H crochet hook and a Knitting Worsted, make 25ch.

1st row 1sc into 3rd ch from hook, *1ch, skip next ch, 1sc into next ch, rep from * to end. Turn.

2nd row 1ch to count as first sc, 1sc into first 1ch sp, *1ch, 1sc into next 1ch sp, rep from * to last sp, 1ch, 1sc into the turning chain. Turn.

The 2nd row is repeated throughout.

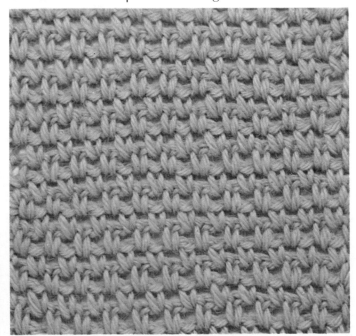

To add the loops Cut several lengths of yarn each to measure 5 inches.

Using two strands together fold them in half, and with right side of work facing, insert the crochet hook horizontally through the first sc in the mesh, place the two loops of yarn over the hook and draw through the work, place the four cut ends of yarn over the hook. Pull up tightly to secure. Repeat this process into each sc throughout the mesh.

Note As with loop stitch, you can vary the amount of cut loops and their position on the fabric. Also experiment to see how attractive these loops can look and the different designs you can create if you work them in various colors, or in shades of one color, as on our sample.

▼ *Hat in loop stitch and chain fur stitch on jacket*

'Fun fur' carriage cover

Color chart for cover

1 Square =1DC

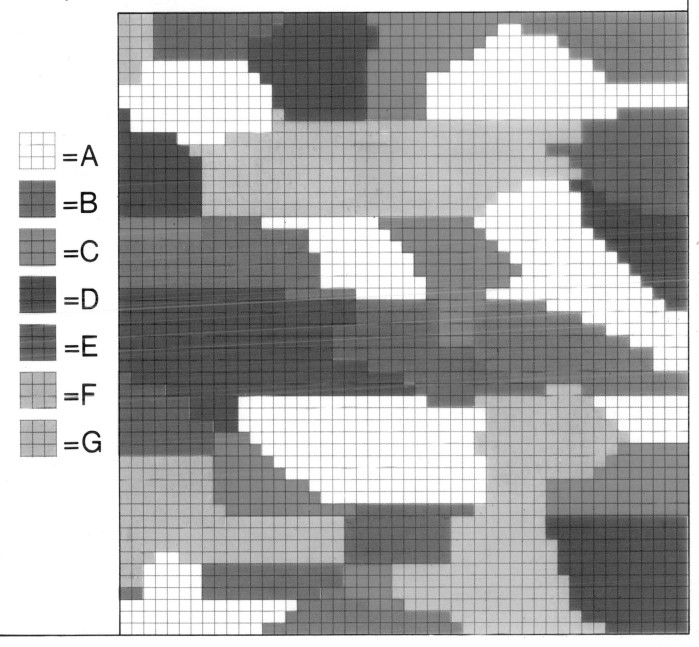

=A
=B
=C
=D
=E
=F
=G

Size
Crochet base measures 23in × 13½in

Gauge
13dc and 9 rows to 4in worked on
size F hook

Materials
4 × 2oz balls Dawn Wintuk Sport Yarn
in main color, A and 2 balls each of

contrast colors B, C, D, E, F and G
One size F crochet hook

Crochet base
Using size F hook and A, make 50
ch.
1st row Into 4th ch from hook work 1dc,
1dc into each ch to end. Turn. 48dc.
2nd row 3ch to count as first dc, skip
first dc, 1dc into each dc, ending with 1dc

into 3rd of 3ch. Turn.
Rep last row 50 times more. Fasten off.

Finishing
Cut rem balls, of all colors into 5in
lengths.
Following chart knot 2 strands together
around every dc on the piece. Trim
strands to desired length or leave
shaggy.

LOOPED BRAIDS AND EDGINGS

In this chapter we shall continue with more variations of the looped stitches you learned in the last chapter. More advanced techniques are illustrated, including working with beads, and suggestions are made as to how you might use these stitches.

Here the methods, because they are so decorative, are used as a trim rather than an all-over design. To get the greatest contrast when using these trimmings on a crochet garment, you should use very basic stitches, such as single or double crochet.

Accordion braid

This is formed by working many double crochets into a small space on a background fabric of treble crochet to give a fluted effect.

Using size H crochet hook and Knitting Worsted, make 23ch.

1st row 1tr into 5th ch from hook, work 1tr into every ch to end. Turn.

2nd row 4ch to count as first tr, skip first st on previous row, 1tr into each st to end, 1tr into the turning chain. Do not turn.

3rd row 3ch, work 6dc down side of first tr, 1dc into st at base of this tr, *work 7dc up side of next tr on row, 1dc into st at top of this tr, work 7dc down side of next tr on row, 1dc into st at base of this tr, rep from * to end of row. Fasten off.

Work in this manner along the first row of tr that was made.

This braid can be incorporated into a garment or applied to one that has been completed. It looks very effective around the outer edges of a long, simple evening coat, its bulkiness counteracting the length of the coat.

Accordion braid used to trim an evening coat

Triple loops worked over a bar

This is an unusual technique for making very thick loops. To be most effective it should be worked into the garment you are making as single rows or no more than three rows at the most. You might also try spacing single rows at varying distances, as in our illustrations.

Work up to the point in your garment where you wish to include triple loops, ending with a right side row.

Take a separate ball of yarn and wind it in a single strand several times over a ruler or a rug wool gauge used for cutting yarns for rug making and which has a groove down one side.

Next row Holding the yarn-covered ruler or gauge behind your work, and beginning at opposite end to the ball of yarn, *insert hook into next st, then insert hook behind first 3 loops on ruler, yo and draw beneath the 3 loops of yarn and through the st of the previous row, yo and draw through both loops on hook, rep from * to end of row, taking care to remove the yarn from the ruler in consecutive order. Remove the ruler from the loops now and cut the loop yarn at the end of the row. Work one row in single crochet before starting another triple loop row.

Vertical beaded loops
These are ideal for working a jabot around the front opening of an evening top.

Make sure that you buy beads that have the correct size hole for the yarn that you are using. Usually the beads will already be threaded on a coarse string when you purchase them, but you will need to transfer them onto the crochet yarn with which you will be working before you start to work. To do this, make an overhand knot in one end of the bead thread, place the crochet yarn through this knot as in the diagram and carefully slide the beads from the thread on to the crochet yarn. Work to the position where a beaded row is desired, ending with a right side row.

Next row Sl st into the first st, *yo and draw through a loop extending it for 6 inches, push up the required number of beads on the yarn and draw through the extended stitch, draw the enlarged st over the beaded loop and pull yarn tightly to secure (there is now no loop on the hook), insert hook into next st, yo and draw through a st, sl st into next st, *, rep from * to * until the desired number of beaded loops have been worked. Use this same method to work beaded fringes, varying the number of beads used in a loop to give different depths.

ARAN CROCHET
BASIC STITCHES

Aran is usually considered to be a knitting technique, but in this and following chapters we explain how you can achieve a similar effect working in crochet. It is a satisfying technique for those who prefer to crochet, for it gives quicker results, and the same range of garments and items for the home can be made as with the knitted patterns.

Traditional Aran work is usually seen in natural or off-white shades of yarn, although today many wool manufacturers make a special, very thick Aran yarn, in a variety of shades. The samples here explain how to work those basic patterns in crochet, which resemble the knitted versions quite closely.

Sample 1

Rib stitch This is the crochet version of the knitted rib. The fabric is used from side to side across a garment, so that the foundation chain forms the side seam rather than the hem. If you are making a garment, this stitch is suitable for the waistband. Using a smaller hook size than that used for the rest of the garment, say size H, make a length of chain to give the required depth of rib.

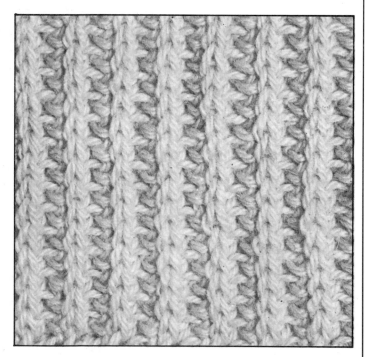

1st row Into 3rd ch from hook work 1sc, 1sc into each ch to end. Turn.
2nd row 1 ch to count as first sc, skip first st, 1sc into each st to end, placing the hook into the horizontal loop under the normal ch loop of the sc, 1sc into turning ch. Turn.

Repeat the 2nd row throughout until the rib is the width of the garment.

To begin work on the main part of the garment, the ribbed fabric is then turned so that the ridges run vertically. The loops formed by the row ends are now used as a base for the first row of the main fabric. A larger hook, size 1, is used for the main part and it may

be necessary to increase the number of stitches by working 2sc into some loops. In the following photograph the rib stitch is shown complete, followed by several rows of single crochet. This forms the base of many Aran styles.

Even moss stitch

The following attractive stitches could be used as an over all pattern or as a panel within an Aran design. Make a length of chain with multiples of 2 stitches.

1st row Skip first ch, sl st into next ch, * 1hdc into next ch, sl st into next ch, rep from * to end. Turn.

2nd row 1ch, skip first st, 1 hdc into next st, sl st into next st, rep from *, ending with last sl st worked into turning ch. Turn.

The 2nd row is repeated throughout.

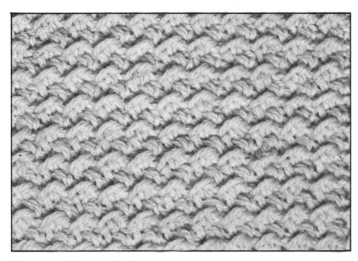

Uneven moss stitch

Make a length of chain and work 1st and 2nd rows as given for even moss stitch.

3rd row 2ch to count as first hdc, skip first st, sl st into next st, * 1hdc into next st, sl st into next st, rep from * to end, 1hdc into turning ch. Turn.

4th row As 3rd.

5th row As 2nd.

6th row As 2nd.

The 3rd through 6th rows are repeated throughout.

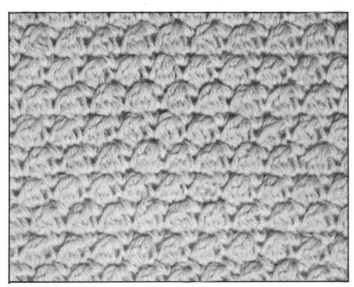

Even berry stitch

Make a length of chain with multiples of 2 stitches.

1st row Into 3rd ch from hook work 1sc, 1sc into each ch to end. Turn.

2nd row 1ch to count as first sl st, skip first st, *yo and insert hook into next st, yo and draw through a loop, yo and draw through first loop on hook, yo and insert hook into same st, yo and draw through a loop, yo and draw through all 5 loops on hook, 1ch to secure st—called berry st—, sl st into next st, rep from *

ending with last sl st worked into turning ch. Turn.

3rd row 1ch to count as first sc, skip first st, *sl st into next berry st, 1sc into next sl st, rep from * to end. Turn.

4th row 1ch to count as first sl st, * 1 berry st into next sl st, sl st into next sc, rep from * to end. Turn. The 3rd and 4th rows are repeated throughout.

Uneven berry stitch

Make a length of chain and work 1st to 3rd rows as given for even berry stitch.

4th row 1ch to count as first sl st, 1 berry stitch into first sc, sl st into next sl st, * 1 berry st into next sc, sl st into next sl st, rep from * to end. Turn.

5th row As 3rd.

The 2nd through 5th rows are repeated throughout.

RAISED DESIGNS

We have already shown you how to work the basic background effects necessary for Aran crochet, where the single crochet or double crochet stitches are very important. Here you will see how the background can be decorated with raised designs which are added after the main fabric has been completed.

Practice our samples first on a piece of double crochet fabric before attempting to start your own designs.

Sample 1

Raised lines may run horizontally, vertically or diagonally. For all samples of raised work begin at the lower edge and hold the crochet hook on top of the crochet (right side of work) with the yarn to be used held in the usual way, under the work. Using size I hook, make a slip loop on the hook, insert hook into first hole on the foundation chain, yo and draw through a loop, drawing it through loop on hook, * insert hook into same hole as last st, yo and draw through a loop (2 loops on hook), insert hook into next hole above last insertion, yo and draw through a loop, drawing it through both loops on hook—called one raised double crochet—, rep from * to end of the row.

Other crochet stitches, such as slip stitch or double crochet may be substituted for the raised single crochet, depending on the depth of stitch required.

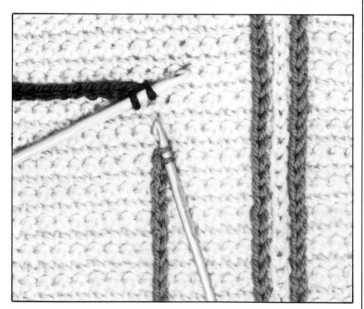

Sample 2

This sample depicts a variety of designs worked on a single crochet background. From left to right across the design there are 2 vertical rows of single crochet, then, looking at the illustration, there is a row of twisted raised single crochet (work black line first),

2 lines of twisted single crochet which form a diamond pattern, another line of twisted raised single crochet and finally 2 more vertical lines of crochet.

These designs can be used as a pattern panel on a garment, or on household articles such as the pillow cover given in the instructions.

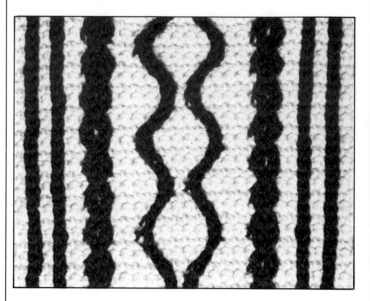

Aran pillow cover
Size
22inches × 15inches, excluding fringe

Gauge
13sts and 8 rows to 4in in dc worked on size F crochet hook

Materials
One size F crochet hook
One size I crochet hook
¾ yard cotton lining material
Material for filling
1 × 20in zipper

Pillow cover (make 2)
Using size F crochet hook, make 72ch loosely.
1st row Into 4th ch from hook work 1dc, 1dc into each ch to end. Turn. 70dc.
2nd row 3ch to count as first dc, skip first dc, 1dc into each dc ending with last dc into 3rd of 3ch. Turn. Rep last row 28 times more. Fasten off.
Surface crochet This can be worked on either one or both sides as desired. Using size I hook and double yarn throughout, follow the chart and work in raised slip stitch following the direction of the arrows throughout, and noting that in row C the

cable patt should be worked first by following the arrows, then in the opposite direction indicated by the dots.

Finishing

With WS tog and using size I hook and double yarn, join 2 short sides and 1 long side by working a row of sc through both thicknesses, working 1sc into each dc, 1sc into each row end and 3sc into each corner. On 4th side, work in sc along one side only, leaving an opening for the zipper. Sew in zipper. Finish pillow pad to required size using lining material and stuffing. Insert into pillow cover.

Fringe Cut yarn into 12-inch lengths and, using 3 strands tog, knot through each sc along both short edges.

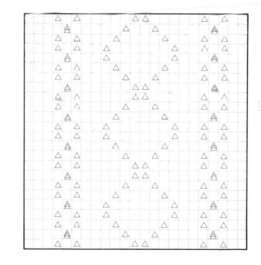

☐ = one space between single crochet

△ = one raised single crochet

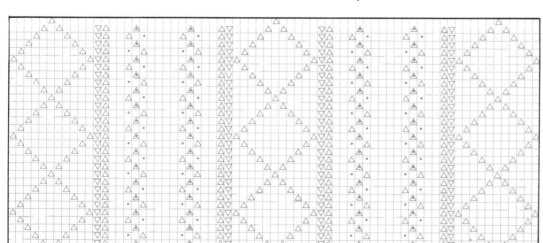

☐ one space between doubles

△ = one raised slip stitch

• = one raised slip stitch in opposite direction to arrows

BERRY STITCH MOTIFS

This chapter shows in detail how berry stitch, which was previously explained as an all-over design, can be worked into motifs on a single crochet background. The motifs are then outlined with raised single crochet to form a panel which could be incorporated into an Aran style garment.

Sample 1

This illustrates one method of grouping berry stitches. Using size I hook and an Aran yarn, make a length of chain with multiples of 8 +4 stitches.

1st row Into 3rd ch from hook work 1sc, 1sc into each ch to end. Turn.

2nd row 1ch to count as first sc, skip first st, 1sc into each st to end. Turn.

3rd row 1ch, skip first st, 1sc into each of next 3 sts, *sl st into next st, yo and insert hook into next st, yo and draw through a loop, yo and draw through first loop on hook, yo and insert hook into same st, yo and draw through a loop, yo and draw through all loops on hook, 1ch to secure st – called berry st –, sl st into next st, 1sc into each of next 5 sts, rep from * ending last rep with 1sc into each of next 4 sts. Turn.

4th row 1ch, skip first st, 1sc into each of next 3 sts, *1sc into next sl st, sl st into next berry st, 1sc into next sl st, 1sc into each of next 5 sts, rep from * ending last rep with 1sc into each of next 4 sts. Turn.

5th row 1ch, skip first st, 1sc into each of next 2 sts, * sl st into next sc, berry st into next sc, sl st into next sl st, berry st into next sc, sl st into next sc, 1sc into each of next 3 sts, rep from * to end. Turn.

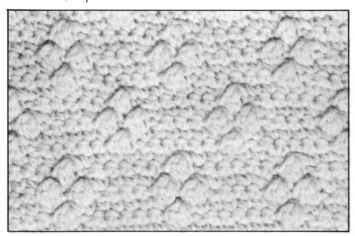

6th row 1ch, skip first st, 1sc into each of next 3 sts, *sl st into next berry st, 1sc into next sl st, sl st into next berry st, 1sc into each of next 5 sts, rep from * ending last rep with 1sc into each of next 4 sts. Turn.

7th–8th rows As 3rd and 4th rows.

9th row 1ch, skip first st, berry st into next sc, sl st into next sc, *sc into each of next 5 sts, sl st into next sc, berry st into next sc, sl st into next sc, rep from * to end. Turn.

10th row 1ch, skip first st, sl st into next berry st, *1sc into each of next 7 sts, sl st into next berry st, rep from * ending with 1sc into last st. Turn.

11th row 1ch, skip first st, *sl st into next sl st, berry st into next sc, sl st into next sc, 1sc into each of next 3 sts, sl st into next sc, berry st into next sc, rep from * to last 2 sts, sl st into next sl st, 1sc into last st. Turn.

12th row 1ch, skip first st, 1sc into next sl st, sl st into next berry st, *1sc into each of next 5 sts, sl st into next berry st, 1sc into next sl st, sl st into next berry st, rep from * to last 3 sts, sl st into next berry st, 1sc into next sl st, 1sc into last st. Turn.

13th–14th rows As 9th and 10th rows.

The 3rd through 14th rows are repeated to form the pattern.

Sample 2

This is a sample design where berry stitches in a diamond pattern have been included in a single crochet background and then the entire design has been outlined with lines of raised single crochet. The technique of working raised single crochet was explained in detail previously and in our sample the rows are worked in varying colors to give them definition.

Using size I hook and an Aran yarn, make 23ch.

1st row Into 3rd ch from hook work 1sc, 1sc into each ch to end. Turn.

Continue working in single crochet until one row before the position for starting the berry stitch motif.

Next row Work across first 7 sts marking last st with a colored thread, work across next 7 sts – this is the pattern area for the berry st motif, work across last 8 sts marking first st with a colored thread. Turn.

1st patt row Work to marked position, 1sc into each of next 2 sts, sl st into next st, berry st into next st, sl st into next st, 1sc into each of next 2 sts, work to end. Turn.

Note From this point the instructions refer only to the center 7 sts involved in the berry st design.

2nd patt row 1sc into each of next 3 sts, sl st into next st, 1sc into each of next 3 sts.

3rd patt row 1sc into next st, (sl st into next st, berry st into next st) twice, sl st into next st, 1sc into next st.

4th patt row 1sc into each of next 2 sts, (sl st into next st, 1sc into next st) twice, 1sc into next st.

5th patt row Sl st into next st, (berry st into next st, sl st into next st) 3 times.

6th patt row 1sc into next st, (sl st into next st, 1sc into next st) 3 times.

7th–8th patt rows As 3rd–4th rows.

9th–10th rows As 1st–2nd rows.

Continue working in single crochet for the desired depth, making more motifs if required. Complete the design by working the lines in raised single crochet from the chart.

Work in same way as for sample 2, marking a center panel to cover 7 sts. Repeat 1st through 6th patt rows, 3rd through 6th, 3rd through 4th and then 1st through 2nd rows. Following the chart in that order work the rows of raised single crochet.

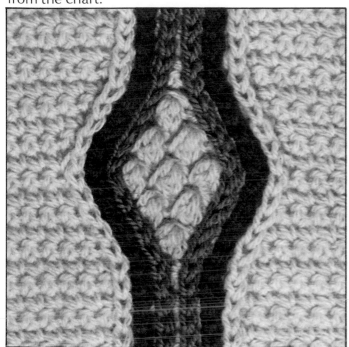

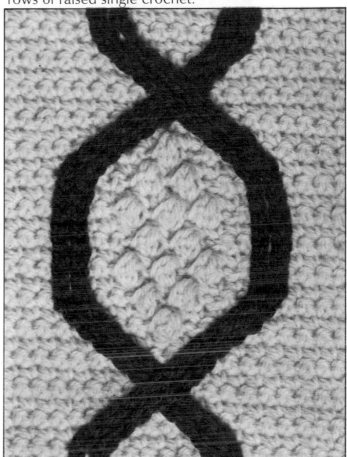

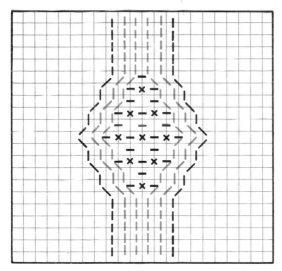

KEY

Each vertical line on each square = 1 single crochet

Each horizontal line on each square = one row

‒ = one berry stitch in place of a single crochet stitch

| = one slip stitch in place of a single crochet stitch

/ = one raised single crochet worked vertically

/ = one raised single crochet worked diagonally

Sample 3

This is a variation of the previous sample with an enlarged berry stitch motif and double lines of raised single crochet crossing each other.

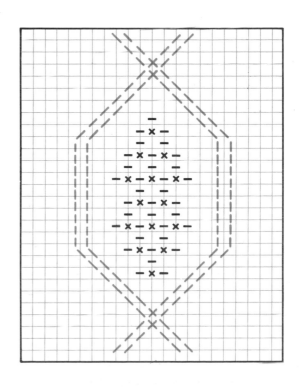

IRISH CROCHET
BASIC TECHNIQUES

Irish crochet, also known as Honiton crochet, is a form of lace which originated as a copy of the Guipure laces of Spain. The lace background and various motifs, such as the rose, leaf, shamrock and other flowers and curves, are both major characteristics of this work.

This introductory chapter to the craft will cover some of the techniques used for working the background, and also a selection of some of the more simple motifs. In this work, the motifs may either be applied directly on to the background, or the lace mesh may be worked around the finished motifs.

The samples shown here were worked with a No.5 cotton yarn with a No.1 crochet hook. Once you understand the basic techniques, try experimenting with some more unusual yarns and see what different effects can be achieved. Any of the net backgrounds seen here, for example, would make an attractive evening shawl, if you worked with one of the new mohair yarns.

Sample 1
To work the net background Make 50ch loosely.
1st row Into 10th ch from hook work 1sc, *6ch, skip 3ch, 1sc into next ch, rep from * to end of row. Turn.
2nd row 9ch, 1sc into first ch sp, *6ch, 1sc into next ch sp, rep from * to end of row. Turn.
The 2nd row is repeated throughout.

To work the rose motif Wrap the yarn 20 times around a pencil.
1st round Remove yarn carefully from the pencil, work 18sc into the ring. Join with a sl st into first sc.
2nd round 6ch, skip 2sc, 1hdc into next sc, *4ch, skip 2sc, 1hdc into next sc, rep from * 3 times more, 4ch. Join with a sl st into 2nd of 6ch.
3rd round Into each 4ch sp work 1sc, 1hdc, 3dc, 1hdc and 1sc to form a petal. Join with a sl st into first sc.
4th round Sl st into back of nearest hdc of 2nd round, *5ch, passing chain behind petal of previous round, sl st into next hdc of 2nd round, rep from * 5 times.
5th round Into each 5ch sp work 1sc, 1hdc, 5dc, 1hdc and 1sc. Join with a sl st into first sc.
6th round Sl st into back of sl st of 4th round, *6ch, passing chain behind petal of previous round, sl st into next sl st of 4th round, rep from * 5 times more.
7th round Into each 6ch sp work 1sc, 1hdc, 6dc, 1hdc and 1sc. Join with a sl st into first sc. Fasten off.

Sample 2
To work the net background Make 58ch loosely.
1st row Into 16th ch from hook work 1sc, 3ch, 1sc into same ch as last sc, *9ch, skip 5ch, 1sc into next ch, 3ch, 1sc into same ch as last sc, rep from * to end of row. Turn.
2nd row 13ch, 1sc into first ch sp, 3ch, 1sc into same sp, *9ch, 1sc into next ch sp, 3ch, 1sc into same sp,

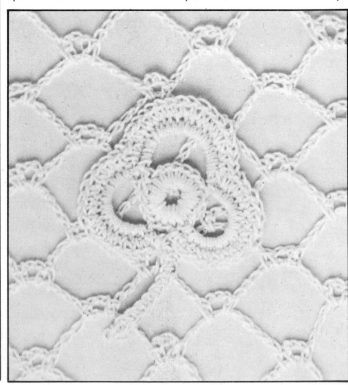

rep from * to end of row. Turn.
The 2nd row is repeated throughout.
To work the motif Wrap yarn 12 times around a pencil.
1st round Remove yarn carefully from the pencil, work 18sc into the ring. Join with a sl st into first sc.
2nd round 8ch, skip 4sc, sl st into next sc, 10ch, skip 4sc, sl st into next sc, 8ch, skip 4sc, sl st into next sc, work 12ch for stem, into 3rd ch from hook work 1sc, 1sc into each of next 9ch, turn.
3rd row Into first ch sp work 16sc, 20sc into next ch sp and 16sc into next ch sp. Turn.
4th row 3ch to count as first dc, skip first sc, 1dc into each sc to end of row. Fasten off.

Sample 3

To work the net background This background incorporates an attractive picot design. Make 47ch loosely.
1st row Work 4ch, sl st into 4th ch from hook – called a picot –, 2ch, into 12th ch from picot work 1sc, *4ch, work a picot, 2ch, skip 4ch, 1sc into next ch, rep from * to end of row. Turn.
2nd row 6ch, work a picot, 2ch, 1sc into first ch sp, *4ch, work a picot, 2ch, 1sc into next ch sp, rep from * to end of row. Turn.
The 2nd row is repeated throughout.
To work the motif Wrap yarn 14 times around the little finger of your left hand.
1st round Remove yarn carefully from finger, work 38sc into the ring. Join with a sl st into first sc.
2nd round *9ch, skip 6sc, sl st into next sc, rep from * 4 times more, sl st into each of next 3sc.
3rd round Into each 9ch sp work 12sc, work 14ch for stem, into 3rd ch from hook work 1sc, 1sc into each of next 11ch. Join with a sl st into first sc.
4th round 3ch to count as first dc, skip first sc, 1dc into each sc on all 5 loops. Fasten off.

Sample 4
Here our sample has the same net background as sample 2, but it is worked with ordinary household string and the raffia motif is made in the same way as the motif on sample 3. Use different colored motifs to decorate a string tote bag.

Sample 5
Use the rose motif described in sample 1 to decorate a wedding veil. This rose is worked in an extremely fine yarn and has beads sewn on to the motif over the background. The net shown here is a commercial one, but you could, with time and patience, make a valuable family heirloom if you worked the veil itself in a crochet net.

ADVANCED DESIGNS

To continue our series about Irish crochet we here provide ideas for a more complicated background net, and for several different motifs.

The crochet lace background could be used for a scarf or evening shawl, made either into a straight stole shape or a large triangle trimmed with a fringe. Instead of the traditional cotton used for Irish crochet, try working with mohair, lurex or a novelty cotton for an unusual effect. By working the motifs illustrated here you will learn the two techniques which are most common in this type of work. They both give a raised look to the work, each in a different way. One is worked over several thicknesses of yarn, and the other is made by inserting the hook into the horizontal loop under the two loops where it is usually placed.

Shawl incorporating net background, rose and leaf motifs

1st row Into 4th ch from hook work a sl st – one picot formed –, 8ch, sl st into 4th ch from hook, 2ch, 1sc into 8th ch from first picot worked, *6ch, sl st into 4th ch from hook, 8ch, sl st into 4th ch from hook, 2ch, skip 4ch, 1sc into next ch, rep from * to end. Turn.

2nd row 9ch, sl st into 4th ch from hook, 8ch, sl st into 4th ch from hook, 2ch, 1sc into first ch sp (between the 2 picots), *6ch, sl st into 4th ch from hook, 8ch, sl st into 4th ch from hook, 2ch, 1sc into next ch sp, rep from * to end. Turn.

The 2nd row is repeated throughout.

To work the rose motif Repeat the instructions given for the rose in the last chapter, but do not fasten off. Continue as follows:

Next round *7ch, passing chain behind petal of

The samples in this chapter were worked with a very fine No.30 cotton yarn and a fine crochet hook, although the size of the hook will vary with the type of yarn you decide to use.

Sample 1
To work the net background Make 57ch loosely.

previous round sl st between the 2sc of next adjoining petals, rep from * 5 times more.

Next round Into each 7ch sp work 1sc, 1hdc, 8dc, 1hdc, 1sc. Join with a sl st into first sc. Turn work.

Next round Into each 7ch sp work 1sc, 1hdc, 8dc, 1hdc, 1sc into each st around placing the hook each time into the horizontal loop of the st on the previous row –

this st gives a raised effect on the right side of the work. Fasten off.

To work the leaf motif All the single crochet stitches from a given point in the pattern are worked over four thicknesses of yarn to give a ridged effect. Cut four lengths of yarn, each 16 inches long, and when the first sc to be worked in this way is indicated, place the yarn behind the work on a level with the stitch into which the hook is to be placed.

Make 16ch. Into 3rd ch from hook work 1sc, 1sc into each ch to last ch, 5sc into last ch to form tip of leaf, then work 1sc into each st along the other side of chain. Work 3sc over the 4 thicknesses of yarn, still working over the yarn and continuing towards tip of leaf, work 1sc into each of next 12sc, working into back loop only of each st. Turn work, 1ch, skip first sc, working down one side of leaf and up the other side, work 1sc into each sc to within 4sc of tip of leaf. Turn work, *1ch, skip first st, 1sc into each sc of previous row to last 4sc of row and working 3sc into sc at base of leaf. Turn work. * Repeat from * to * until the leaf is the desired size.

Sample 2

Wrap yarn 14 times around a pencil.

1st round Remove yarn carefully from pencil, work 21sc into ring. Join with a sl st into first sc.

2nd round 1ch to count as first sc, skip first st, 1sc into each sc around. Join with a sl st into first ch.

3rd round 1ch to count as first sc, skip first sc, 1sc into each of next 6 sts, (12ch, 1sc into each of next 7 sts) twice, 14ch. Join with a sl st into first ch.

4th round 1ch to count as first sc, skip first sc, 1sc into each of next 4 sts, (22sc into next 12ch sp, 1sc into each of next 5 sts) twice, 24sc into next 14ch sp. Join with a sl st into first ch.

5th round Sl st into each of next 4 sts, *4ch, skip 2 sts, sl st into next st, * rep from * to * 6 times more, skip next 3 sts, sl st into each of next 3 sts, rep from * to * 7 times, skip next 3 sts, sl st into each of next 3 sts, rep from * to * 8 times. Join with a sl st into first sl st.

6th round 1ch to count as first sc, skip first st, 1sc into each of next 2 sts, (6sc into next 4ch sp) 7 times, sl st into next st, work 18ch for stem, into 3rd ch from hook work 1sc, 1sc into each of next 15ch, sl st into next st on main motif, (6sc into next 4ch sp) 7 times,

1sc into each of next 3 sts, (6sc into next 4ch sp) 8 times. Join with a sl st into first ch. Fasten off.

Sample 3

Make 40ch.

1st row Into 3rd ch from hook work 1sc, 1sc into each ch to last ch, 5sc into last ch. Do not turn.

2nd row 1sc into each ch along opposite side of 1st row. Turn.

3rd row The petals are worked individually down each side of the stem beginning from the tip where the last sc was worked as follows: *12ch, sl st into st at base of ch, 3ch, skip 2sc, sl st into next sc, turn, work 25dc into 12ch sp, sl st into first sc on row 1, turn, 1ch to count as first sc, skip first dc, 1sc into each dc around petal, sl st into same sl st as last sl st – one petal has been completed –, rep from * to give the desired number of petals noting that when the 25dc have been worked, the sl st is placed in front of the previous petal by inserting the hook into the 3rd sc up from the base of the petal being worked. Fasten off.

To complete the other side, rejoin yarn at the tip and work the petals in the same way, joining the last of the 25dc behind the previous petal.

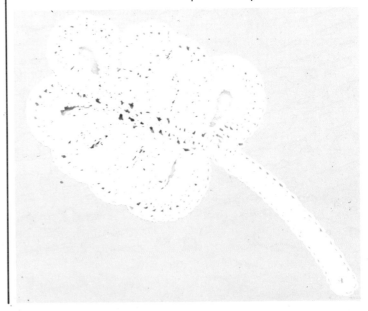

COMBINING MOTIFS AND BACKGROUNDS

In our previous chapters on Irish crochet instructions have been given for working the background and motifs separately. This chapter will deal with the alternative techniques of producing the background and motifs together.

Sample 1

This is a six-sided figure where the net background has been worked around the central motif. The shapes may eventually be joined together to form a large piece of fabric (see the chapter on joining square and circular motifs) which would serve as an attractive bedcover of tablecloth.

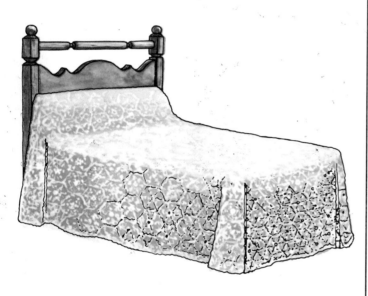

To work the sample Using a No.1 crochet hook and a No.30 cotton yarn, make a rose motif in the same way as that explained earlier.

Next round Sl st into each of next 3 sts of first petal, *(5ch, skip 2 sts, sl st into next st) twice, 5ch, skip 3 sts, sl st into next st, rep from * 5 times more.

Next round Sl st into each of next 2 sts, 6ch, *1sc into next 5ch sp, 5ch, rep from * 16 times more. Join with a sl st into 2nd of 6ch.

Next round *Into next 5ch sp work 1sc, 1hdc, 5dc, 1hdc and 1sc, (5ch, 1sc into next 5ch sp) twice, 5ch, rep from * 5 times more. Join with a sl st into first sc.

Next round Sl st into each of next 5 sts, 6ch, (1sc into next 5ch sp, 5ch) 3 times, *1sc into center dc of next petal gr, (5ch, 1sc into next 5ch sp) 3 times, 5ch, rep from * 4 times more. Join with a sl st into 2nd of 6ch.

Next round Sl st into each of next 2 sts, 6ch, *1sc into next 5ch sp, 5ch, rep from * 22 times more. Join with a sl st into 2nd of 6ch.

Next round Sl st into each of next 2 sts, 6ch, (1sc into next 5ch, sp, 5ch) twice, into next 5ch sp work 1sc, 1hdc, 5dc, 1hdc and 1sc, *(5ch, 1sc into next 5ch sp) 3 times, 5ch, into next 5ch sp work 1sc, 1hdc, 5dc, 1hdc and 1sc, rep from * 4 times more, 5ch. Join with a sl st into 2nd of 4ch.

Next round Sl st into each of next 2 sts, 6ch, 1sc into next ch sp, 5ch, 1sc into next ch sp, 5ch, 1sc into center dc of next petal gr, *(5ch, 1sc into next ch sp) 4 times, 5ch, 1sc into center dc of next petal gr, rep from * 4 times more, 5ch, 1sc into next ch sp, 5ch. Join with a sl st into 2nd of 6ch.

Next round Sl st into each of next 2 sts, 6ch, *1sc into next ch sp, 5ch, rep from * 28 times more. Join with a sl st into 2nd of 6ch.

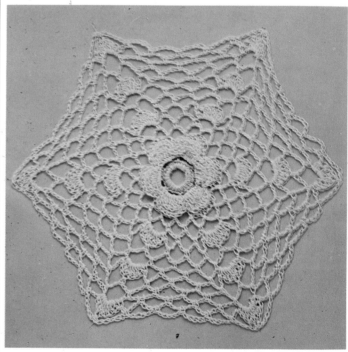

Next round Sl st into each of next 2 sts, 6ch, 1sc into next ch sp, 5ch, into next ch sp work 1sc, 1hdc, 5dc, 1hdc, and 1sc, *(5ch, 1sc into next ch sp) 4 times, 5ch, into next ch sp work 1sc, 1hdc, 5dc, 1hdc and 1sc, rep from * 4 times more, (5ch, 1sc into next ch sp) twice, 5ch. Join with a sl st into 2nd of 6ch.

Next round Sl st into each of next 2 sts, 6ch, 1sc into next ch sp, 5ch, 1sc into center dc of next petal gr, *(5ch, 1sc into next 5ch sp) 5 times, 5ch, 1sc into center dc of next petal gr, rep from * 4 times more, (5ch, 1sc into next ch sp) 3 times, 5ch. Join with a sl st into 2nd of 6ch. Fasten off.

Sample 2

The technique shown here is the method of working motifs and placing them onto paper so that a chain stitch may be worked to join the motifs together to form a fabric.

To work the ring Wrap yarn 20 times around a pencil.

1st round Remove yarn carefully from pencil, work 24sc into ring. Join with a sl st into first sc.

2nd round 8ch, skip 2sc, *1dc into next sc, 5ch, skip 2sc, rep from * 6 times more. Join with a sl st into 3rd of 8ch.

3rd round 3ch to count as first dc, 3dc into first ch sp, 4ch, sl st into 4th ch from hook – called 1 picot –, 4dc into same ch sp, 1 picot, *(4dc, 1 picot) twice into next ch sp, rep from * 6 times more. Join with a sl st into 3rd of 3ch. Fasten off.

To work the curve Cut ten lengths of yarn, each 7 inches long. Work 60sc over cut yarn. Turn work and leave extra yarn to hang freely.

Next row 1ch, sl st into 2nd sc, 3ch, skip 3sc, 1hdc into next sc, (3ch, skip 3sc, 1dc into next sc) 5 times, (3ch, skip 2sc, 1dc into next sc) 8 times, (3ch, skip 2sc, 1hdc into next sc) 3 times, 3ch, sl st into last sc. Join with a sl st into sc below 3rd dc worked at beg of row to make a ring plus a small length of work. Turn.

Next row Into ch sp work 5sc, (4sc into next ch sp, 1 picot) 16 times, 4sc into next ch sp, double back the extra 10 lengths of yarn and work 4sc very tightly over the double length, 1sc into end loop, 1ch. Fasten off working yarn. Pull ten lengths of yarn tight to finish, then cut away.

To join the motifs Make the desired number of motifs and tack on to a firm paper background. The green tacking stitches may be seen in the illustration and further tacks, rather than pins which tend to fall out, should be used as the filling-in progresses.

Our sample shows a ring and four curves, but any of the previous motifs which you have learned could be incorporated into this method of working. Only half of the filling-in has been completed so that the working method may be clearly seen.

A dress pattern of an evening bodice could be used as the paper backing and the various motifs would then be joined together to give the appearance of lace. It would be necessary to make a lining for this lace.

Chain stitches are used for filling-in which starts at the top right hand corner of the work. At random intervals a picot is worked by making four chain and slip stitching into the first of these. It is easiest to work back and forth in rows, joining the motifs together and slip stitching back across a few chain stitches where necessary, or even breaking off the yarn and rejoining it at a new position on the work. When all the motifs are joined, the tacks may be removed and all the cut ends of yarn should be woven in on the wrong side of the work.

IRISH MOTIFS ON SQUARES

Our illustration shows a long evening skirt which is made up of simple crochet squares, some of which are decorated with Irish crochet motifs. To make the skirt, which has no side seams or opening, work 80 squares with a Knitting Worsted weight and a size H crochet hook, making the squares as described later in this chapter. When done, they are to be joined, by the same method described in the chapter on Square and Wheel motifs, into ten lines of eight squares each.

Use the crochet motifs, also described in this chapter to decorate squares, using a matching yarn and tiny stitches. Finish the waist with a round of loosely worked double treble crochets and then thread elastic, dyed to a matching shade if necessary, through the trebles. Two motifs may be placed at the center front of the waistband to be used as buckles.

To work the square motif Make 6ch. Join with a sl st into first ch to form a ring.

1st round 3ch to count as first dc, work 19dc into the ring. Join with a sl st into 3rd of 3ch.

2nd round 1ch to count as first sc, 1hdc into next st, 1dc, 3ch, and 1dc into next st, 1hdc into next st, 1sc into next st, *1sc into next st, 1hdc into next st, 1dc, 3ch and 1dc into next st, 1hdc into next st, 1sc into next st, rep from * twice more. Join with a sl st into first ch.

3rd round 3ch to count as first dc, 1dc into each of next 2sts, into corner 3ch sp work 2dc, 3ch and 2dc, *1dc into each of next 6 sts, into corner 3ch sp work 2dc, 3ch and 2dc, rep from * twice more, 1dc into each of next 3 sts. Join with a sl st into 3rd of 3ch.

4th round 3ch to count as first dc, 1dc into each of next 4 sts, into corner 3ch sp work 2dc, 3ch and 2dc, *1dc into each of next 10 sts, into corner 3ch sp work 2dc, 3ch and 2dc, rep from * twice more, 1dc into each of next 5 sts. Join with a sl st into 3rd of 3ch.

5th round 3ch to count as first dc, 1dc into each of next 6 sts, into corner 3ch sp work 2dc, 3ch and 2dc, *1dc into each of next 14 sts, into corner 3ch sp work 2dc, 3ch and 2dc, rep from * twice more, 1dc into each of next 7 sts. Join with a sl st into 3rd of 3ch. Fasten off. You now have a firm crochet square, as used in samples 1 and 2, where the corners are emphasized by the diagonal line of holes. Samples 3 and 4 have the same square as a base, but are made more solid by replacing the 3ch at each corner with 1ch.

Sample 1

To work the wheel motif Wrap yarn 20 times around first finger of left hand.

1st round Remove yarn carefully from finger, work 20sc into ring. Join with a sl st into first sc.

2nd round 12ch, into 3rd ch from hook work 1sc, work 11sc over complete length of chain instead of into each ch, skip next sc on ring, sl st into next sc, *10ch, join with a sl st into 6th sc up from circle of last "petal", 1ch, work 12sc over the complete chain, skip next sc on ring, sl st into next sc, rep from * 7 times

more, 10ch, join with a sl st into 6th ch up from ring of last "petal," 1ch, work 6sc over the complete chain, join with a sl st into free end of first "petal", work 6 more sc over complete chain. Join with a sl st into a ring. Fasten off.

To work a stem Make 14ch. Into 3rd ch from hook work 1sc, work 14sc over the complete length of chain. Fasten off.
Arrange the rings and stem on the square to give the desired effect and sew in place.

Sample 2
This is known as the Clones knot and it is often seen in Irish lace. Here we use a very different yarn from the traditional since it is easier to work with, but you will need to practice to achieve a perfect knot.

To work the knots Make 10ch. Hold the length of chain firmly between thumb and first finger of left hand, *yo, bring hook towards you, under the length of chain and draw through a loop, rep from * approx 18 times, being careful that the yarn passing over the hook and length of chain is loosely but evenly placed to give a good looped knot. When the required number of loops have been worked, yo and draw through all the loops on the hook, sl st into the ch just behind the looped knot. Continue by making as many lengths of chain and knots as desired.
A stem may be added to complete the motif by working 14ch after the last knot has been completed, into 3rd ch from hook work 1sc, work 14sc over complete length of chain, sl st into last knot. Fasten off. Arrange the knots in position on the square and sew in place.

Sample 3
This is a simple design achieved by making several small rings.
To work the rings Wrap yarn 12 times around first finger of left hand.
Next round Remove yarn carefully from finger, work 14sc into ring. Join with a sl st into first sc. Fasten off. Make as many rings as desired, then work a stem to complete the design.

Sample 4
This is known as coiled work. Take 8 thicknesses of yarn, approx 20 inches long, to form a filling core. We worked approximately 25sc over the entire core, but you can experiment with any number you desire, then take the beginning of the work, twist it behind the hook to form a ring, sl st into 5th sc worked, continue by working another 25sc over the core, forming it into a ring as before.
Continue in this way until the desired shape is achieved. Fasten off yarn and arrange in place on the square.

Glittering Irish crochet bolero

Sizes

Directions are to fit 32/36in bust
Changes for 37/40in bust are in brackets
[ ]
Length to center back, 16[17]in
Sleeve seam, 12in

Gauge

$4\frac{1}{2}$ shells and 16 rows to 4in in patt worked with size B crochet hook

Materials

10[11] × 20grm balls Reynolds Feu d'Artifice
One size B crochet hook
One button

Note

It is easier to work with Feu d'Artifice if the ball of yarn is first placed on a central spool. This can be done by rolling up a piece of cardboard, about 5in square, and anchoring the end with Scotch tape.

Jacket

Using size B crochet hook make 90[99]ch and start at neck edge.
Base row Into 3rd ch from hook work 1sc, 1sc into each ch to end. Turn. 89 [98]sc.
1st inc row 1ch to count as first sc, 1sc into each of next 7sc, *2sc into next sc, 1sc into each of next 8sc, rep from * to end, working last sc into turning ch. Turn. 98[107]sc.
Next row 1ch, *1sc into next sc, rep from * to end. Turn.
2nd inc row (buttonhole row) 1ch, 1sc into each of next 2sc, 3ch, skip 3sc, 1sc into each of next 2sc, *2sc into next sc, 1sc into each of next 9[10]sc, rep from * to end. Turn. 107[116]sc.
Next row 1ch, 1sc into each sc to end, working 3sc into 3ch loop of previous row. Turn.
3rd inc row 1ch to count as first sc, 1sc into each of next 7sc, *2sc into next sc, 1sc into each of next 10[11]sc, rep from * to end. Turn. 116[125]sc.
Next row 1ch, 1sc into each sc to end.

Turn.
Start lace patt.
Base row 1ch to count as first sc, 1sc into each of next 6sc for right front border, *5ch, skip 2sc, 1sc into next sc, rep from * to last 7sc, turn and leave these 7sc for left front border. 34[37] 5ch loops.
1st row 1ch, *into next 5ch loop work (2sc, 3ch, sl st into last sc to form picot, 3sc, 1 picot, 2sc) – called 1 shell –, sl st into next sc, rep from * to end, working 1sc into last sc. Turn.
2nd row 7ch, 1sc into center sc between first 2 picots, *5ch, 1sc into center sc between 2 picots on next shell, rep from * to end, 3ch, 1tr into last sc. Turn.
3rd row 1ch to count as first sc, into next 3ch loop work (1sc, 1 picot, 2sc), sl st into next sc, *1 shell into next 5ch loop, sl st into next sc, rep from * to end, ending with 2sc, 1 picot, 2sc into 7ch loop, 1sc into 4th of 7ch. Turn.
4th row 1ch to count as first sc, *5ch, 1sc into center sc between 2 picots on next shell, rep from * to end, 3ch, 1tr into last sc. Turn.
These 4 rows form patt, noting that on subsequent 1st patt rows the first shell will be worked into 3ch loop and last sc will be worked into 3rd of 5ch loop. Rep the four rows once more, then first one again.
Shape yoke
****1st inc row** Patt 6[7] loops, (always counting $\frac{1}{2}$ loops at ends of rows as 1 loop), (5ch, skip next picot and 2sc, 1sc into sl st between shells, 5ch, 1sc between next 2 picots – called inc 1), patt 6[6] loops, inc 1, patt 7[8] loops, inc 1, patt 6[6] loops, inc 1, patt to end. 39[42] loops.
Patt 3 rows without shaping.
2nd inc row Work as given for 1st inc row, working 11[12] loops in center-back instead of 7[8] loops. 43[46] loops.
Patt 3 rows without shaping.
3rd inc row Patt 3[4] loops, *inc 1, patt 5 loops, rep from * ending last rep with 3[5] loops.
Patt 3 rows without shaping.
4th inc row Patt 3[5] loops, *inc 1, patt 5

loops, rep from * ending last rep with 3[5] loops.
Patt 3 rows without shaping.
5th inc row Patt 2[3] loops, *inc 1, patt 5 loops, rep from * ending last rep with 1[3] loops. 68[71] loops.
Patt 3 rows without shaping.
Divide for underarm
Next row Patt 12[13] loops, *work 15[18]ch, skip 11[12] shells, 1sc between next 2 picots, *, patt 19[20] loops, rep from * to * once more, patt to end. Turn.
Next row Patt 12[13] loops, *1sc into each of next 15[18]ch, *, patt 19[20] loops, rep from * to * once more, patt to end. Turn.
Next row Patt 12[13] loops, *5ch, skip first of 15[18]sc at underarm, 1sc into next sc, (5ch, skip 3sc, 1sc into next sc) 3[4] times, 5ch, 1sc between next 2 picots, *, patt 18[19] loops, rep from * to * once more, patt to end. Turn. 51[56] loops.
Maintaining patt, cont without shaping until 13[15] picot rows in all have been worked from underarm. Fasten off.
Sleeves
Using size B hook and with WS of work facing, rejoin yarn to center sc at 15 underarm sc for 1st size and between 2 center sc of 18sc for 2nd size.
Next row (5ch, skip 3sc, 1sc into next sc) once[twice], 5ch, 1sc into next sc, (5ch, 1sc between next 2 picots) 11[12] times, 5ch, 1sc into next sc before underarm, (5ch, skip 3sc, 1sc into next sc) twice. Turn. 16[18] loops.
Cont in patt until 14 picot rows in all have been worked from underarm, ending with a picot row.
New row (inc) Patt 1 loop, inc 1 as given for yoke, patt 5[6] loops, inc 1, patt 6[7] loops, inc 1, patt to end. Turn. 19[21] loops.
Patt 7[9] more rows without shaping. Fasten off.

Finishing

Do not block. Join sleeve seams.
Edging Using size B hook and with WS of left front facing, rejoin yarn to 7sc at neck, 1ch, 1sc into each sc to end. Turn.
Next row 1ch, 1sc into each sc to end. Turn.
Rep this row until border, slightly stretched, fits down left front to lower edge. Fasten off.
Work other side in same way. Sew borders into place.
With RS of work facing, rejoin yarn to right front at neck edge and work 1 row around neck edge. Fasten off.
Sl st around neck edge. Fasten off.
Sew on button to correspond to buttonhole.

Irish motif pillows

Sizes
Each pillow measures 16in square

Gauge
Brown and orange motif measures 3in square, worked with No.1 crochet hook

Turquoise and lemon motif measures 4½in between widest points worked with No.1 crochet hook

Materials
Both pillows 3 × 53yd balls DMC No.5 Pearl Cotton in each of two colors, A and B
One No.1 steel crochet hook
½yd of 36in wide gingham material
16in square pillow form

Brown and orange motifs
1st motif
Using No.1 hook and A, make 8ch. Join with a sl st into first ch to form a ring.
1st round 4ch, leaving last loop of each st on hook work 2tr into ring, yo and draw through all loops on hook – called 1st cluster –, *4ch, leaving last loop of each st on hook work 3tr into ring, yo and draw through all loops on hook – called 1 cluster –, rep from * 6 times more, 4ch. Join with a sl st to top of 1st cluster. Break off A.
2nd round Join B with a sl st into any 4ch loop, work 1st cluster into this loop, (4ch and 1 cluster) twice into same loop, *3ch, 1sc into next 4ch loop, 3ch, 1 cluster into next 4ch loop, (4ch and 1 cluster) twice into same loop, rep from * twice more, 3ch, 1sc into next 4ch loop, 3ch. Join with a sl st to top of first cluster. Break off B.
3rd round Join A with a sl st to next 4ch loop, 1sc into same loop, *9ch, 1sc into next 4ch loop, (5ch, 1sc into next 3ch loop) twice, 5ch, 1sc into next 4ch loop,

rep from * 3 times, omitting last sc. Join with a sl st into first sc.
4th round Using A work *7dc, 5ch and 7dc into 9ch loop, 1sc into next 5ch loop, 3sc, 3ch and 3sc into next 5ch loop, 1sc into next 5ch loop, rep from * 3 times more. Join with a sl st into top of first dc. Fasten off.

2nd motif
Work as given for 1st motif until 3rd round has been completed.
4th round Work 7dc into first 9ch loop, 2ch, sl st into corresponding 5ch loop on 1st motif, 2ch, 7dc into same 9ch loop on 2nd motif, 1sc into next 5ch loop, 3sc into next 5ch loop, 1ch, sl st into corresponding 3ch loop on 1st motif, 1ch, 3sc into same 5ch loop on 2nd motif, 1sc

into next 5ch loop, 7dc into next 9ch loop, 2ch, sl st into corresponding 5ch loop on 1st motif, 2ch, 7dc into same 9ch loop on 2nd motif, complete as given for 1st motif. Fasten off.
Make and join the 3rd and 4th motifs in the same way so that they form a square.
5th motif
Work as given for 1st motif, using B instead of A and A instead of B and joining to one free side of 1st motif on 4th round.
6th motif
Work as given for 5th motif and join on the 4th round to other free side of 1st motif, also joining to 5th motif at one corner.
7th and 8th motifs

around.

3rd round 5ch, *working across back work 1sc round stem of next dc on 1st round, 5ch, rep from * 4 times more. Join with a sl st around last stem, taking in first 5ch.

4th round *Into next 5ch loop work 1sc, 1hdc, 5dc, 1hdc and 1sc, rep from * to end.

5th round *7ch, 1sc into back of sc between petals of previous round, rep from * around, ending with 7ch, 1sc into back of next sc between petals, taking in the base of the 7ch.

6th round *Into next 7ch loop work 1sc, 1hdc, 7dc, 1hdc and 1sc, rep from * all round. Join with a sl st into first sc. Break off A.

7th round Join in B to sc between petals, 1sc into same place, *8ch, 1sc into 4th of 7dc of next petal, 8ch, 1sc between petals, rep from * around. Join with a sl st into first sc.

8th round Sl st into first 4ch, 1sc into 8ch loop, *12ch, 1sc into next 8ch loop, 1sc into next 8ch loop, rep from * omitting sc at end of last rep. Join with a sl st into first sc.

9th round *1sc into each of next 6ch, 3ch, 1sc into each of next 6ch, 1sc between 2sc of previous round, rep from * to end. Join with a sl st into first sc. Fasten off.

2nd motif

Work as given for 1st motif until 8th round has been completed.

9th round 1sc into each of first 6ch, 1ch, sl st into 3ch loop on 1st motif, 1ch, 1sc into each of next 6ch on 2nd motif, work as given for 1st motif, joining as before in the next 3ch loop, complete as given for 1st motif. Fasten off.

Make 7 more motifs, joining as before into 3 rows with 3 motifs on each.

Small motif

Using No.1 hook and A, make 5ch. Join with a sl st into first ch to form a ring.

1st round 3ch, 11dc into ring. Join with a sl st into 3rd of 3ch.

2nd round 1sc into sp between 3ch and next dc, *8ch, skip next 2 sp between dc, 1sc into sp between next 2dc, rep from * to end. Join with a sl st into same sp as first sc.

3rd round Sl st into first 4ch, 1sc into 8ch loop, *6ch, 1sc into join of large motif, 6ch, 1sc into next 8ch loop on small motif, rep from * 3 times more, working last sc into first sc.

Fasten off. Make 3 more small motifs and join to large motifs in the same way.

Finishing

Complete as given for other pillow.

Work as given for 5th motif, but join to the two free sides of 3rd motif and to each other at one corner.

Small flowers

Using A only, work as given for 1st motif until 1st round has been completed.

2nd round Work 3sc, 3ch and 3sc into each 4ch loop to last loop, 3sc into last loop, 1ch, sl st to free 5ch loop of motif of opposite color, 1ch, 3sc into same 4ch loop. Join with a sl st to first sc. Fasten off. Make 3 more motifs in A and 2 in B.

Finishing

Cut a piece of gingham 34in square, fold in half and seam along 3 edges, leaving ½in turnings. Turn to RS and insert a piece of cardboard into the case to make pinning the motifs easier. Pin crochet in position on cover, then sew in place using a matching color. Place pad in cover, turn in raw edges and sew together with an overcast st.

Turquoise and lemon motifs

1st motif

Using No1 hook and A, make 8ch. Join with a sl st into first ch to form a ring.

1st round 6ch to count as first dc and 3ch, 1dc into ring, *3ch, 1dc into ring, rep from * 3 times more, 3ch. Join with a sl st into 3rd of 6ch.

2nd round *Into next 3ch loop work 1sc, 1hdc, 3dc, 1hdc and 1sc, rep from *

COLORED PATTERNS
ZIGZAG STRIPES

Zigzag crochet designs

The technique of working this very attractive form of patterning is very different from those learned in previous chapters. Crochet formed in this way with a knitting worsted yarn gives a very decorative, thick fabric which is suitable for jackets and vests. The same technique could be worked in Lurex for evening bags and belts, or in straw yarns for more casual accessories. Instructions for working the technique and several variations of the design are given here.

Sample 1

Two colors of knitting worsted yarn, A and B, have been used for this sample. Using size F hook and A, make a chain with multiples of 10 + 2 stitches.

1st row Into 3rd ch from hook work 1sc, 1sc into each ch to end. Turn.

2nd row 1ch to count as first sc, skip first st, 1sc into each st, ending with last sc into turning ch. Turn.

3rd–6th rows As 2nd. Do not break off A.

7th row Using B, 1ch to count as first sc, *1sc into next st skipping 1 row, noting that each time the hook is inserted into a stitch skipping a row the yarn forming the loop on the hook must be extended to meet the

previous st of the working row, 1sc into next st skipping 2 rows, 1sc into next st skipping 3 rows, 1sc into next st skipping 4 rows, 1sc into next st skipping 5 rows , 1sc into next st skipping 4 rows, 1sc into next st skipping 3 rows, 1sc into next st skipping 2 rows, 1sc into next st skipping 1 row, 1sc into next st, rep from * to end. Turn.

8th–12th rows Using B, as 2nd.

13th row 1ch (this does not count as first st), 1sc into first st skipping 5 rows, .1sc into next st skipping 4 rows, 1sc into next st skipping 3 rows, 1sc into next st skipping 2 rows, 1sc into next st skipping 1 row, 1sc into next st, 1sc into next st skipping 1 row, 1sc into next st skipping 2 rows, 1sc into next st skipping 3 rows, 1sc into next st skipping 4 rows, 1sc into next st skipping 5 rows, rep from * to end. Turn.

14th–18th rows Using A, as 2nd.

The 7th through 18th rows inclusive are repeated throughout.

Note At the beginning of a row when changing color it is a good adea to wind the working color around the yarn not in use in order to give a neat edge.

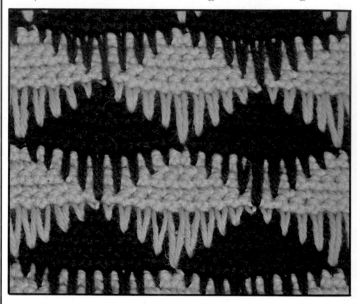

Sample 2

Here we have used three colors of Knitting Worsted A, B and C. Using size F hook and A, make a chain with multiples of 14 + 4 stitches.

1st–6th rows As 1st–6th rows of sample 1. Do not break off A.

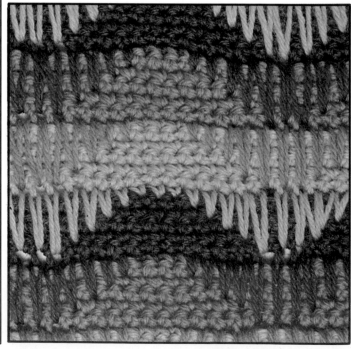

7th row Using B, 1ch to count as first sc, 1sc into of next 2 sts, * 1sc into next st skipping 1 row, 1sc into next st skipping 2 rows, 1sc into next st skipping 3 rows, 1sc into next st skipping 4 rows, 1sc into each of next 3 sts skipping 5 rows, 1sc into next st skipping 4 rows, 1sc into next st skipping 3 rows, 1sc into next st skipping 2 rows, 1sc into next st skipping 1 row, 1sc into each of next 3 sts, rep from * to end. Turn.

8th–12th rows Using B, as 2nd row of sample 1. Do not break off B.

13th–18th rows Using C, as 7th–12th rows. Do not break off C.

19th–24th rows Using A, as 7th–12th rows. The 7th through 24th rows are repeated throughout.

Sample 3

The four colors of knitting worsted yarn used here are noted as A, B, C and D. Using size G hook and A, make a chain with multiples of 6 + 1 stitches.

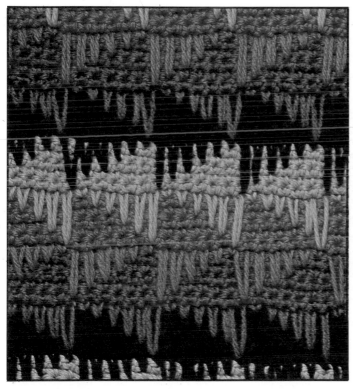

1st–6th rows As 1st–6th rows of sample 1. Do not break off A.

7th row 1ch to count as first sc, *1sc into next st skipping 1 row, 1sc into next st skipping 2 rows, 1sc into next st skipping 3 rows, 1sc into next st skipping 4 rows, 1sc into next st skipping 5 rows, 1sc into next st, rep from * to end, omitting 1sc at end of last rep. Turn.

8th–12th rows Using B, as 2nd row of sample 1. Do not break off B.

13th row Using C, 1ch (this does not count as first st), *1sc into first st skipping 5 rows, 1sc into next st skipping 4 rows, 1sc into next st skipping 3 rows, 1sc into next st skipping 2 rows, 1sc into next st skipping 1 row, 1sc into next st, rep from * to end. Turn.

14th–18th rows Using C, as 2nd row of sample 1. Do not break off C.

19th–24th rows Using D, as 7th–12th rows. Do not break off D.

25th–30th rows Using A, as 13th–18th rows. The 7th through 30th rows inclusive form the pattern and color sequence for this design.

Sample 4

Shiny and mat straw in four colors, A, B, C and D have been used for this sample. Using size F hook and A, make a chain with multiples of 6 + 2 stitches.

1st–4th rows As 1st–4th rows of sample 1. Do not break off A.

5th row Using B, 1ch (this does not count as first st),

1sc into first st, *1sc into next st skipping 1 row, 1sc into next st skipping 2 rows, 1sc into next st skipping 3 rows, 1sc into next st skipping 2 rows, 1sc into next st skipping 1 row, 1sc into next st, rep from * to end. Turn.

6th–8th rows Using B, as 2nd row of sample 1. Do not break off B.

9th row Using C, 1ch (this does not count as first st), 1sc into first st skipping 3 rows, *1sc into next st skipping 2 rows, 1sc into next st skipping 1 row, 1sc into next st, 1sc into next st skipping 1 row, 1sc into next st skipping 2 rows, 1sc into next st skipping 3 rows, rep from * to end. Turn.

10th–12th rows Using C, as 2nd row of sample 1. Do not break off C.

13th–16th rows Using D, as 5th–8th rows. Do not break off D.

17th–20th rows Using A, as 9th–12th rows.

The 5th through 20th rows inclusive are repeated throughout.

CHEVRON DESIGNS AND BRAIDS

More zigzag designs in crochet

A different kind of zigzag design which is very simple to work is illustrated in this chapter. Both wavy lines and pronounced zigzags are formed by this method, either an over-all patterned fabric or a strip of crochet braid.

If knitting worsted yarn is used, this crochet work makes beautiful bed covers, afghans and pillow covers or could be used as a pattern on a fashion garment such as a jacket where a scalloped edge is desired as a design feature. More unusual yarns, like string and straw in particular, could be used to make bags, belts and slippers.

Our samples show different stitches for you to experiment with before starting a design of your choice.

Sample 1

Using size G hook and Knitting Worsted in various colors, make a length of chain with multiples of 17 + 4 stitches.

1st row Into 4th ch from hook work 3dc, **1dc into each of next 5ch, *yo and insert hook into next ch, yo and draw through a loop, yo and draw through first 2 loops on hook, yo and insert hook into next ch, yo and draw through a loop, yo and draw through first 2 loops on hook, yo and draw through all 3 loops on hook – called dec 1dc –, *, rep from * to * twice more, 1dc into each of next 5ch, 4dc into next ch, rep from ** to end. Turn.

2nd row 3ch to count as first dc, skip first 2 sts, 3dc into next st, *1dc into each of next 5 sts, dec 3dc over next 6 sts, 1dc into each of next 5 sts, 4dc into next st, rep from * ending last rep with 4dc into 3rd of 3ch. Turn.

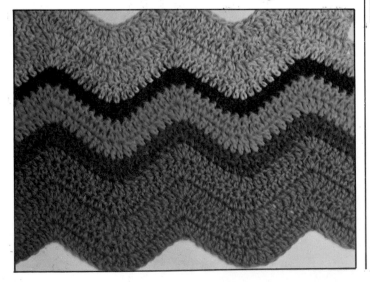

Repeat 2nd row throughout, alternating the colors as desired. You will see that the pattern gives a flowing, wavy line.

Sample 2

This design, which gives a very ribbed zigzag pattern, has been worked throughout in four rows each of two colors of Knitted Worsted, A and B. Using size G hook and A, make a length of chain with multiples of 16 + 4 stitches.

1st row Insert hook into 3rd ch from hook, yo and draw through a loop, insert hook into next ch, yo and draw through a loop, yo and draw through all 3 loops on hook, **1sc into each of next 6ch, 3sc

into next ch, 1sc into each of next 6ch, *insert hook into next ch, yo and draw through a loop, *, rep from * to * twice more, yo and draw through all 4 loops on hook – called dec 2sc –, rep from ** to end. Turn.

Note From this point, insert hook into back loop only of each st throughout.

2nd row 2ch, insert hook into st at base of ch, yo and draw through a loop, insert hook into next st, yo and draw through a loop, yo and draw through all loops on hook, *1sc into each of next 6 sts, 3sc into next sc, 1sc into each of next 6 sts, dec 2sc over next 3 sts, rep from * ending last rep by working into 2nd of 2ch. Turn. The 2nd row is repeated throughout the design.

Sample 3

Two colors of Knitting Worsted, A and B, have been used for this sample. Using size G hook and A, make a length of chain with multiples of 13 + 6 stitches.

1st row Yo and insert hook into 4th ch from hook, yo and draw through a loop, yo and draw through first 2 loops on hook, *yo and insert hook into next ch, yo and draw through a loop, yo and draw through first 2 loops on hook, *, rep from * to *, yo and draw through 4 loops on hook, **1dc into each of next 4ch, 4ch into next ch, 1dc into each of next 4ch, rep from * to * 4 times, yo and draw through all 5 loops on hook – called dec 3dc –, rep from ** to end, 2ch. Fasten off A. Do not turn.

2nd row Join B to 3rd of 3ch at beg of previous row, 1ch to count as first sc, 1sc into front loop of each st to end. Fasten off B. Do not turn.

3rd row Join A to first ch at beg of previous row, 3ch, working into back loop only of each st in previous alternate row, *yo and insert into next st, yo and draw through a loop, yo and draw through first 2 loops on hook, *, rep from * to * twice more, yo and draw through all loops on hook, **1dc into each of next 4 sts, 4dc into next st, 1dc into each of next 4 sts, dec 3dc over next 4 sts, rep from ** to end, 2ch. Fasten off A. Do not turn.

The 2nd and 3rd rows complete the design and are repeated throughout.

Sample 4

Sometimes zigzag designs require at least one straight edge, as on a belt. Here our sample illustrates this method of work with two zigzag lines between the straight edges. Two colors of Knitting Worsted, A and B, have been used so that it is easy to distinguish between the straight lines and the zigzag.

Using size G hook and A, make a length of chain with multiples of 13 + 4 stitches. The 4 extra chains are not turning chains but are for the 4 slip stitches at each end of the pattern repreat.

1st row Skip first ch, sl st into each of next 3ch, *1sc into next ch, 1hdc into next ch, 1dc into next ch, 1 tr into next ch, 1dtr into next ch, 1tr into next ch, 1dc into next ch, 1hdc into next ch, 1sc into next ch, sl st into each of next 4ch, rep from * to end. Turn. Break off A.

2nd row Join B to first st, 3ch, *yo and insert hook into next st, yo and draw through a loop, yo and draw through first 2 loops on hook, *, rep from * to * twice more, yo and draw through all loops on hook, **1dc into each of next 4 sts, 4dc into next st, 1dc into each of next 4 sts, rep from * to * 4 times, yo and draw through all loops on hook, rep from ** to end. Turn.

3rd row As 2nd, working a 4dc group between 2nd and 3rd dc of 4dc group of previous row. Fasten off B.

4th row This shows how to end a zigzag design with a straight edge. Join A to last st worked on previous row, 4ch to count as first dtr, *tr into next st, 1dc into next st, 1hdc into next st, 1sc into next st, sl st into each of next 4 sts, 1sc into next st, 1hdc into next st, 1dc into next st, 1tr into next st, 1dtr into next st, rep from * to end. Fasten off.

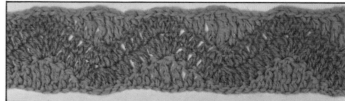

Sample 5

Here is one of the many interesting effects that can be achieved by using the techniques given here. Make two lengths of crochet by working the first two rows as given for sample 2, using only 4sc between each increase and decrease, then twist the lengths around each other to give this braided effect which could be used as trim or as a belt.

Crochet dress
with chevron skirt

Sizes
Directions are to fit 32in bust. Changes for 34, 36, 38 and 40in bust are in brackets [ ].
Length to shoulder, 37½[38:38½:39:39½]in
Long sleeve seam, 16[16½:16½:17:17]in
Short sleeve seam, 4in

Gauge
20 sts and 24 rows to 4in in sc worked with size E crochet hook

Materials
Dress with long sleeves 16[17:18:19:20] × 1oz balls Brunswick Fairhaven Fingering Yarn in main color, A
4[4:4:5:5] × 1oz balls of contrast color, B
Dress with short sleeves 14[15:16:17:18] × 1oz balls Brunswick Fairhaven Fingering Yarn in main color, A
3[3:4:4:5] × 1oz balls of contrast color, B
One size D crochet hook
One size E crochet hook
One size F crochet hook
One 22in zipper

Dress
(worked in one piece to underarm)
Using size F hook and A, make 224[260:276:292:308] ch for entire lower edge.
1st row (RS) Into 4th ch from hook work 1dc, *1dc into each of next 6ch, skip 3ch, 1dc into each of next 6ch, 3dc into next ch, rep from * ending last rep with 2dc into last ch instead of 3. Turn.
2nd row 3ch to count as first dc, 1dc into st at base of ch, *dc into each of next 6dc, skip 2dc, 1dc into each of next 6dc, 3dc into next dc, rep from * ending last rep with 2dc into 3rd of 3ch instead of 3. Turn.
The 2nd row forms the patt. Cont in patt until work measures 6in from beg.
Next row 3ch, skip first dc, 1dc into each of next 6dc, *skip 2dc, 1dc into each of next 13dc, rep from * to last 9dc, skip 2dc, 1dc into each of next 6dc, 1dc into 3rd of 3ch. Turn.
Next row 3ch, 1dc into st at base of ch,

*1dc into each of next 5dc, skip 2dc, 1dc into each of next 5dc, 3dc into next dc, rep from * ending last rep with 2dc into 3rd of 3ch. Turn.
The last row forms the patt. Cont in patt until work measures 12in from beg.
Next row 3ch, skip first dc, 1dc into each of next 5dc, *skip 2dc, 1dc into each of next 11dc, rep from * to last 8dc, skip 2dc, 1dc into each of next 5dc, 1dc into 3rd of 3ch. Turn.
Next row 3ch, 1dc into st at base of ch, *1dc into each of next 4dc, skip 2dc, 1dc into each of next 4dc, 3dc into next dc, rep from * ending last rep with 2dc into 3rd of 3ch. Turn.
Cont in patt as now set until work measures 18in from beg.
Next row 3ch, skip first dc, 1dc into each of next 4dc, *skip 2dc, 1dc into each of next 9dc, rep from * to last 7dc, skip 2dc, 1dc into each of last 4dc, 1dc into 3rd of 3ch. Turn.
Next row 3ch, 1dc into st at base of ch, *1dc into each of next 3dc, skip 2dc, 1dc into each of next 3dc, 3dc into next dc, rep from * ending last rep with 2dc into 3rd of 3ch. Turn.
Cont in patt as now set until work measures 21in from beg, ending with a WS row. Change to size E hook.

Shape waist
1st row 1ch to count as first sc, skip first st, *1sc into next dc, 1hdc into next dc, 1dc into next dc, 1tr into each of next 2dc, 1dc into next dc, 1hdc into next dc, 1sc into next dc, skip next dc, rep from * to end working 1sc into 3rd of 3ch. Turn. 122[130:138:146:154] sts.
2nd row (eyelet hole row) 3ch to count as first dc, skip first st, 1dc into next st, *1ch, skip next st, 1dc into each of next 3 sts, rep from * to end. Turn.
3rd row 1ch to count as first sc, skip first st, work 1sc into each dc and ch sp to end. Turn.
4th row 1ch to count as first sc, skip first st, 1sc into each sc to end. Turn.
Join in B. Using B, rep 4th row twice.

Using A, rep 4th row twice. The last 4 rows form the stripe patt for the bodice which is repeated throughout.
Shape bodice
Next row 1ch, skip first st, 1sc into each of next 28[30:32:34:36]sc, 2sc into each of next 2sc, 1sc into each of next 60[64:68:72:76]sc, 2sc into each of next 2sc, 1sc into each of next 29[31:33:35:37]sc. Turn.
Next row Work in sc.
Next row 1ch, skip first st, 1sc into each of next 29[31:33:35:37] sts, 2sc into each of next 2sc, 1sc into each of next 62[66:70:74:78]sc, 2sc into each of next 2sc, 1sc into each of next 30[32:34:36:38]sc. Turn.
Cont inc 4sc in this way on foll alt rows until there are 138[146:158:166:178] sts, then on every foll 4th row until there are 166[174:186:194:206] sts. Cont without shaping until work measures 31in from beg, ending with a WS row.
Divide for back and front armholes
Next row 1ch, skip first st, 1sc into each of next 38[40:43:45:48]sc, turn.
Cont on these 39[41:44:46:49] sts for left back.
Next row 1ch, skip first 2 sts, 1sc into each sc to end. Turn.
Next row 1ch, skip first st, 1sc into each sc to last 2sc, skip next sc, 1sc into last st. Turn.
Rep last 2 rows 3[3:4:4:5] times more. 31[33:34:36:37] sts. Cont without shaping until armhole measures 6½[7:7½:8:8½]in from beg, ending at back edge.
Shape shoulder
Next row Patt to last 8 sts, turn.
Next row Sl st into each of next 8[10:11:13:14] sts, patt to end. Fasten off.
With RS of work facing, return to part where stitches were divided, skip 5sts for underarm, rejoin yarn to next st and work 1ch, 1sc into each of next 77[81:87:91:97]sc, turn. Cont on these 78[82:88:92:98] sts for front.
Next row 1ch, skip first 2 sts, 1sc into each sc to last 2sc, skip next sc, 1sc into last st. Turn.

Rep last row 7[7:9:9:11] times more. 62[66:68:72:74] sts. Cont without shaping until work measures 14 rows less than back to shoulder shaping.

Shape Neck
Next row Patt across 23[25:26:28:29] sts. Turn.
Next row 1ch, skip first 2 sts, patt to end. Turn.
Next row Patt to last 2 sts, skip next sc, 1sc into last st. Turn.
Rep last 2 rows twice more, then first row again. 16[18:19:21:22] sts. Cont without shaping until work measures same as back to shoulder, ending at armhole edge.

Shape shoulder
Next row Sl st into each of next 8 sts, patt to end. Fasten off.
With RS of work facing return to rem sts at front, skip center 16 sts for front neck, rejoin yarn to next st, 1ch, patt to end. Turn. Complete to correspond to first side of neck, reversing shapings.
With RS of work facing return to part where sts were divided, skip 5sts for underarm, rejoin yarn to next st, 1ch, patt to end for right back. Complete to correspond to left back, reversing shaping.

Long sleeves
Using size D hook and A, make 39 [41:43:45:47]ch.
1st row Into 3rd ch from hook work 1sc, 1sc into each ch to end. Turn. 38[40:42:44:46] sts.
2nd row 1ch to count as first sc, skip first st, 1sc into each sc to end, ending with last sc into turning ch. Turn.
Join in B. Using B, rep 2nd row twice. Using A, rep 2nd row twice more. These 4 rows form the striped patt which is repeated throughout. Cont in patt until work measures 2in from beg.
Change to size E hook. Cont in patt, inc one sc at each end of next and every foll 6th row until there are 60[64:68:72:76] sts. Cont without shaping until work measures 16[16½:16½:17:17]in from beg.

Shape top
1st row Sl st into each of next 4 sts, 1ch, patt to last 3 sts, turn.
2nd row Patt to end. Turn.
3rd row 1ch, skip 2 sts, 1sc into each st to last 2 sts, skip next sc, 1sc into last st. Turn.
Rep 2nd and 3rd rows until 36[36:40:40: 44] sts rem, then rep 3rd row until 14 sts rem. Fasten off.

Short sleeves
Using size E hook and A, make 53[57:61:65:69]ch.

1st row Into 3rd ch from hook work 1sc, 1sc into each ch to end. Turn. 52[56:60: 64:68] sts.
2nd row As 2nd row of long sleeves. Join in B and working in stripe sequence as given for bodice, inc one sc at each end of next and every foll 6th row until there are 60[64:68:72:76] sts. Cont without shaping until work measures 4in from beg.

Shape top
Work as given for long sleeves.

Finishing
Block each piece under a damp cloth with a warm iron. Join shoulder and sleeve seams. Set in sleeves.
Neck edging Using size D hook and A, work 5 rows sc evenly around neck edge.
Sew in zipper, joining rem back seam. Using 6 strands of A tog, make a twisted cord approx 60in long and thread through eyelet holes at waist. Block seams.

CHECK PATTERNS

Checked pattern in crochet

Effective checked crochet patterns in one or more colors may be worked, and they, because of the method used, form a thick fabric suitable for warm outer garments such as coats, jackets and skirts. The stitches used to form the checks pass over previous rows thus forming a double fabric in some designs. Many of these can be reversible, and this should be taken into account when deciding on the kind of garment which you are going to make.

Knitting Worsted and a size G crochet hook are recommended for the samples you see illustrated. Samples 2 and 3 are worked from one side, therefore the crochet could be worked in continuous rounds without turning the work or breaking the yarn at the end of each row. This technique would be ideal for making a skirt, since it avoids side seams.

Sample 1

Make 26ch.

1st row Into 4th ch from hook work 1dc, 1dc into each ch to end. Turn. 24dc.

2nd row 3ch to count as first dc, skip first dc (1dc into next dc, inserting hook from the front of the work horizontally from right to left under the vertical bar of the dc on the previous row so that the hook is on the front of the work) 3 times, (1dc into next dc inserting the hook from the back of the work from right to left over the vertical bar of the dc on the previous row so that the hook is on the back of the work) 4 times. Cont in this way, working 4dc to the front and 4dc to the back of the work to the end of the row, working last dc in 3rd of the 3ch. Turn.

3rd row As 2nd.

4th row 3ch to count as first dc, skip first dc, work 1dc to the back of each of the next 3dc, work 1dc to the front of each of the next 4dc. Cont in this way, reversing the checked effect to the end of the row, working the last dc into 3rd of the 3ch. Turn.

5th row As 4th.

Rows 2 through 5 form the pattern.

Sample 2

This is worked in 2 colors, A and B. With A, make 26ch.

1st row Into 3rd ch from hook work 1sc, 1sc into each ch to end. 25sc. Fasten off yarn. Do not turn.

Note Unless otherwise stated, work into the back loop only of each st to end of design.

2nd row Join B to beg of previous row, 1ch to count as first sc, skip first st, 1sc into each st to end. Fasten off yarn. Do not turn work.

3rd and 4th rows As 2nd.

5th row Join A to beg of previous row, 1ch to count as first sc, skip first st, insert hook under horizontal front loop of next st, yo and draw through a loop, (insert hook under horizontal front loop of st immediately below st just worked into, yo, and draw

through a loop) 3 times, (yo and draw through first 2 loops on hook) 4 times – 1 connected quad dc has been worked –, *1sc into each of next 3 sts, 1 connected quad dc into next st, rep from * to last 2 sts, 1sc into each of next 2 sts. Fasten off yarn. Do not turn work.

6th to 8th rows As 2nd.

9th row Join A to beg of previous row, 1ch to count as first sc, skip first st, 1sc into each of next 3 sts, *1 connected quad dc into next st, 1sc into each of next 3 sts, rep from * to last st, 1sc into last st. Fasten off yarn. Do not turn.

Rows 2 through 9 form the pattern and are repeated throughout.

Sample 3

Three colors are used for this sample, A, B and C. Unless otherwise stated, insert the hook into the back loop only of each st. With A, make 26ch.

1st row Into 3rd ch from hook work 1sc, 1sc into each ch to end. 25sc. Fasten off yarn. Do not turn.

2nd row Join A to beg of previous row. 1ch to count as first sc, skip first st, 1sc into each st to end. Fasten off yarn. Do not turn.

3rd row As 2nd.

4th row Join B to beg of previous row. 1ch to count as first sc, skip first st, 1sc into next st, yo 3 times, insert hook under horizontal front loop of next st in 4th row below, yo and draw through a loop, (yo and draw through first 2 loops on hook) 4 times – 1 surface dtr has been worked –, 1 surface dtr into each of next 2 sts, *1sc into each of next 3 sts, 1 surface dtr into each of next 3 sts, rep from * to last 2 sts, 1sc into each of next 2 sts. Fasten off yarn. Do not turn.

5th and 6th rows With B, as 2nd.

7th row Join C to beg of previous row. 1ch to count as first sc, skip first st, 1sc into each of next 4 sts, *1 surface dtr into each of next 3 sts, 1sc into each of next 3 sts, rep from * to last 2 sts, 1sc into each of last 2 sts.

Fasten off yarn. Do not turn.

8th and 9th rows With C, as 2nd.

10th to 12th rows With A, as 4th to 6th rows.

13th to 15th rows With B, as 7th to 9th rows.

16th to 18th rows With C, as 4th to 6th rows.

Rows 1 through 18 form the pattern and color sequence for this sample.

Sample 4

Two colors, A and B, are used for this sample. With A, make 22ch.

1st row Into 3rd ch from hook work 1sc, 1sc into each ch to end. Turn. 21sc.

2nd row 1ch to count as first sc, skip first sc, 1sc into front loop only of each st to end. Turn. Fasten off yarn.

3rd row Join in B. 2ch to count as first hdc, skip first st, 1hdc into each st to end placing hook each time under both loops. Fasten off yarn. Do not turn.

4th row Join A to beg of previous row. 1ch to count as first sc, (1tr into front loop only of next st in 3rd row below) twice, 1sc into back loop only of next 3 sts, *1tr into each of next 3 sts placing the hook as before, 1sc into back loop only of next 3 sts, rep from * to last 3 sts, 1tr into each of next 2 sts, 1sc into last st. Fasten off yarn. Do not turn work.

5th row As 3rd.

6th row Join A to beg of previous row. 1ch to count as first sc, 1sc into back loop only of next 2 sts, *(1tr into front loop only of next st in 3rd row below) 3 times, 1sc into back loop only of next 3 sts, rep from * to end. Fasten off. Do not turn.

7th row As 3rd.

Rows 4 through 7 form the pattern.

CROCHET WITH LEATHER AND SUEDE

In this chapter we have used circular leather motifs and crochet stitches together to give some interesting results. This type of work lends itself especially to the making of belts, bags and vests. A firm, good quality leather, suede or grain skin should be chosen to withstand the pull of the crochet work. Most local handicraft shops will sell off-cut leather pieces suitable for this purpose. First mark the shape on the wrong side of the skin by drawing around a circular object with a pencil. Cut out the circles with a sharp pair of scissors to avoid making a rough edge. You will need a special tool, called a leather punch, to make the holes, which must be evenly spaced around the circle, but not too near the edge. Also make sure that the holes are the correct size to accommodate the yarn and crochet hook you are using.

We have worked with various sized circles decorated with a Knitting Worsted, string and a lurex yarn, and a No.1 steel crochet hook. We show a number of methods for working crochet around leather circles here, along with instructions for joining the circles.

Sample 1

This illustrates a 1½ inch leather circle with the holes cut out ready to start work.

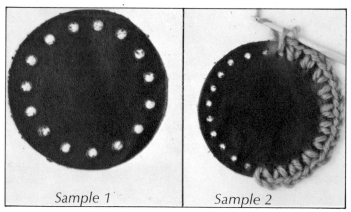

Sample 1   Sample 2

Sample 2

This is a 2¼ inch circle with the surrounding crochet in progress.

To work the crochet Hold the leather circle so that the right side is facing you and place the working yarn behind the circle, insert hook through any hole, yo and draw through hole, yo and draw through loop on hook, 2ch, *insert hook into next hole, yo and draw yarn through hole, yo and draw yarn through both loops on hook – 1sc has been worked into the hole –, 1ch, rep from * until you have crocheted around the circle. Join with a sl st into first ch to finish. Fasten off.

Sample 3

The single crochet edging around this circle is now complete.

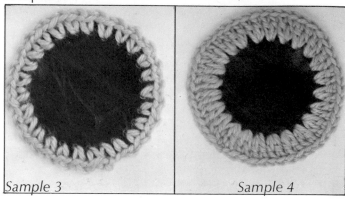

Sample 3   Sample 4

Sample 4

Using the same technique as described in sample 2, work 3ch at the beginning of the edging and work 1dc into the same hole, *2dc into next hole, rep from * to the end of the circle. Join with a sl st into 3rd of 3ch. Fasten off.

Sample 5

Here is a grouping of circles ranging in sizes from 1 inch to 2¼ inches. The surrounding stitches vary in depth to give a "clam" appearance.

Begin by working 2ch into the first hole, 1sc into each of next 2 holes with 1ch between them, then continue by working 2 sts into each hole and increase the stitch depth by working into the same number of holes with hdc, dc and hdc, then decrease the st size in the same way. The number of sts in each group will have to be varied according to the size of the circle and number of holes.

Samples 6, 7, 8 and 9 show a more experimental way to edge the leather. These would make ideal edgings for a plain leather vest.

Sample 6

1st round Begin with 2ch and 1sc into first hole, 2sc into each hole around. Join with a sl st into 2nd of 2ch.

2nd round 2ch (yo and insert hook into st at base of ch, yo and draw through a loop extending it for $\frac{3}{8}$ inch) twice, yo and draw through all 5 loops on hook, 1ch, skip next st, *yo and insert hook into next st, yo and draw through a loop extending it for $\frac{3}{8}$ inch, (yo and insert hook into same st as last, yo and draw through an extended loop) twice, yo and draw through all 7 loops on hook, 1ch, skip next st, rep from * to end of circle. Join with a sl st into 2nd of 2ch.

3rd round 1ch to count as first sc, *2sc into next sp between bobbles, 1sc into top of next bobble, rep from * to end, 2sc into next sp. Join with a sl st into first ch. Fasten off.

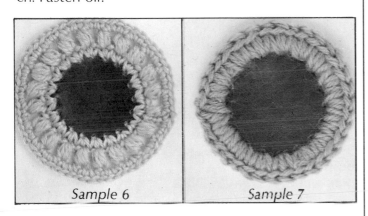
Sample 6   *Sample 7*

Sample 7

Cut 8 thicknesses of yarn to fit around the outer edge of the circle.

Next round Working over 8 thicknesses of yarn to produce a rounded effect, begin with 2ch and 1sc into first hole, 2sc into each hole to end of round. Join with a sl st into 2nd of 2ch. Fasten off.

Sample 8

Two colors, A and B, were used for this sample.

1st round Using A, beg with 3ch and 1dc into first hole, 2dc into each hole to end of round. Join with a sl st into 3rd of 3ch.

2nd round Join in B. Work 1sc into each st, working from left to right (working backwards around circle) instead of from right to left. Fasten off.

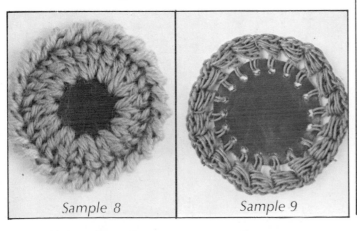
Sample 8   *Sample 9*

Sample 9

Green parcel string was used for this sample.

1st round Begin with 4ch into first hole, (yo and take hook in front of chain, around to the back and yo) 3 times, yo and draw through all 7 loops on hook, 1ch, *1dc into next hole, (yo and take hook in front of dc, around to the back and yo) 3 times, yo and draw through all 7 loops on hook, 1ch, rep from * to end of round. Join with a sl st into 3rd of 4ch. Fasten off.

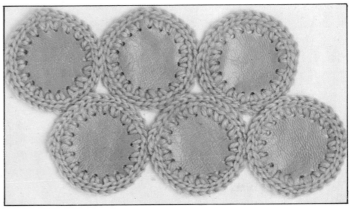

Sample 10

1st round Begin with 2ch, then work 1sc and 1ch into each hole to end of round. Join with a sl st into 2nd of 2ch.

2nd round Sl st into back loop only of each st to end of round.

To join the circles At the point where two circles are to be joined on the 2nd round, insert the hook into the next st of the circle on which you are working and then into any stitch of the circle to be joined, yo and draw through all loops on hook. In our sample three stitches were used at each joining point. Our circles were all the same size, but even if there were a variety of sizes they could be joined in the same way.

Sample 11

This gold belt illustrates the method of edging used in sample 7. Twelve circles, each 2 inches in diameter were used to fit a 27-inch waist. Work around half the circle in crochet before joining onto the next circle, and when the complete length has been worked, the return crochet is worked on the second half of each circle.

Brass rings are used as a fastening with a cord worked in double chain threaded through to link them.

PROJECTS WITH LEATHER AND VINYL

The technique of working crochet around leather circles was dealt with in the last chapter, and now we shall show you more ideas for using this technique with a variety of shapes and different materials.

Vinyl is an interesting fabric to work with as it has a very glossy surface which is a good contrast to most crochet yarns. Also it has the additional advantage of being able to be cut without the edges fraying in the same way as they do with leather. There are two types of vinyl available, one with a light backing fabric and one without. Both are suitable to use.

To make the suitcase

You will need four pieces of vinyl, two measuring 8 inches by 10½ inches for the outer piece and lining and another two measuring 16 inches by 10½ inches. The two larger pieces are for the back allowing for a fold-over flap, and the corners of these pieces should be rounded. Only the corners of the lower edge on the smaller front piece need to be rounded.

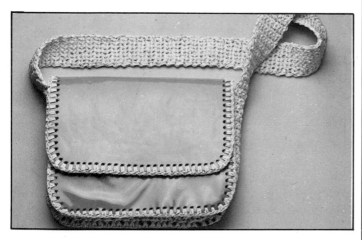

A middle layer of thick bonded interfacing is attached with a suitable fabric adhesive between the outer vinyl and the lining. The three layers are then treated as one. Holes are punched evenly around the vinyl pieces about ¼ inch in from the edge.

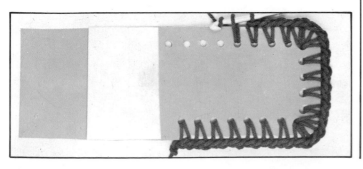

The back and front are then linked with a crochet gusset which extends to form the handle.

To work the gusset Using size F crochet hook and a very strong knitting yarn or string make 9ch.

Next row Into 3rd ch from hook work 1sc, 1sc into each ch to end. Turn.

Next row 1ch to count as first sc, 1sc into each st to end. Turn.

Rep last row until work measures 57 inches from beg. Fasten off. Join 2 short ends to form a circle.

To work the edging and join the sections together

Begin with a slip loop on the hook and hold the bag section with RS towards you, insert hook from front to back into first hole at right hand side of flap, yo and draw through a loop, yo and draw through both loops on hook – 1sc has been worked into the hole –, *1ch, work 1sc into next hole, rep from * to halfway down first long side (where back begins), then join bag onto gusset by placing hook through next hole as before and also through edge of gusset and complete the st in the usual way. Cont in this way until all the back and flap section has been worked. Work around the front section and join to the gusset in the same way.

To make the leather belt

The same techniques have been incorporated into the making of a belt. Depending on the size needed, you will need approximately ten rectangles of leather each 1¾ inches by 2½ inches. To these a strong bonded interfacing is again adhered to the wrong side of each shape.

To work the crochet Using a size E hook, a lurex yarn and with the RS of the work facing you, insert the hook from front to back into a hole, yo and draw through hole, yo and draw through a loop – 1ch has been worked –, *insert hook into next hole, yo and draw through hole, yo and draw through first loop on hook, yo and draw through both loops on hook, rep from * around shape, working 3 sts into each corner hole. Fasten off and finish ends.

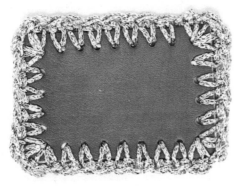

To join the parts Place two pieces with right sides together so that the chain of each stitch is uppermost on the right side thus giving a pronounced ridge effect. Sew together.

To fasten the belt Two large eyelets, available at most chain stores, are placed at either side of the center front opening. A double chain tie is then made to lace through the eyelets; this needs to be long enough to allow the belt to open enough for the wearer to slip the belt over her hips. Four loops of beads are then added to each end of the tie for trim.

To make the slippers
Another use for this form of work is for attractive slippers which are easy to make. Our size fits a size 5–6 foot. The pattern for the upper portion is divided into five pieces and each piece is cut out in both suede and a heavy bonded interfacing, which is then adhered to the suede. Holes are then punched around each piece.

To work the crochet Using size E crochet hook, a chenille yarn (or any other type of heavy yarn) and with the RS of the work facing you, insert hook into hole from front to back, yo and draw through hole, yo and insert hook into same hole, yo and draw through a loop, yo and draw through all 4 loops on hook, cont in this way around work, working 3 sts into each corner hole.

To join the parts together When the 5 pieces are completed, sew them firmly together on the wrong side. A lining fabric can also be sewn into place at this point, if desired.
The insole is cut from a plastic fabric and has a bonded interfacing backing adhered to it. Holes are punched around the sole. The stitches described for the suede shapes are then worked into the holes, noting that 1ch should be worked between the stitches at the heels and toes and also that the upper portions should be joined to the insoles between the marked positions by inserting the hook into the upper part and then into the insole, completing the stitch in the usual way. At this point the completed work is then adhered to a main rubber sole with a suitable adhesive. These instructions are repeated for the second slipper, making sure that the pattern pieces are reversed.

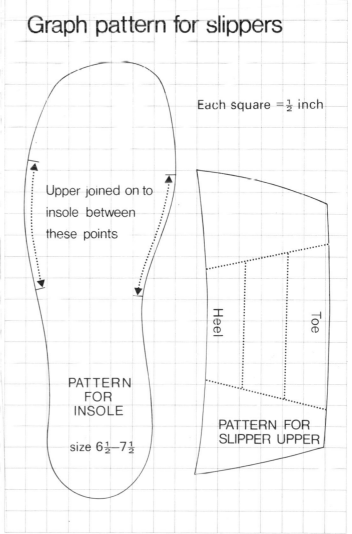

Graph pattern for slippers

Each square = ½ inch

Upper joined on to insole between these points

Heel

Toe

PATTERN FOR INSOLE

size 6½–7½

PATTERN FOR SLIPPER UPPER

COVERED RINGS
BASIC TECHNIQUES

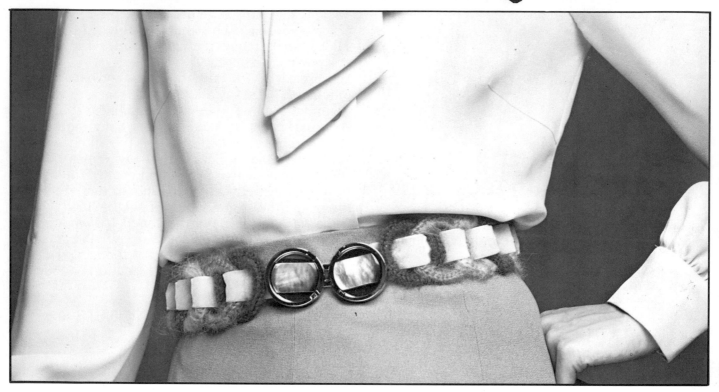

Crochet covered rings can be used in a variety of ways, ranging from belt fastenings to window hangings. There are several different methods of covering rings, some of which have already been illustrated, as, for example, covering them with a looped or buttonhole stitch or with simple crochet stitches.

This chapter develops the technique further and shows what can be done by using several rings on a belt. Any kind of curtain ring, obtainable from the drapery counters of your local department or large store, may be used. The type of yarn depends on the item being made, although this is largely a question of choice. The crochet hook should be one size smaller than usual in order to obtain a close stitch which will cover the ring completely.

To make the belt

For a belt which is approximately 28 inches long, you will need 23 rings each 1½ inches in diameter, five different shades of mohair yarn, a length of 1 inch wide velvet ribbon, a clasp and a size C crochet hook.

Before starting work on covering the ring note that the cut end of yarn at the beginning can be laid along the ring and worked over in order to finish it. Remember to keep the stitches close together so that the ring will be completely covered. Hold the yarn in the left hand in the usual way and place the ring over the yarn and, holding it between the thumb and first finger of left hand, insert the hook from front to back into the center of the ring, yo and draw through a loop, place the hook over the top of the ring, yo and draw yarn through loop on hook, *insert hook from front to back into the center of the ring, yo and draw through a loop, place hook over top of the ring, yo and draw through both loops on hook, rep from * until the ring is completely covered. Join with a sl st into first st. Break off the yarn and darn in the cut end.

Slot ribbon through the rings as shown in the illustration to form a continuous belt and attach a clasp at either end.

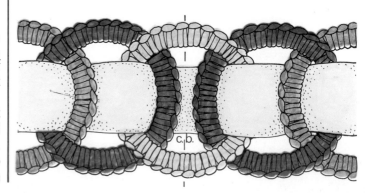

Alternative methods of working and joining rings suitable for belts

(a) Here the method of work is the same as that used for the belt rings, except that the rings are covered and joined continuously in one operation. Using size C hook, Knitting Worsted and 1¼-inch in diameter rings, work 14 stitches as previously shown to cover half the ring, then work the same number of stitches in a semi-circle around the next ring. Continue in this way until the required number of rings are joined and half covered in crochet. Work completely around the last ring and continue back along the other side of the rings.

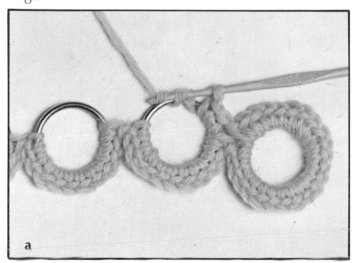

a

(b) Using size C crochet hook, a cotton yarn and 1¼-inch rings, work in the same way as given for

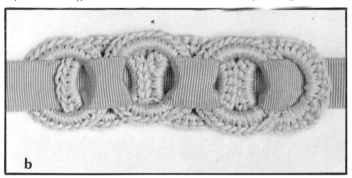

b

the belt and cover each ring individually. Thread grosgrain ribbon through the rings as shown in the illustration.

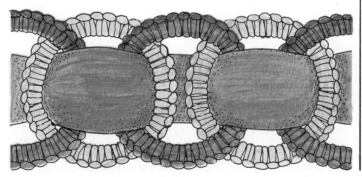

Alternative methods of covering individual rings

Each ring here is 2 inches in diameter and a size C hook is used for all the work.

(a) Here 34 stitches worked in straw yarn are needed to cover the ring. The straw gives a distinct chain edging to the circumference.

(b) Chenille yarn gives a softer appearance to this ring. You will need to work 46 stitches to cover the ring completely. The reverse side of the work is illustrated since this shows more of a looped effect.

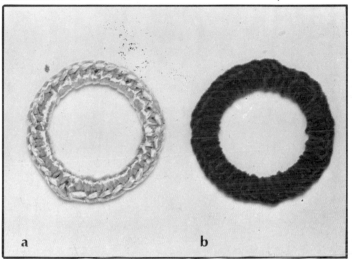

a   b

(c) Two rounds in two different yarns are worked over this ring. Using Knitting Worsted, work 50 stitches into the ring as given for the belt. Lurex yarn is used for the 2nd round where single crochet is worked into each stitch on the 1st round, working from left to right instead of from right to left.

(d) Work in the same way as for the previous sample until the 1st round has been completed. For the 2nd round, instead of working into all the stitches of the previous round, the hook is inserted into the center of the ring at various intervals. In this sample, using lurex yarn, work *1sc into each of next 3 sts, 1sc inserting hook into center of ring, 1sc into each of next 3 sts, 3sc inserting hook into center of ring, repeat from * to end of round. Join with a sl st into first st. Fasten off.

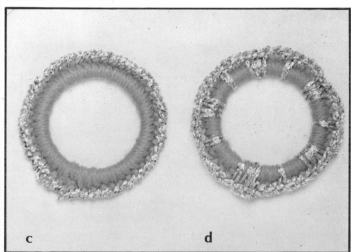

c   d

LARGE CIRCULAR MOTIFS

In this chapter, by telling you how to work our attractive window hanging, we hope to increase your knowledge of working circular motifs and to combine it now with two new techniques which we will give in these instructions. One is the method of covering a large ring and making loops so that crochet work may be attached to the ring; and the other is the method of making small circles by wrapping yarn around the fingers to form the base of the ring.

Window hangings are a popular continental form of decoration. Usually white yarn is used for this kind of work, this making more effective the many designs which are based on snowflake patterns. Once you know the new methods of working described in this chapter, use them with the various techniques and stitches with which we have dealt in previous chapters, and in this way you will be able to enjoy designing your own circular motifs.

To cover the ring

The most suitable ring to use is a plastic covered lampshade ring. Ours is 12 inches in diameter and the use of the plastic is practical, since it is rust proof and the white yarn will not stain.

Work eleven pair of reserve half hitch knots, making a picot between each group of eleven knots by leaving ½ inch of yarn free before working the next knot. Continue in this way until 24 picots have been made, join to first knot and fasten off. The covered ring will next be used in the final round of the crochet work.

To work the window hanging

Using size B crochet hook and a cotton yarn, wrap yarn 20 times around first two fingers of your left hand, insert hook under all the strands of yarn, yo and draw through a loop which now becomes your working st.

1st round 1ch to count as first sc, work 47sc into the circle of yarn. Join with a sl st into first ch.

2nd round 3ch, 1dc into same place as sl st, * 11ch, skip 5sc, leaving the last loop of each on hook, work 2dc into next sc, yo and draw through all 3 loops on hook, rep from * 6 times more. 11ch. Join with a sl st into 3rd of the 3ch.

3rd round * 13sc into next 11ch sp, sl st into top of pair of dc in previous round, rep from * 7 times more.

4th round ** Sl st into each of next 5sc, 5ch, skip 3sc, yo 4 times and insert hook into next sc, yo and draw through a loop, (yo and draw through first 2 loops on hook) 5 times—called a quad dc—, * 8ch, work a ring as foll: wrap yarn 10 times around second finger of left hand, insert hook under all the strands of yarn, yo and draw a loop through the working st on the hook, remove yarn from finger, work 23sc into the ring, join with a sl st into first st, (10ch, skip next 5sc on ring, sl st into next sc) twice, 8ch, sl st into top of pair of quad dc's at base of previous 8ch, * , 17ch, 1 quad dc into 5th sc of next sp, skip 3sc, 1 quad dc into next sc, rep from * to *, work 5 sl st down side of

next quad dc, sl st into each of next 5sc of sp, 21ch and now work 1sc into 3ch from hook, 1sc into each ch just worked, **. Rep from ** to ** 3 times more. Join with a sl st into first sl st of round. Fasten off.

5th round * Rejoin yarn into the top of the length of ch just worked, 6ch, 6sc into first 10ch sp above next ring, 6sc into next 10ch sp above same ring, 5ch, leaving the last loop of each st on hook work 3dc into next 17ch sp, yo and draw through all 4 loops on hook, 5ch, (6sc into next 10ch sp above ring) twice, 6ch, sl st into top of next length of 20ch, rep from * 3 times more.

6th round * 1ch, 6sc into next 6ch sp, sl st into each of next 12sc, (6sc into next 5ch sp) twice, sl st into each of next 12sc, 7sc into next 6ch sp, rep from * 3 times more working 7sc at beg of each rep instead of 1ch, 6sc. Join with a sl st into first ch.

7th round 3ch to count as first dc, 1dc into same place, * 5ch, skip next 4 sts, leaving the last loop of each st on hook, work 2dc into next st, yo and draw through all 3 loops on hook, rep from * around, ending with 5ch. Join with a sl st into 3rd of the 3ch.

8th round This is the round where the crochet motif is joined into the circle. Work 1ch, 5sc into first 5ch sp, 6sc into each sp to end of round, *at the same time* after every 10th st, remove hook from working loop, insert it into the picot on ring from front to back, reinsert it into the working loop and draw through picot. Join with a sl st into first ch.

A window hanging

Our last chapter dealt with the basic techniques involved in working large circular motifs which are popularly used as window hangings. The intricate design shown here involves three more complicated techniques in crochet. These show how to cover a narrow tube, enclose spheres with crochet, and one more way of covering and joining a center motif into a ring.

Follow our step by step instructions for making the window hanging and learn these new methods. You will enjoy making the pieces and will also find them useful for other forms of crochet work. The spheres, for example, could be very handsomely used as a decorative fringe on a lampshade. Once again, a plastic covered lampshade ring 12 inches in diameter was used for the large circle. Also used were a fine cotton yarn and a size B crochet hook.

To cover the tube

Make a slip loop on the hook, * holding the tube between thumb and first finger of left hand and having the yarn behind the tube, insert hook inside tube from top to lower edge, yo and draw through tube, taking hook behind tube, yo and draw through both loops on hook, rep from * 47 times more. Join with a sl st into first st. Fasten off.

Move the chain ridge formed by the previous row to give a zig-zag pattern with 3 points at each edge of the tube.

To work the center motif

1st round Join yarn into one of the zig-zag points, * 6ch, sl st into next point at same edge, rep from * twice more.

2nd round 12dc into first 6ch sp, 12ch into each of next 2 sps.

3rd round * 6ch, skip 5 sts, sl st into next st, rep from * 5 times more.

4th round Work 1sc into each sc worked on 2nd round. 36sc. Join with a sl st into first sc.

5th round * 4ch, sl st into next 6ch sp, 4ch, sl st into 6th sc of previous round (behind the joining point of two 6ch sp), rep from * 5 times more.

6th round Work 5sc into each 4ch sp around. Join

108

with a sl st to first sc.

7th round 9ch, skip 4sc, sl st into next sc, sl st into next to last ch just worked, *7ch, skip 4sc, sl st into next sc, sl st into next to last ch just worked, rep from * 9 times more, 5ch. Join with a sl st into 2nd of first 9ch.

8th round Work 7sc into each 5ch sp around. Join with a sl st into first sc.

9th round 3ch to count as first dc, 2dc into st at base of ch, *7ch, skip 6sc, 2tr into next sc, 7ch, skip 6sc, 3dc into next sc, rep from * 4 times more, 7ch, skip 6sc, 2tr into next sc, 7ch, skip 6sc. Join with a sl st into 3rd of first 3ch.

10th round 1ch to count as first sc, 1sc into each of next 6 sts, 10ch, skip 8 sts, *1sc into each of next 11 sts, 10ch, skip 8 sts, rep from * 4 times more, 1sc into each of next 4 sts. Join with a sl st into first ch. Fasten off. Rejoin yarn into one of the zig-zag points at the other end of the tube and repeat the 1st through 10th rounds, thus giving a 3-dimensional effect to the work.

To cover the small spheres

These are made from a crochet casing filled with cotton wool which forms a firm ball shape approximately 1½in in diameter. You will need six balls for our window hanging.

Using the same yarn and crochet hook, leave a length of yarn 14in long and then make 3ch. Join with a sl st into the first ch to form a ring.

1st round 1ch to count as first sc, work 9sc into ring. Join with a sl st into first ch.

2nd round 1ch to count as first sc, 2sc into next sc, *1sc into next sc, 2sc into next sc, rep from * to end. Join with a sl st into first ch. 15sc.

3rd round 2ch to count as first cluster st, *yo and insert hook into next sc, (yo and draw through a loop extending it for ⅜in) 4 times, yo and draw through all loops on hook—called 1 cluster st —, 1ch to secure the st, rep from * into each sc around. Join with a sl st into 2nd of the 2ch.

4th round 2ch to count as first cluster st, work 1 cluster st and 1ch into each cluster st around. Join with a sl st into 2nd of the 2ch.

Keeping the right side of the work on the outside, insert the cotton wool into the ball at this point.

5th round 1ch, (yo and insert hook into next cluster st, yo and draw through a loop) twice, yo and draw through all 5 loops on hook—thus dec 1sc. Rep from * around. Join with a sl st into first ch.

6th round 1ch to count as first sc, 1sc into each st of previous round. Join with a sl st into first ch. Thread yarn carefully through each st of last round and draw through the last st on the hook. Leave a length of yarn 14in long for attaching the sphere on to the work.

To cover the ring and join in the center motif

To work the covering of our lampshade ring, we used a size D crochet hook and a slightly thicker cotton. First place a slip loop on to the crochet hook, keeping the yarn behind the ring, insert the hook into the ring, from top to lower edge, yo and draw through both loops on hook. Repeat this stitch until the ring is completely covered. You will need 258 stitches if you are using the same size ring as in our directions. Fasten off.

Next round Rejoin yarn into any st and draw through, thus making a st. Work 1sc into each st around. Join with a sl st into first st.

Next round *36ch, skip 42sc, sl st into next sc, rep from * 5 times more.

Next round Sl st into each of next 2ch, 3ch, 1dc into st at base of 3ch, (2ch, skip next 2ch, leaving the last loop of each st on hook, work 2ch into next ch, yo and draw through all 3 loops on hook—called a joint dc—, 5 times, 1ch, remove hook from working loop and insert it from back to front into any of the 10ch sp of 10th round of either section of center motif, *pick up the working loop and work 1ch, skip 2ch, (a joint dc into next ch, 2ch, skip 2ch) 5 times, a joint dc into next ch, skip 2ch, a joint dc into next ch, (2ch, skip 2ch, a joint dc into next ch) 5 times, remove hook from working loop and insert it into next 10ch sp of same section as before*. Repeat from * to * 4 times more, pick up the working loop and work 1ch, skip 2ch, (a joint dc into next ch, 2ch, skip 2ch) 5 times, a joint dc into next ch. Join with a sl st into 3rd of the 3ch.

To join the spheres

Using the 10ch sp of the other part of the center motif, attach one end of the sphere firmly to the center of the space. At the other end of the sphere, crochet 4ch and attach to the point where two joint double crochet meet at the point of a star on the ring.

CROCHET ON MESH
CROCHET ON NET

This is an unusual and unexpected use for crochet—working on to net to create a design, which can eventually be completed to give the appearance of lace. The samples in this chapter demonstrate the basic techniques and are worked in straight rows. These need to be practiced first, however, before attempting anything more complicated.

Several types of net are available, usually made from nylon, silk or rayon. Although colored nets are easy to obtain, white still is the most popular, one reason being that it is available in very wide yardages which makes it ideal for wedding veils.

For beginners the usual commercial net is rather fine to work with at first, consequently for our samples we have used one with a larger hole. Work with a size B hook and Knitting Worsted when practicing. If you cannot obtain net with the larger holes, we suggest that you use the plastic net often found in supermarkets for covering oranges and other fruits. You may find it easier to work the crochet if the net is placed in an embroidery ring, holding it taut in this way to ease the insertion of the hook.

Sample 1

The chain on net is the first basic stitch, and all the other designs are variations of this, therefore it is important to master this technique first. Place the net firmly in the ring. Begin working from the outer edge of the ring and plan to work in an upward direction. This is the easiest way to start, but when you are more familiar with this technique you will be able to work in any chosen direction. Holding the yarn under the net or the ring and the hook over the net on the ring, insert the hook into one hole, yo and draw through a loop, * insert the hook into the next hole above (as shown in the illustration), yo and draw

through a loop, drawing it through the loop already on the hook—one chain st has been worked over one hole in the net. Repeat from * for the desired length.

Note It is important to keep your chain stitches fairly loose, otherwise the net will pucker.

Sample 2

Chain stitch is used again, but the hook is placed into alternate holes.

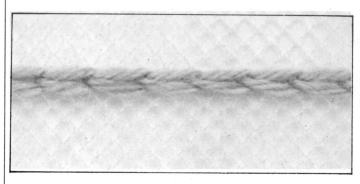

Sample 3

This is worked in the same way as for sample 2, but in 8 rows of 4 colors to give a striped effect. The chain is worked back and forth, and you turn the ring for each new row and cut the yarn only when changing colors.

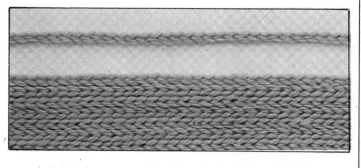

Sample 4

Straight lines have been used again here, but a zigzag effect has been achieved by, *working 8 sts into alternate diagonal holes in a left to right direction, then another 8 sts into alternate diagonal holes in a right to left direction, rep from * for the required length. Two rows have been worked in a variety of colors, leaving a space of two rows of holes between each new color.

Sample 5

Here a variety of stitches has been worked using the same technique. First place the net in the ring as given for sample 1.

(a) Insert hook into one hole on the edge of the ring,

and again working upward, yo and draw through a loop extending it to reach 3rd hole on right, insert hook into this hole, yo and draw through a loop drawing it through loop on hook, *insert hook into adjacent hole above last st on left, yo and draw through a loop extending it as before, insert hook into 3rd hole on the right, yo and draw through all loops on hook, rep from * to end of the row.

(b) Following the illustration work in a similar way to previous sample, but extend the stitches alternately two and three spaces to the right.

(c) You will see from the illustration that this sample has been worked over 3 sts in a zigzag direction.

(d) Two rows of sts as given for sample (a) have been worked side by side (work one row as on sample (a), then turn the ring so that the completed row is on the right and work a second row as the first thus working the chain sts in adjacent rows).

Sample 6

These stitches are all a zigzag variation of chain stitch.

(a) Place net in ring as given for sample 1. Working upward as before, insert hook into hole at left edge, yo and draw through a loop, skip one hole on the right, insert hook into next hole on the right, yo and draw through a loop drawing it through loop on hook, *insert hook into next hole above last st on the left, yo and draw through a loop drawing it through loop on hook, skip one hole on the right, insert hook into next hole above last st on the right, yo and draw through a loop drawing it through loop on hook, rep from * to end of row.

(b) This is worked in the same way as sample (a), but slightly more spaced (there is one hole skipped between each st worked on the left and on the right).

(c) Here is another variation where the hook is inserted to give a diamond effect.

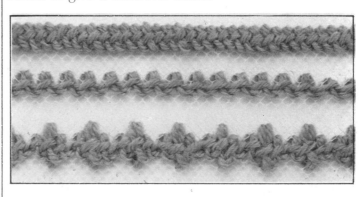

CROCHET ON RUG CANVAS

Crochet on rug canvas

Most stitches on canvas are worked with a needle, but many interesting effects will be illustrated in this chapter where crochet techniques are used.

In the last chapter we demonstrated how crochet is worked onto net where the holes do not come immediately one above the other, but rather to either side on each new row. With canvas, however, the holes are immediately next to and above each other, consequently your designs can easily be worked out on ordinary squared graph paper.

Both double and single weave canvas can be used for this technique, and very delicate work can be achieved by using a finer canvas with more holes to the square inch. Choose a hook which will easily enter the holes in the canvas and a yarn which will completely cover the weave when the stitches are worked. Too fine a yarn used with a thick canvas will result in gaps in the finished work.

No frame is necessary if you are using a stiff canvas. If a large amount of work is being done and a finer canvas is being used, an embroidery frame is recommended, which can be obtained from any good crafts supplier or shop. For our samples we have used an ordinary rug canvas, a bulky knitting yarn and a size E crochet hook. This combination of materials is suitable for making shoulder bags, carryalls and chair seat covers.

Sample 1

At the top of the sample a straight line of chain stitch has been worked in every adjacent hole. This was worked upward from the lower edge of the canvas and then turned to give a horizontal row of stitches. Two rows have been completed and the third is in the process of being worked.

To work the stitches Holding the yarn under the canvas in the usual way and the hook above the right side of the canvas, insert hook into one hole on the line of canvas to be worked, yo and draw loop through hole, *insert hook into next hole upwards, yo and draw through a loop drawing it through loop on hook, rep from * for the desired length of chain.

To the left of the photograph the same chain stitches have been worked vertically. The canvas is turned at the end of every row in order to keep working in an upward direction.

The remaining sample shows chain stitches worked into a zigzag design. Again work up the canvas and follow the chart which shows where to insert the hook.

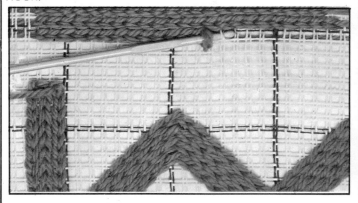

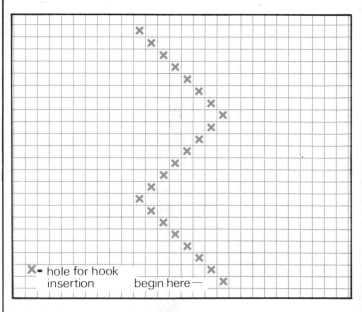

× - hole for hook insertion   begin here —

Sample 2

This is a square design worked in chain stitch which can be either enlarged to form one pattern, or on a smaller gauge, used together as motifs.

Each new round of our sample has been worked in a different color and a different yarn, including straw. Follow the diagram for the order of working, beginning with the 1st round which is to be worked over the four holes at the center.

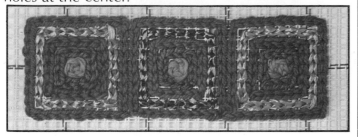

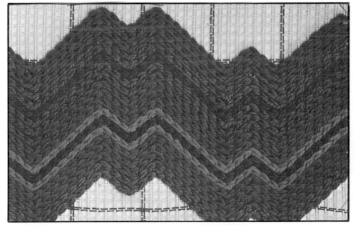

○ = 1st round

□ = 2nd

△ = 3rd

◇ = 4th

▽ = 5th

Sample 3

This is a copy of Florentine embroidery, the zigzag stitchery which is often seen on canvas. Careful color selection is necessary for this and the work can be made much more effective by varying the number of rows worked in each color. The chart illustrates our design, but it is quite easy to adapt your own ideas into zigzag patterns.

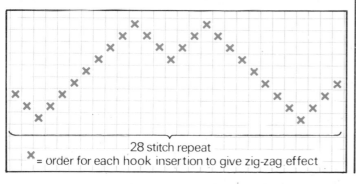

28 stitch repeat
× = order for each hook insertion to give zig-zag effect

Sample 4

This illustrates three stitches which can be used on rug canvas in place of chain stitch. Follow the instructions given here to learn how to work these stitches.

(a) Holding the yarn and hook as given for sample 1 and working in an upward direction, insert hook into one hole on the row of work, yo and draw through a loop, insert hook into next hole up, yo and draw through a loop, drawing it through loop on hook, *insert hook into next hole up on 2nd row to the left, yo and draw through a loop extending it to meet the next hole above last st worked on the right, insert hook into that hole, yo and draw through a loop drawing it through both loops on hook. Rep from * for the desired length.

(b) Holding the yarn and hook as given for sample 1 and working in an upward direction, insert hook into one hole on the row of work, yo and draw through a loop, insert hook into next hole up, yo and draw through a loop drawing it through loop on hook, insert hook into next hole up on 2nd row to the left, *yo and draw through a loop extending it to meet the next hole above last st worked on the right, insert hook into that hole, yo and draw through a loop drawing it through both loops on hook, *, — one long st has been worked. Insert hook into next hole up on the next row to the left and rep from * to * to form a short st. Cont working a long and a short st alternately to end of the line. Turn work and repeat a second row of crochet opposite the first, working a long st next to a short st and a short st next to a long st.

(c) Holding the yarn and hook as given for sample 1 and working in an upward direction, insert hook into one hole on row of work, *insert hook into next hole up to the left, yo and draw through a loop drawing it through loop on hook, insert hook into next hole to the right, yo and draw through a loop drawing it through loop on hook, rep from * for the desired length.

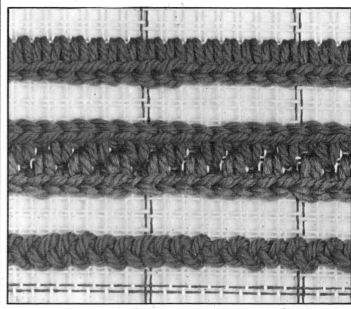

EMBROIDERY ON CROCHET

Crochet plus stitchery

A background of simple crochet lends itself attractively to decorative stitchery and many of the traditional embroidery stitches can be worked onto crochet fabrics.

To work the crochet background This is a basic mesh which is quick and simple to work. Vary the size of the mesh by working a smaller or larger crochet stitch with additional or fewer chain stitches between as desired. Any yarn may be used but for these samples we have used a size E crochet hook and Knitting Worsted. Make a length of chain with multiples of 4 plus 11 stitches.

1st row Into 11th ch from hook work 1tr, *3ch, skip next 3ch, 1tr into next ch, rep from * to end. Turn.

2nd row 7ch to count as first tr and 3ch, skip first tr, 1tr into next tr, *3ch, 1tr into next tr, rep from * ending with last tr into 4th of turning ch. Turn.

Rep the 2nd row for the required depth of work. Throughout these samples we have used an embroidery stitch which is a form of darning. Again any yarn can be used, but choose it carefully and work a trial piece before beginning work since different yarns make stitches which can look entirely different. Many varied and attractive designs can be made with this basic stitch technique including table linen, bedcovers and curtains. A more delicate effect can be made by using a finer cotton yarn and a smaller sized crochet hook.

Sample 1

Here is a design which is suitable for an over-all pattern. Certain squares on the background have been

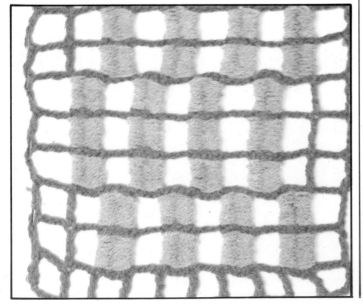

filled in with the darning or weaving stitch as shown on the illustration. The chart shows which squares are to be filled in.

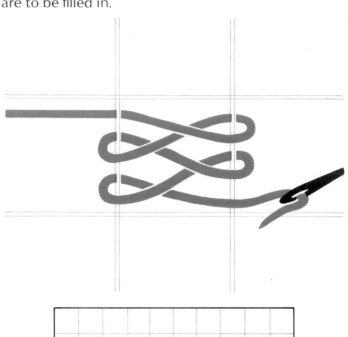

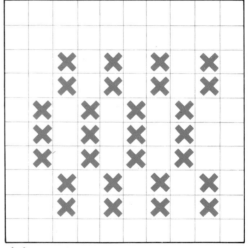

X = sq. to be filled in with 'darning' stitch

Sample 2

This basic background has a shaped edge and the finished piece of work could be used as a window valance or as an edging on a window shade.

To work the background Work 3 rows as given for the basic background.

4th row Sl st across first 4 sts to dec one square, 7ch, patt to end. Turn.

5th row Patt to last square, turn to dec one square.

6th row 8ch to count as first tr of this row and space at end of next row, sl st into each of first 4ch, 3ch, patt to end. Turn.

7th row Patt to end, working last tr into last sl st of previous row to inc one square. Turn.

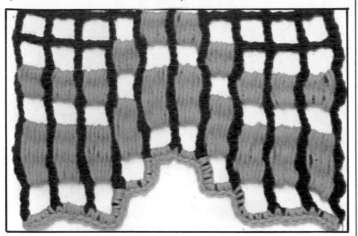

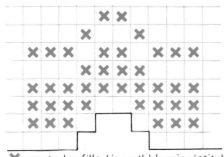

✕ - sq. to be filled in with 'darning' stitch

8th row 10ch to inc one square, 1tr into first tr, patt to end. Turn.

9th–10th row Patt to end. Turn.

These 10 rows form the basic pattern which can be repeated for the desired length.

Darn the appropriate squares as shown in the chart and then, using the same yarn as for the darning, complete the shaped edge by working 3sc into each square and 1sc into each tr or corner of a square.

Sample 3

Circular motifs have been added to the basic background. Using two strands of a 4 ply yarn together,

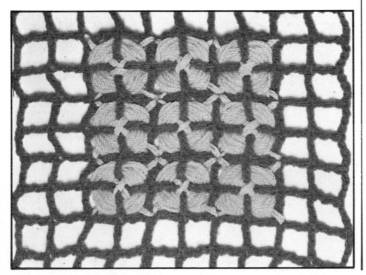

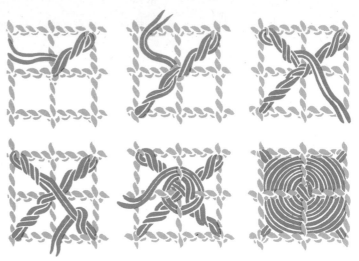

thread the motifs over four squares as shown in the illustration. The photograph shows the motifs worked over adjacent groups of four squares.

Sample 4

Here a single flower motif has been worked onto a basic background using a bulky yarn. After working the four basic lines as shown in the illustration twice, weave the thread around the center by passing the needle (under the blue line, over the green, under the red and over the brown) six times in all. All the cut ends of yarn should then be finished on the wrong side of the work.

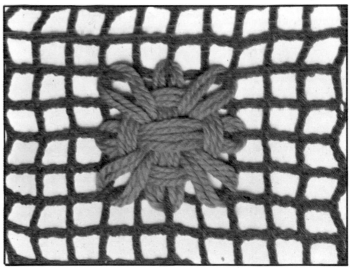

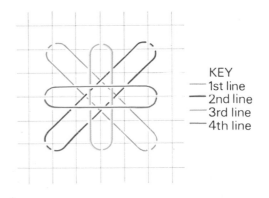

KEY
— 1st line
— 2nd line
— 3rd line
— 4th line

MORE EMBROIDERY DESIGNS

This is a continuation of our chapter about weaving designs onto a crochet mesh background. We also give instructions for working an unusual and decorative shawl, which is simple to make and employs the techniques shown in recent chapters. Practice the samples shown here before starting to work on the shawl.

Sample 1

To work the background Using size D crochet hook and a 4 ply yarn, make a length of chain with multiples of 4 +11 stitches.
1st row Into 11th ch from hook work 1tr, *3ch, skip 3ch, 1tr into next ch, rep from * to end. Turn.
2nd row 7ch to count as first tr and 3ch, skip first sp, 1tr into next tr, *3ch, 1tr into next tr, rep from * to end with last tr into 4th of turning ch. Turn.
The 2nd row is repeated throughout.

Sample 2

Work the mesh as given for sample 1, then weave the flower with a double thickness of contrasting yarn as in the illustration for sample 4 of previous chapter.

To work the flower Using double thickness of a contrasting yarn and a large blunt-ended needle, follow the diagram and work the yarn through the crochet mesh.

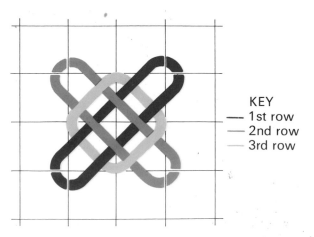

KEY
— 1st row
— 2nd row
— 3rd row

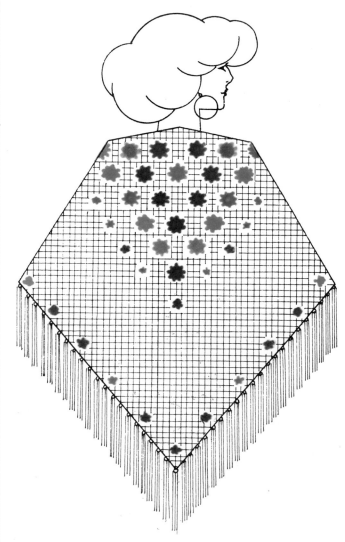

116

Crochet shawl

Size

Triangle measures approximately 45 inches across top and 30 inches from center of top edge to point

Gauge

5ch sp and 6 rows to 3 inches in patt worked with size C crochet hook

Materials

10 × 30grm balls Reynolds Parfait
Small amounts of six contrasting colors
One size C crochet hook

Shawl

Using size C hook and A, make 327ch loosely.

1st row Into 11th ch from hook work 1tr, *3ch, skip 3ch, 1tr into next ch, rep from * to end. Turn. Eighty 3ch sp.

2nd row 7ch to count as first tr and 3ch, skip first sp, 1tr into next tr, *3ch, 1tr into next tr, rep from * ending with last tr into 4th of turning ch. Turn.

3rd and 4th rows As 2nd.

5th row (dec row) 7ch to count as first tr and 3ch, skip first sp, (1tr into next tr) twice – i.e. skip the 3ch between tr, so dec one sp –, *3ch, 1tr into next tr, rep from * to last 2 sp, 1tr into· next tr, 3ch, 1tr into 4th of turning ch. Turn. 2 sp decreased.

6th and 7th rows As 2nd.

8th row As 5th.

Cont in this way, dec 2 sp on every foll alt row, until 46 sp rem, then on every row until 2 sp rem. Fasten off.

Finishing

Using the contrasting colors, apply motifs as shown in the illustration. Care should be taken to finish all the cut ends neatly on the wrong side of the work.

Fringe Cut 10 strands of yarn each 13 inches long, fold in half and using crochet hook pull folded end through first space at side of shawl, pull cut ends through loop thus made and pull tight to form a knot. Rep these knots into each space along 2 sides of the triangle. Trim fringe ends evenly.

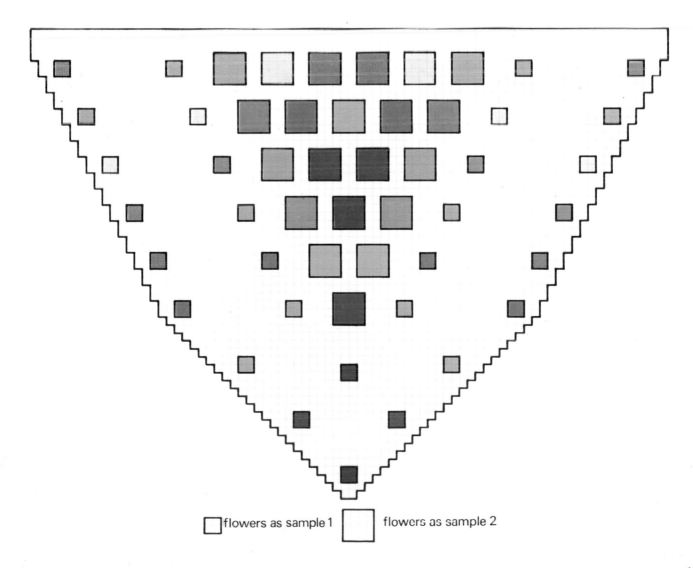

☐ flowers as sample 1   ☐ flowers as sample 2

BEADED DESIGNS

Beaded designs may easily be incorporated into crochet work during the process of making an article. There are numerous types of beads, normally made of glass, china or wood, available in most large department or chain stores.

The size of beads varies considerably, but any type can be used for this kind of work providing that the hole in the bead is large enough to take the yarn which is being used. To thread the beads onto the yarn, see the second chapter on Loopy Stitches. Each bead is positioned so that it forms part of a design and care must be taken to see that the beads are placed on the right side of the work.

It should be remembered too that beads are quite heavy if they are used in large quantities. Therefore small articles are really the most suitable, or border pattern areas. Even these articles will need to be lined to strengthen the work and to accomodate the weight of the beads.

Beads are particularly popular for evening wear. Very attractive patterns using beads may be designed and applied to evening jackets and bags, or used as a border around the hem of a long evening coat or skirt. There are two distinct methods of applying the beads. One way is to thread the beads onto the yarn which you will be using, before you start working. The bead is then pushed up and positioned as it is needed and the next stitch is then worked in the usual way. This technique is illustrated in samples 1 and 2. Another method, used in sample 3, is to thread the beads onto a separate ball of yarn. When a bead row is being worked, the yarn on either side of the bead is caught into place during the working of the crochet by looping the working yarn around the yarn holding the beads. Our samples show some simple designs which follow the two methods described above. If you practice these samples from our instructions you will soon become familiar with the art of beaded crochet.

Sample 1

Using a fine yarn and No.0 crochet hook, make 40ch.

1st row Into 3rd ch from hook work 1sc, 1sc into each ch to end. Turn.

2nd–7th rows 1ch to count as first sc, 1sc into each sc to end. Turn.

8th row 1ch to count as first sc, 1sc into each of next 6 sts, *push up one bead, placing it at back of the work which will be the right side, 1sc into next st – called 1 Bsc –, 1sc into each of next 7 sts, rep from * 3 times more. Turn.

9th row 1ch to count as first sc, 1sc into each of next 6 sts, *noting that beads are placed at the front of the work, 1Bsc into each of next 2 sts, 1sc into each of next 6 sts, rep from * 3 times more. Turn.

10th row 1ch to count as first sc, 1sc into each of next 5 sts, *1Bsc into each of next 3 sts, 1sc into each of next 5 sts, rep from * 3 times more, ending last rep 1sc with each of next 6 sts. Turn.

11th row 1ch to count as first sc, 1sc into each of next 5 sts, *1Bsc into each of next 4 sts, 1sc into each of next 4 sts, rep from * 3 times more, ending last rep 1sc with each of next 5 sts. Turn.

12th row 1ch to count as first sc, 1sc into each of next 4 sts, *1Bsc into each of next 5 sts, 1sc into each of next 3 sts, rep from * twice more, 1Bsc into each of next 5 sts, 1sc into each of next 5 sts. Turn.

13th row As 11th.

14th row As 10th.

15th row As 9th.

16th row 1ch to count as first sc, 1sc into each of next 2 sts, *1Bsc into next st, 1sc into each of next 3 sts, rep from * 8 times more. Turn.

17th row 1ch to count as first sc, 1sc into each of next 2 sts, *1Bsc into each of next 2 sts, 1sc into each of next 6 sts, rep from * 3 times more, 1Bsc into each of next 2 sts, 1sc into each of next 2 sts. Turn.

18th row 1ch to count as first sc, 1sc into next st, *1Bsc into each of next 3 sts, 1sc into each of next 5 sts, rep from * 3 times more, 1Bsc into each of next 3 sts, 1sc into each of next 2 sts. Turn.

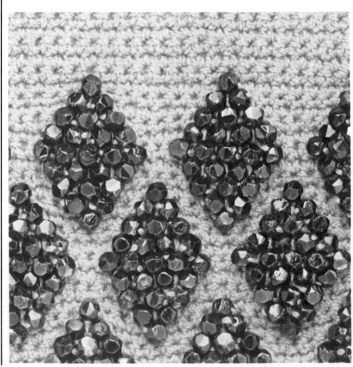

19th row 1ch to count as first sc, 1sc into next st, *1Bsc into each of next 4 sts, 1sc into each of next 4sc, rep from * 3 times more, 1Bsc into each of next 4 sts, 1sc into last st. Turn.

20th row 1ch to count as first sc, *1Bsc into each of next 5 sts, 1sc into each of next 3 sts, rep from * 3 times more, 1Bsc into each of next 5 sts, 1sc into last st. Turn.

21st–24th rows As 19th–16th rows, in that order. The 9th row is then repeated to complete the pattern and to start the next diamond shape.

Sample 2

Using a cotton yarn and No.0 crochet hook, make 40ch.

1st row Into 3rd ch from hook work 1hdc, 1hdc into each ch to end. Turn.

2nd row 2ch to count as first hdc, 1hdc into each of next 6 sts, *push up one bead, placing it at back of work which will be the right side, 1hdc in the next st – called 1Bhdc –, 1hdc into each of next 7 sts, rep from * 3 times more. Turn.

3rd row 2ch to count as first hdc, *1hdc into each of next 5 sts, 1Bhdc into next st, 1hdc into next st, 1Bhdc into next st, rep from * 3 times more, 1hdc into each of next 6 sts. Turn.

4th row 2ch to count as first hdc, 1hdc into each of next 4 sts, *1Bhdc into next st, 1hdc into each of next 3 sts, rep from * 7 times more, 1Bhdc into next st, 1hdc into each of next 2 sts. Turn.

5th row 2ch to count as first hdc, 1hdc into each of next 3 sts, *1Bhdc into next st, 1hdc into each of next 5 sts, 1Bhdc into next st, 1hdc into next st, rep from * 3 times more, 1hdc into each of next 3 sts. Turn.

6th row 2ch to count as first hdc, 1hdc into each of next 2 sts, *1Bhdc into next st, 1hdc into each of next 7

sts, rep from * 3 times more, 1 Bhdc into next st, 1hdc into each of next 3 sts. Turn.

7th–10th rows As 5th–2nd rows, in that order. The 2nd through 10th rows form the pattern.

Sample 3

Wooden beads, approximately $\frac{3}{4}$ inch long, were used for this sample. Thread them on to a separate ball of yarn.

Using a cotton yarn and size C crochet hook, make 33ch.

1st row Into 3rd ch from hook work 1sc, 1sc into each ch to end. Turn.

2nd–8th rows 1ch to count as first sc, 1sc into each sc to end. Turn.

9th row 1ch to count as first sc, 1sc into next st, *hold the yarn with the beads behind the work, place the working yarn round the yarn holding the beads, work 1sc into next st, work 1sc into each of next 3 sts using the main yarn, push up one bead into position behind the work, *, rep from * to * 9 times more, ending last rep with 1sc into each of next 2 sts. Turn. Cut off yarn holding beads.

10th row Work in sc.

11th row 1ch to count as first sc, 1sc into each of next 3 sts, rep from * to * of 9th row to complete the row. The 9th and 11th rows show the sequence of working the beads so that they lie in alternate spaces. You may make your own designs by using this sequence, but remember that the beads are always placed from the opposite side of the work, so that you will have to cut the yarn after each bead row.

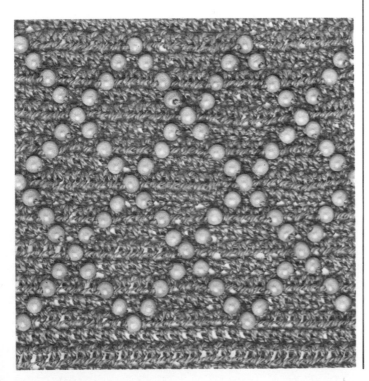

NEEDLEWEAVING
BASIC DESIGNS

Crochet with needleweaving

This chapter gives instructions for working a crochet background into which various materials may be woven to produce a solid fabric. The background is formed by working in double crochets with one chain separating each one, and on subsequent rows the double crochets are worked into those on the previous row to give a straight vertical line. The chains of each space or the double crochets worked between the spaces, form bars over or under which the weaving threads may pass, according to the design.

A crochet hook or blunt-ended needle is used to pass the threads vertically, horizontally or diagonally across the fabric, breaking off the yarn after each row. It is interesting to experiment with different yarns and ribbons for weaving. We have used four thicknesses of the same yarn, rug wool, various ribbons and strips of plastic. Strips of fur could also be used to produce a very expensive-looking fabric.

The weaving threads help to keep the crochet in position and, as the fabric formed is thick and warm, it is especially suitable for outer garments such as jackets, coats, scarves and skirts. The fabric made by this technique is also ideal for pillows and rugs.

Follow the instructions for our samples before experimenting with your own designs and yarns.

Sample 1

This is the basic open background for needle weaving. Using size F hook and Knitting Worsted, make 30ch.

1st row Into 6th ch from hook work 1dc, *1ch, skip next ch, 1dc into next ch, rep from * to end. Turn.

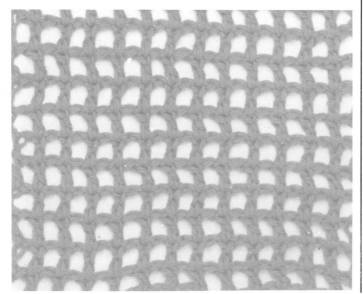

Note A firmer fabric is produced by placing the hook under three loops of each dc, instead of the usual one or two loops.

2nd row 4ch to count as first dc and 1ch, skip first ch sp, 1dc into next dc, *1ch, skip next ch sp, 1dc into next dc, rep from * to end, working last dc into 4th of 5ch. Turn.

The 2nd row is repeated throughout, noting that each subsequent row will end with last dc worked into 3rd of 4ch.

One attractive item to make entirely in this stitch is a bag. It is quick and easy to work in one piece which is folded in half and seamed at the sides. A row of crochet chain gathers the top edges and at the same time joins them to wooden handles.

Sample 2

Work a basic background as given for sample 1. Ribbon, $\frac{1}{4}$ inch wide, is then woven vertically through the spaces.

1st weaving row Draw the ribbon under the ch of the foundation row and up into the first space, *skip the next space and insert ribbon from front to back into the next space, draw ribbon from back to front into the next space, *, rep from * to * to end of fabric.

2nd weaving row Insert ribbon from front to back into first space of next row, then draw ribbon from back to front into second space, rep from * to * of 1st weaving row to end of fabric.

3rd weaving row Insert ribbon from front to back into second space of next row, then draw ribbon from back to front into third space, rep from * to * of 1st weaving row to end of fabric.

The 3 weaving rows are repeated vertically across the fabric.

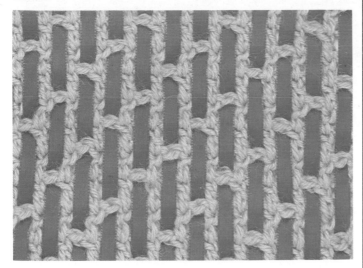

Sample 3

Green household string has been used for the background of this sample. Using size H hook make 31ch.

1st row Into 7th ch from hook work 1tr, *1ch, skip next ch, 1tr into next ch, rep from * to end. Turn.

2nd row 5ch, skip next sp, 1tr into next tr, *1ch, 1tr into next tr, ending with last tr into 5th of 6ch. Turn.

The 2nd row is repeated throughout, noting that each subsequent row will end with last tr worked into 4th of 5ch.

$\frac{3}{4}$ inch wide grosgrain ribbon is woven horizontally through each space on the first row, and then through alternate spaces on the next row.

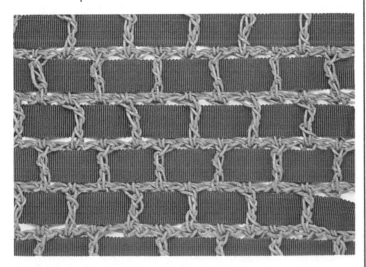

Sample 4

Work a basic background as given for sample 1. There are two types of weaving involved in this design. First, thick rug wool is placed vertically around each treble crochet working up the fabric. Instead of working in and out of the crochet fabric, the rug wool is placed under each treble from left to right working upwards on the first row and on

alternate rows. On the remaining rows the rug wool is threaded in the same way, but it is passed from right to left.

Strips of plastic $\frac{1}{4}$ inch wide, matching the background color, and ribbon $\frac{1}{4}$ inch wide, matching the rug wool are then woven alternately between each row of treble crochets. The plastic is threaded so that on the right side the strip passes completely over one space, while the ribbon goes into alternate spaces.

Sample 5

Work a basic background as given for sample 1.

The weaving is worked in two different colors, A and B, of Knitting Worsted, using four thicknesses together each time. With A work into alternate horizontal spaces on the first row. Continue with A into each horizontal row throughout the fabric, alternating the spaces worked into with those on the previous row. Color B is woven vertically into each row in the same way as A, weaving in and out of the strands of A as well as the bars of the background fabric.

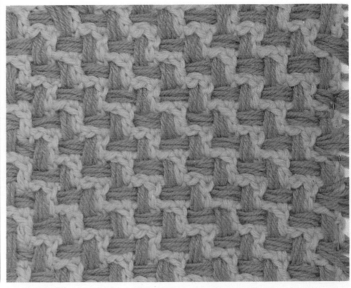

EXPERIMENTAL TECHNIQUES

The basic methods of needle weaving were dealt with in the last chapter, and now we shall illustrate some more experimental uses of this technique with different yarns and with other methods of weaving. Two of the samples are checked fabrics worked onto the basic background and they are thick and warm because of the way in which they are worked. Other samples are worked in different crochet stitches to form a background. Most of these samples of needle weaving are suitable for an over-all fabric, but some (such as sample 4) can be adapted very well to the making of an attractive border for a jacket or long skirt.

Sample 1
To work the background This is worked in two colors of Knitting Worsted, A and B. Using size H hook and A, make 30ch.

1st row Into 6th ch from hook work 1dc, *1ch, skip 1ch, 1dc into next ch, rep from * to end. Turn.

2nd row 4ch to count as first dc and 1ch, skip 1ch sp, 1dc into next dc, *1ch, skip 1ch sp, 1dc into next dc, rep from * finishing with last dc into 5th of 6ch. Turn.

Join in B and rep 2nd row twice more, noting that on subsequent rows the last dc is worked into 3rd of 4ch. Continue in this way, working 2 rows in each color, for the desired length.

To work the weaving Using 4 thicknesses of A together, weave in and out of each vertical space on the first row. Then using A again, work into each space on the next row alternating where the yarn passes over or under a bar. Alternating A and B, repeat this process in two row stripes throughout the fabric.

C. Note also that colors A and C will have to be cut at the end of the row so that the yarn will be in the correct position for the repeat of color sequence.

To work the weaving This is worked in the same way as sample 1, but with one vertical row in A, two rows in B and three rows in C.

Sample 3
Two colors of Knitting Worsted are used for this sample, color A for the background and B for the needle weaving.

To work the background Using size H hook and A, make 27ch.

1st row Into 5th ch from hook work 4dc leaving last loop of each st on hook, yo and draw through all loops on hook, 1ch, skip 1ch, 1sc into next ch, *1ch, skip 1ch, into next ch work 4dc leaving last loop of each on hook, yo and draw through all loops on hook, 1ch, skip 1ch, 1sc into next ch, rep from * to end. Turn.

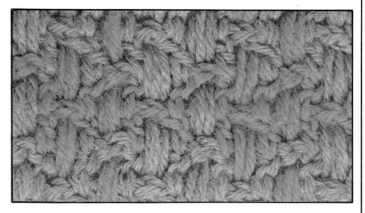

Sample 2
To work the background This is worked in three colors of Knitting Worsted, A, B and C. Using size H hook make a background as given for sample 1, but work one row in A, two rows in B and three rows in

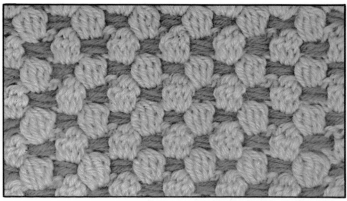

2nd row 3ch, into first sc work 3dc leaving last loop of each on hook, yo and draw through all loops on hook, 1ch, *1dc into top of next 4dc gr, 1ch, into next sc work 4dc leaving last loop of each on hook, yo and draw through all loops on hook, 1ch, rep from *

finishing with last 4dc gr into turning ch. Turn.

3rd row 2ch, *into next sc work 4dc leaving last loop of each on hook, yo and draw through all loops on hook, 1ch, 1sc into top of next 4dc gr, 1ch, rep from * to end, omitting 1ch at end of last rep. Turn. The 2nd and 3rd rows are repeated throughout.

To work the weaving Four thicknesses of color B are placed horizontally across every row by weaving them under each four double crochet group, and over each single crochet.

Sample 4

This crochet background illustrates an attractive stitch made up of blocks and spaces.

To work the background Using size G hook and Knitting Worsted, make 29ch.

1st row Into 5th ch from hook work 2tr, skip 2ch, 1sc into next ch, *3ch, skip 3ch, 3tr into next ch, skip 2ch, 1sc into next ch, rep from * to end. Turn.

2nd row 4ch, 2tr into first sc, 1sc into next 3ch sp, *3ch, 3tr into next sc, 1 sc into next 3ch sp, rep from * ending with last sc into turning ch. Turn.

The 2nd row is repeated throughout.

To work the weaving Following the illustration, thread the ribbon and four thicknesses of yarn in alternate strips over the vertical bars formed by the three chain in the background.

 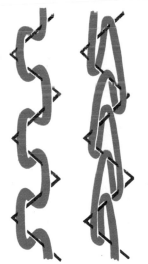

Sample 5

To work the background Using size G hook and a mohair yarn, make 29ch.

1st row Into 7th ch from hook, work 1sc, 2ch, skip next ch, 1dc into next ch, *2ch, skip next ch, 1sc into next ch, 2ch, skip next ch, 1dc into next ch, rep from * to end. Turn.

2nd row 3ch to count as first sc and 2ch, *1dc into next sc, 2ch, 1sc into next dc, 2ch, rep from * to end, working last sc into 3rd of turning ch. Turn.

3rd row 5ch to count as first dc and 2ch, 1sc into first dc, 2ch, 1dc into next sc, 2ch, rep from * to end, working last dc into 2nd of 3rd ch. Turn.

The 2nd and 3rd rows are repeated throughout.

To work the weaving Diagonal lines of alternate strips of velvet ribbon and four thicknesses of a contrasting shade of mohair are worked over the diagonal chain bars and under the double crochet stitches in each row.

This fabric is very light, warm and luxurious and would be very suitable for a long evening skirt, straight evening stole or an area rug.

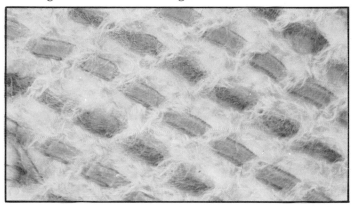

Sample 6

This beautiful evening belt is simple to make by following the needle weaving techniques. Using Size E hook and a lurex yarn, make a length of chain long enough to fit around your waist or hips less the combined diameters of the two rings used for fastening. Into the chain work 6 rows as given for the basic needle weaving background. Two colors of

soutache are threaded through the background to give a raised effect. Secure the ends of the belt over the fastening rings (ours are large brass rings, 2in in diameter) and crochet a length of cord to bind the rings together.

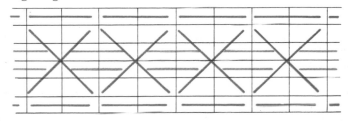

A woven crochet rug

rep from * to end. Turn. 95 sps.

1st row 3ch to count as first dc, *1dc into next dc, 1ch, rep from * to last sp, skip 1ch, 1dc into 4th of first 5ch. Turn. The last row forms the patt. Rep last row 3 times more. Break off A. Continuing in patt work a striped sequence of 5 rows B, 5 rows C and 5 rows A throughout. Rep this striped sequence 6 times more. Fasten off.

Finishing

Sew in ends. Block lightly with a cool iron under a dry cloth.

Weaving Cut 70 lengths of A, 60 lengths of B and 60 lengths of C, all 88in long. Take 2 strands of A and, being careful not to twist the strands, weave vertically over and under 1ch bars separating the dc, beg with 1st row of sps and leaving 6in hanging free.
A firmer edge will be obtained if the needle is passed through the first ch on the lower edge rather than into sp, and also through the final ch in the top edge. Do not pull yarn too tightly, but weave at a tension that will leave 6in hanging free at the top edge. Work another 4 rows in A, weaving over alternate bars from those woven on the preceding row.

Continue in same way as for striped sequence on rug.

Fringe Cut two 13in lengths of color required for each sp along both short ends of rug. Fold strands to form a loop. Insert hook into first sp at lower edge, draw loop through, draw woven ends through loop then draw fringe ends through loop and draw up tightly. Rep along lower edge and upper edge, taking care to keep same side of rug uppermost while knotting fringe. Trim fringe ends evenly.

Size
60in × 52in excluding fringe

Gauge
10dc and 10 sps and 10 rows to 6½in patt worked on size J crochet hook

Materials
15 × 1 oz balls Dawn Sayelle Knitting Worsted in main color, A
13 balls each of contrast colors, B and C
One size J crochet hook

Large tapestry needle

Note
To obtain an even background always insert the hook under 3 top strands of the dc of previous row working into body of st

Rug
Using size J hook and A make 194ch.

Base row Into 6th ch from hook work 1dc, *1ch, skip 1ch, 1dc into next ch,

CROCHET TRIMMINGS
INSERTIONS

Crochet as an insertion

An insertion is usually thought of as a decorative open work strip which joins two pieces of fabric together, often used to add a pretty, patterned panel to a dress, or along the side seams of slacks. In this chapter we deal with making straight insertions which are applied directly onto straight pieces of fabric, working the crochet and joining the pieces together in one easy stage. Dress patterns with simple seams could easily employ this method, remembering though that the crochet has a certain depth and therefore the appropriate amount of the fabric should first be cut away from your pattern (half the width of the total insertion could be removed from both pattern pieces being joined), before starting work. When working on a sample, turn under a 2 inch seam allowance, or for a garment, press back the seam on the fitting line, then follow our instructions to learn the techniques and some interesting new designs.

Sample 1

This sample shows the seam pressed back and ready for work to begin. As a crochet hook cannot be inserted directly into the majority of dress fabrics, an even back stitch has been worked along the

fitting line (this has been emphasized in our sample by the use of green yarn). The size of the sewing stitch should be large enough to allow the crochet hook to pass through it.

Sample 2

Here the first row of crochet is being worked. Make a slip loop on the hook, then working from right to left, with the right side of the work facing, remove hook from loop and insert it into first st on fabric, replace the loop on the hook and draw through the st on the fabric, 2ch, *insert hook into next sewing stitch, yo and draw through a loop, yo and draw through both loops (1sc has been worked), 1ch, rep from * to end of work. Fasten off.

Note Our sample illustrates 1sc followed by 1ch, but if the back stitches are smaller there is no need for 1ch between stitches.

Sample 3

This is the completed insertion. First work along the edges of fabrics, A and B, as described in sample 2. With RS of work facing and working from right to left, insert hook into first ch of fabric A, work 5ch, slip hook out of st and insert into first ch of fabric B again with RS facing, *replace st on the hook and draw through the st on B, yo 3 times, insert hook into next ch of fabric A, yo and draw through a loop, (yo and draw through first 2 loops on hook), 4 times – 1dtr has been worked –, remove hook from st and insert into next ch on fabric B, rep from * to end. Fasten off yarn by replacing st and draw through the ch sp on fabric B, then yo and draw through cutting the end.

Note When joining two pieces of fabric together in this way, it is important that the two rows of back stitches are exactly the same in size and number.

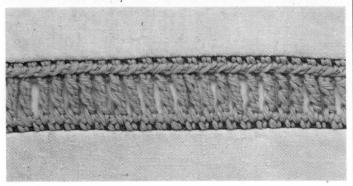

Sample 4

This sample has been made in the same way as sample 3, with one more addition to its design. A cord has been worked through pairs of dtr's – denoted as A and B. To do this, follow our diagram and place first dtr – A over second dtr – B and then take the cord under B and over A. Repeat over each pair of dtr's. Here the insertion has been used vertically as it would be on a pants seam.

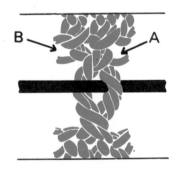

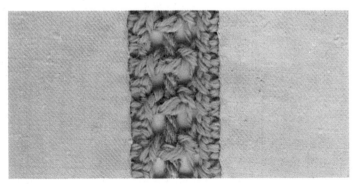

Sample 5

Work a row of sc along two pieces of fabric, A and B, as given for sample 2. To work the crochet joining the two pieces together, with RS of work facing and working from right to left, join yarn to first st on fabric A, work 9ch, slip hook out of st and insert it into first st on fabric B, then still with RS of work facing, *replace the st on the hook and draw through the st on fabric B, yo 8 times, insert hook into next st on fabric A, yo and draw through a loop, (yo and draw through first 2 loops on hook) 9 times – called 1dc8 –, remove st from hook and insert hook into next ch on

fabric B, rep from * to end. Fasten off yarn by replacing st on hook, then draw through the st on fabric B, yo and draw through yarn, then cut off the end. The illustration shows the method of threading the cord through the stitches.

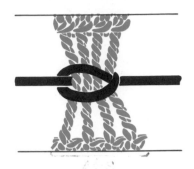

Sample 6

Work as given for sample 5, working 10ch at the beginning and working a 1dc9 by placing yarn over the hook 9 times and (yo and draw through first 2 loops on hook) 10 times.

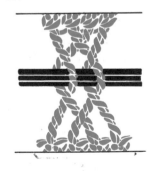

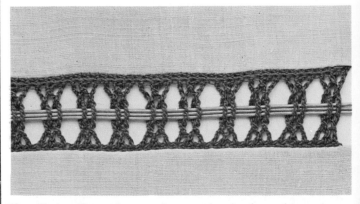

The illustration shows the method of working three rows of cord through the stitches.

EDGINGS

One of the neatest and most attractive ways of finishing off the outer edges of a garment, whether it is knitted or worked in crochet, is with the use of a crochet edging.

The edging may be worked in rounds or rows. It normally consists of only one row or round of crochet, but it is sometimes necessary to work a foundation row or round of single crochet before the actual edging in order to give a firmer edge to it. Our edgings are worked into the stitches around the outer edges of a garment or piece of crochet work after the main part has been completed and sewn together. Edgings can either be a subtle finishing or an important feature of the design, depending on the piece that is to be trimmed. A decorative edging can liven up a plain jacket, while a very simple edging may be all that is needed to finish a heavily patterned piece of work. Choose a yarn that is applicable to the type of work you are doing. You will probably want to use the same yarn as you used for the rest of the garment, perhaps in a different color to add contrast. Should you want to make more of a feature of the edging however and decide to use an entirely different yarn, remember the type of yarn being used for the rest of the work, and do not, for instance, pick a thick, heavy yarn to be worked on a piece of delicate baby's clothing.

There are an infinite number of edgings and below we give instructions for some of the most unusual ones including basic picots, shells and clusters.

Edging 1 Into first st work 1sc, *3ch, skip next st, 1sc into next st, rep from * to end.

Edging 2 This is called cord stitch. It is worked with just a single crochet into every stitch, working, however, from left to right instead of the usual right to left.

Edging 3 This is the most usual way of working a picot. Work 1sc into each of first 3 sts, *4ch, remove hook from st and insert it into first ch worked from front to back, pick up the st that was left and draw through the loop on the hook – 1 picot has been made –, 1sc into each of next 3 sts, rep from * to end.

Edging 4 Here is a more decorative picot edging. Work 1sc into each of first 3 sts, *4ch, 1sc into 3rd ch from hook, 1ch, skip next st, 1sc into each of next 3 sts, rep from * to end.

Edging 5 The picots worked here form a very thick edge. Sl st into first st, *4ch and work a picot into 4th ch from hook as described in edging 3, sl st into next st, rep from * to end.

Edging 6 This is an easy way of making a looped edging. *Work 1sc into first st, extend loop on hook and transfer it to a No.11 knitting needle, keeping the needle at the back of the work, reinsert hook into last sc worked, yo and draw through a loop, 1sc into next st, rep from * to end.

Edging 7 Sl st into each of first 2 sts, *1sc into next st, 3ch, sl st into same st where last sc was worked, sl st into each of next 2 sts, rep from * to end.

Edging 8 The group of stitches in this edging form a decorative scallop shape. Work 3ch, into st at base of ch work (1hdc, 1ch, 1dc, 1ch and 1tr), *skip next 2 sts, sl st into next st, (1hdc, 1ch, 1dc, 1ch and 1tr) into same st as sl st, rep from * to end.

Edging 9 More loops, but this time formed by chain stitches. Work 1sc into first st, *3ch, sl st into same st where last sc was worked, skip next st, 1sc into next st, rep from * to end.

Edging 10 The stitches in each group form a shell. Join in yarn and into 3rd st from hook work (2dc, 1ch, 1tr, 1ch, 2dc), *skip next 2 sts, sl st into next st, skip 2 sts, (2dc, 1ch, 1tr, 1ch, 2dc) into next st, rep from * to end.

Edging 11 This edging gives an unusual geometric outline. *Work 7ch, into 3rd ch from hook work 1sc, 1hdc into next ch, 1dc into next ch, 1tr into next ch, 1dtr into next ch, skip next 3 sts, sl st into next st, rep from * to end.

Edging 12 Here a cluster of stitches gives an interesting variation. Work 2ch, skip first st, 1hdc into next st, *(yo and insert hook into the ch sp at right of hdc just worked from front to back, yo and draw through a loop) 3 times, yo and draw through all 7 loops on hook, 1ch, skip next st, 1hdc into next st, rep from * to end.

SIMPLE BRAIDS AND CORDS

Decoration plays an important part in style today, both for the fashions we wear and for our home decor. Interesting types of decoration are braids and cords. Here we shall tell you how to work a number of different kinds of this type of trim, any of them suitable for any type of garment.

A braid is usually considered to be a narrow piece of work made in a chosen yarn to complement that used on the main fabric, and applied either as a binding to cover or finish a raw edge, or as a trim on the fabric. The color, texture and width of the braid should be chosen carefully to coordinate it with the fabric with which it is to be used and the trimming design used should be worked out with thought to the appearance of the total garment.

The cords illustrated in this chapter can be used for any form of tie lacing or decoration and several strips of cord can be applied one alongside of the other to produce an interesting trim of wider proportion.

Sample 1

This is a simple cord made with a size G hook and Knitting Worsted. Work a length of chain, and then slip stitch back along the length by placing the hook into the loop on the reverse side of each chain. chain.

Sample 2

Make a length of chain in the same way as sample 1 and then slip stitch back along the length by placing the hook into the single top loop on the front of each chain. The reverse side of this chain has been illustrated here and shows an attractive knotted effect.

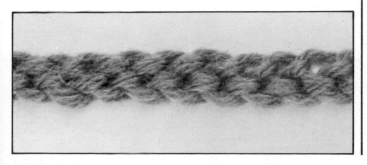

Sample 3

Using size G hook and Knitting Worsted, make a length of chain, working very loosely. When the chain is the desired length, draw four thicknesses of a chenille yarn through the chain stitches.

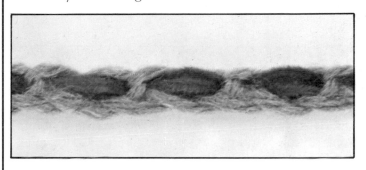

Sample 4

In this sample four thicknesses of chenille yarn are threaded into the cord as you are working it. Using size G hook and Knitting Worsted, make a length of chain, passing the chenille back and forth over the incoming yarn behind the hook between every two stitches worked. The reverse side of this chain has been illustrated.

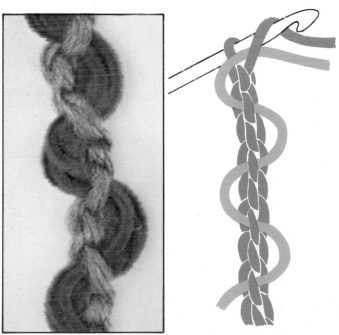

Sample 5

This attractive beaded cord has been worked in a similar way to sample 4. Thread small wooden beads onto a separate length of yarn. Using a size G hook and Knitting Worsted, make a length of chain and while you are working, pass a doubled length of beaded yarn back and forth between every four chain stitches. In the illustrated sample below the beads have been positioned in groups of five followed by groups of three on either side of the chain.

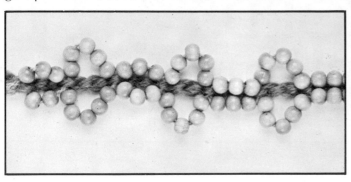

Sample 6

This sample has been worked with a modern interpretation of a "lucet" which is an old-fashioned tool for making a chain type cord. It is usually in the shape of a lyre, and is also known as a "chain fork". However, two crochet hooks placed together, as shown in our illustration, can be used to make this cord.

Rug wool has been used for this particular cord and two size K crochet hooks and one in size B. Place a slip loop on the left hand hook, and then hold the two hooks together. Wrap the yarn behind the right hook and in front of the left hook. Hold the yarn behind the hooks and using the smaller hook slip the loop on the left hook over the yarn. *Place yarn behind the right hook in front of both loops, holding it behind the hooks, then slip the under loop over the top loop on both hooks. *. Repeat from * to * for the required length.

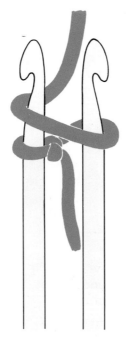

Sample 7

Here the same method as sample 6 is illustrated using two size H hooks in place of the lucet, Knitting Worsted and a size B hook for working the chain.

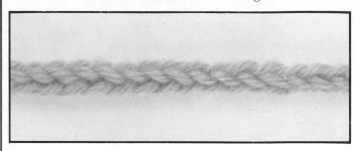

Sample 8

Using two size J hooks in place of the lucet, two thicknesses of Knitting Worsted together and a size B hook, place a slip loop on the left hook behind and then around the left hook from behind as in the illustration. Slip the under loop over the top loop on both hooks. *. Repeat from * to * for the desired length. This forms a very firm cord suitable for a tie belt.

Sample 9

After the completion of a braid made with a lucet, a narrow ribbon has been threaded in and out of the chain, and then it has been drawn through tightly, thus producing a zigzag effect.

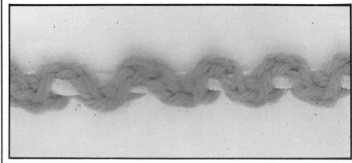

INTRICATE BRAIDS

Here are some braids and trimmings more intricate than the simple cords suitable for lacing and ties described in the last chapter. The samples in this chapter are worked in a different way and produce slightly wider trimmings which are suitable for clothes, as well as lampshades and window blind hems. Again, remember that the choice of yarn you use for working the trimming is very important and that it should complement the fabric on which it will be used.

Sample 1

A very attractive braid is formed by a new technique where the work is turned after each individual stitch has been made. Using a size G hook and Knitting Worsted, make a slip loop on the hook. Yo and draw through loop, insert hook into first loop made, yo and draw through loop, yo and draw through both loops on hook. Turn work. Insert hook from right to left into the small loop on the left hand side, yo and draw through a loop, yo and draw through both loops on hook. Turn work. *Insert hook from right to left into the two loops on the left hand side, yo and draw through a loop, yo and draw through both loops on hook. Turn work. *. Repeat from * to * for required length of braid.

Sample 2

Both sides of this unusual braid are illustrated here, since each has a completely different appearance. Using two thicknesses of Knitting Worsted and a size

H hook, make a slip loop on the hook. Yo and draw through loop, insert hook into first loop made, yo and draw through loop, yo and draw through both loops on hook. Turn work. Insert hook from right to left into the small loop on the left hand side, yo and draw through a loop, yo and draw through both loops on hook. Turn work. *Insert hook from right to left into the two loops on the left hand side as given for sample 1, yo and draw through a loop, yo and draw through both loops on hook. *. Turn work from right to left. Repeat from * to *. Turn work from left to right. Continue in this way, turning work alternately from right to left and then from left to right for the desired length of the cord. One good way of using this braid is for trimming a pocket as shown in our illustration.

Sample 3

This is worked in the same way as sample 1, but in double instead of single crochet. When finished, a double length of mohair yarn has been threaded through the vertical loops on the surface.

Sample 4

Using a very thick embroidery yarn and a size H hook, work in the same way as sample 1, using half double crochets instead of single crochets.

Sample 5

Here is a very pretty shell design which is very easy to make. Using a size G hook and Knitting Worsted, make 8ch. Join with a sl st into first ch to form a ring. 3ch to count as first dc, work 7dc into ring, 6ch, work 1sc into ring. Turn work. *3ch to count as first sc, work 7dc into 6ch sp, 6ch, 1sc into 6ch sp. Turn work. *. Repeat from * to * for the desired length.

Sample 6

Using two thicknesses of Knitting Worsted and a size H hook, make 4ch. Into 4th ch from hook work 1dtr and 1sc. Turn work. *3ch, into sc work 1dtr and 1sc. Turn work. *. Repeat from * to * for the desired length. This produces a thick, chunky accordion type braid.

Sample 7

Straw has been used for this braid to give a shiny and crinkly texture. Using a size H hook work in the same way as sample 1, but instead of single crochet make a 7 loop double by placing (yo insert hook into stitch, yo and draw through a loop) 3 times, yo and draw through all 7 loops.

Sample 8

Bobble stitches give an interesting chunky look to this braid. Using size H hook and two thicknesses of Knitting Worsted, make 2ch. (Yo and insert into first ch worked, yo and draw through a loop) 3 times, yo and draw through all loops on hook, 3ch, 1sc into first ch worked. Turn work. *(Yo and insert into 3ch sp, yo and draw through a loop) 3 times, yo and draw through all loops on hook, 3ch, 1sc into 3ch sp. Turn work. *. Continue in this way for the required length. You will note that the bobbles lie in an alternating

pattern with the outer edges forming gently scalloped lines on either side of the braid.

Sample 9

An interesting frieze has been created by working crochet stitches within a border. Using size G hook and Knitting Worsted, make a chain the desired length with multiples of 4 stitches.

1st row Into 3rd ch from hook work 1sc, 1sc into each ch to end. Turn.

2nd row 4ch, skip first 2sc, *leaving last loop of each on hook work 2tr into next sc, yo and draw through all 3 loops – called a joint tr –, 3ch, work a joint tr into same sc as before, skip next 3sc, rep from * finishing with 1tr into last sc. Turn.

3rd row Work 1sc into each st to end of row. Fasten off.

Sample 10

Two colors of Knitting Worsted, A and B, create an unusual effect in this braid. Using a size G hook and A, make 5ch.

1st row Into 2nd ch from hook work 1sc, 1hdc into next ch, 1dc into next ch, leaving the last loop of each on hook work 3tr into next ch, yo and draw through all loops on hook. Turn.

2nd row Join in B. *Work 1sc into first st, 1tr into next st, 1dc into next st, leaving the last loop of each on hook work 3tr into next st, yo and draw through all loops on hook. Turn. *.

3rd row Join in A. Rep from * to * of 2nd row.

Repeat 2nd and 3rd rows for the desired length.

Note Always work over the color not in use to keep the loose ends of yarn behind the work.

BRAIDS USING RIBBON

Braids using ribbons

Most of the braids illustrated here can be used for either a trimming added to a garment, or a chosen sample could be incorporated as part of the design of a garment and worked in with the regular crochet stitches. They can be used as trimmings around the hemline of a plain skirt, pants or vests. If the braid is placed on the waistline of a garment, then the ribbon can act as a drawstring at the waist.

Sample 1

This demonstrates the basic technique used in this chapter, and the samples following show developments of this method of work.

Using size F hook and a cotton yarn, make a length of chain with multiples of 2 stitches.

1st row Into 3rd ch from hook work 1hdc, 1hdc into each ch to end. Turn.

2nd row 4ch to count as first dc and ch sp, skip first 2 sts, 1dc into next st, *1ch, skip next st, 1dc into next st, rep from * to end. Turn.

3rd row 2ch to count as first hdc, 1hdc into each ch sp and dc, ending with 1hdc into 4ch sp, 1hdc into 3rd of 4ch. Fasten off.

The ribbon has been threaded through alternate double crochet in the 2nd row.

Sample 2

Using size C hook and a cotton yarn, make a chain with multiples of 4 +2 stitches.

1st row Into 3rd ch from hook work 1sc, 1sc into each ch to end. Turn.

2nd row 4ch to count as first tr, 2tr leaving last loop of each st on hook into st at base of ch, yo and draw through all loops on hook, *ch, skip next 3 sts, 3tr leaving last loop of each on hook into next st, yo and draw through all loops on hook rep from * to end. Turn.

3rd row 1ch to count as first sc, 1sc into each st to end. Fasten off.

Velvet ribbon has been threaded in and out of alternate treble groups.

Sample 3

Using size C hook and a cotton yarn, make a length of chain with multiples of 6 +3 stitches.

1st row Into 3rd ch from hook work 1sc, 1sc into each ch to end. Turn.

2nd row 1ch to count as first sc, 1sc into each st to end. Turn.

3rd row As 2nd.

4th row 1ch to count as first sc, 1sc into each st working into same sts as for 3rd row – this gives a very firm ridge. Turn.

5th row 6ch to count as first st and ch sp, skip first 2 sts, *yo 5 times, insert hook into next st, yo and draw through a loop, (yo and draw through first 2 loops on hook) 6 times – called 1dc5 –, (1ch, skip next st, 1dc5 into next st) twice, 1ch, yo twice, take hook in front of last 3 vertical bars worked to the back, yo and draw through a loop, yo and draw through one loop, yo twice, skip next st, insert hook into next st, yo and draw through a loop, (yo and draw through first 2 loops on hook) 6 times, rep from * to end, beg each new rep with first 1dc5 into same st as last 1dc5. Turn.

6th row 1ch to count as first sc, 1sc into each st to end. Turn.

7th row 1ch to count as first sc, 1sc into each st working into same sts as for 6th row. Turn.

8th and 9th rows As 2nd. Fasten off.

Ribbon has been threaded through alternate groups of crossed stitches.

Sample 4

Using size C hook and a cotton yarn, make a length of chain with multiples of 6 + 2 stitches.

1st to 3rd rows As 1st to 3rd rows of sample 3.

4th row 9ch, skip first 6 sts, sl st into next st, *9ch, skip next 5 sts, sl st into next st, rep from * to end. Turn.

5th row 1ch to count as first sc, 10sc into first 9ch sp, 11sc into each 9ch sp to end. Turn. Fasten off.

6th row Join yarn into 3rd st of first sp between half circles, *9ch, sl st into 3rd ch of next sp passing ch length in front of work, rep from * taking the ch length behind and in front of work alternately. Turn.

7th row As 5th.

8th row Make a slip loop on the hook, 2ch, ss into 6th sc of first half circle, *2ch, sl st into 6th sc of next half circle, rep from * to end, 2ch. Turn.

9th row 1ch to count as first sc, 1sc into each st to end. Turn.

10th and 11th rows As 9th.

This braid is reversible and grosgrain ribbon has been threaded through as illustrated.

Sample 5

Using size E hook and Knitting Worsted, make 2ch. (Yo and insert hook into first ch worked, yo and draw through a loop) 3 times, yo and draw through all loops on hook, 3ch, 1sc into first ch worked. Turn. *(Yo and insert hook into ch sp, yo and draw through a loop) 3 times, yo and draw through all loops on hook, 3ch, 1sc into same ch sp. Turn. * Rep from * to * for required length.

Double cord has been threaded in and out of the chain spaces.

Sample 6

Using size E hook and Knitting Worsted, make a length of chain with multiples of 4 + 3 stitches.

1st row Into 5th ch from hook work 1sc, *1ch, skip next ch, 1sc into next ch, rep from * to end. Turn.

2nd row *5ch, 3tr into 4th ch from hook, skip next ch sp, 1sc into next ch sp, rep from * to end. Break off yarn.

3rd row Rejoin yarn to other side of foundation ch and rep 2nd row, working the sc into the sp skipped on that row.

A narrow velvet ribbon has been threaded in a spiral over the center core, working in and out of the spaces below the trebles.

Sample 7

This sample is worked with a size E hook and Knitting Worsted.

1st line *6ch, (yo and insert hook into first ch, yo and draw through a loop) 3 times, yo and draw through all loops on hook, rep from * for required length.

2nd line *3ch, sl working loop off hook and insert into next 6ch sp of first line, pick up working loop and draw through to front of work, 3ch, (yo and insert hook into first ch worked, yo and draw through a loop) 3 times, yo and draw through all loops on hook, rep from * joining each 6ch length to the next 6ch sp of the 1st row. Fasten off. Narrow velvet ribbon has been threaded in and out between the 6 chain spaces.

Hatband with leather trim

Size
1in wide by 23in long

Gauge
12sts to 3.9in and 1 row to 1in worked on size F crochet hook.

Materials
Approximately 9yds of garden twine
Approximately 4yds of leather thonging for trimming
Size F crochet hook

Hatband
Using size F hook and twine, make 72ch.
1st row Into 6th ch from hook work 1dc, 1ch, skip 1ch, 1dc into next ch, rep from * to end.

Fasten off.

To finish
Block with a warm iron under a damp cloth. Darn in ends.
Leather thonging Cut leather thonging into 3 lengths. Thread through holes on hatband, leaving ends to tie at center back.

EDGINGS FOR LINEN

Crochet trimmings for household linens

The theme of this chapter centers around trims on household linens. The samples illustrated are worked in white since traditionally these "laces" would have been used on white linen sheets and pillowcases. Even though the trend today is for colored and patterned bed linen, however, the white trimmings can still make attractive decoration or colored yarn can be used.

Before starting to work you must first decide where the trim is to be placed, and whether it is to be on the edge of the work or within the main fabric. This will determine if you should use a trim with a definite straight edge (the other edge being curved, scalloped, pointed or fringed) which can be sewn onto the edge of an article or a double sided trim (the two edges being exactly the same) which is suitable for an insertion on the main fabric and is usually placed within a border of the hem.

All the designs illustrated may be used as an edging, or can be made into a double sided trim by repeating the design on the opposite side of the foundation chain, as in sample 7. Always remember to wash and block all trimmings before sewing them to the linen to prevent them from shrinking during laundering.

Sample 1

Using size E hook and a cotton yarn, make a length of chain with multiples of 4 + 3 stitches.
1st row Into 3rd ch from hook work 1hdc, 1hdc into each ch to end. Turn.
2nd row 2ch to count as first hdc, 1hdc into next hdc, *6ch, into 4th ch from hook work 1dc, 1dc into each of next 2ch, skip 2hdc, 1hdc into each of next 2hdc, rep from * ending with last hdc into top of turning ch. Fasten off.

Sample 2

Using size E hook and a cotton yarn, make a length of chain with multiples of 6 + 8 stitches.

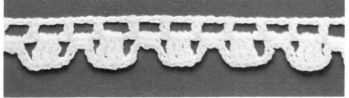

1st row Into 8th ch from hook work 1dc, *2ch, skip next 2ch, 1dc into next ch, rep from * to end. Turn.
2nd row *3ch, 3tr into next ch sp, 3ch, 3sc into next ch sp, rep from * to last ch sp, 3ch, 3tr into last ch sp, 3ch, sl st into ch sp. Fasten off.

Sample 3

Using size E hook and a cotton yarn, make a length of chain with multiples of 6 + 4 stitches.
1st row Into 6th ch from hook work 1dc, *1ch, skip next ch, 1dc into next ch, rep from * to end. Turn.
2nd row Sl st into first ch sp and into next dc, *5ch, skip next ch sp, (sl st into each of next dc and ch sp) twice, sl st into next dc, rep from * finishing with 3 sl st instead of 5 at end of last rep. Turn.
3rd row *Into next 5ch sp work 5dc, 5ch, sl st into 4th ch from hook, 1ch and 5dc, sl st into 3rd of next 5 sl st, rep from * to end. Fasten off.

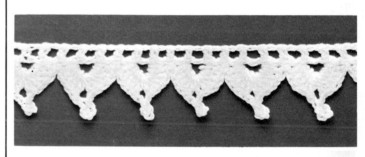

Sample 4

Using size E hook and a cotton yarn, make a length of chain with multiples of 5 + 1 stitches.
1st row Into 3rd ch from hook work 1sc, 1sc into each ch to end. Turn.
2nd row 1ch to count as first sc, skip first st, 1sc into each st to end. Turn.
3rd row As 2nd.
4th row 4ch to count as first tr, 1tr into first st, *skip next 3 sts, leaving last loop of each st on hook work 2tr into next st, yo and draw through all 3 loops on hook – called a joint tr –, 3ch, a joint tr into next st, rep from * to last 4 sts, skip next 3 sts, a joint tr into last st. Turn.
5th row 4ch to count as first tr, 1tr into first st, *3ch, a joint tr into top of next joint tr on previous row, skip next 3 sts, a joint tr into top of next joint tr on previous row, rep from * to last 2tr, 3ch, a joint tr into last 2tr. Turn.
6th–8th rows 1ch to count as first sc, 1sc into each st to end. Turn.
9th row 6ch, skip first 4 sts, sl st into each of next 2 sts, *6ch, skip next 3 sts, sl st into each of next 2 sts, rep from * finishing with a sl st into last st. Turn.

10th row Into each 6ch sp work 3sc, 3ch, 1dc, 3ch and 3sc. Fasten off.

Sample 5

Using size E hook and a cotton yarn, make 13ch.

1st row Into 4th ch from hook work 1dc, 1dc into each of next 3ch, 2ch, skip next 2ch, 1dc into each of next 4ch, 2ch, 1dc into last ch. Turn.

2nd row 3ch, skip ch sp, 1dc into each of next 4dc, 2ch, 1dc into each of next 4dc. Turn.

3rd row 3ch to count as first dc, 1dc into each of next 3dc, 2dc into next 2ch sp, 1dc into each of next 4dc, 5dc into next ch sp at beg of 2nd row, 5dc into next ch sp at end of 1st row. Do not turn.

4th row 1 ch to count as first sc, work 1sc into front loop only of each st to end of row working from left to right instead of right to left. Do not turn.

5th row 3ch to count as first dc, 1dc into each of next 3 sts placing hook into back loop only of each st, 2ch, skip next 2 sts, 1dc into back loop only of next 4 sts, 2ch, 1dc into next st. Turn.

Repeat 2nd through 5th rows for desired length.

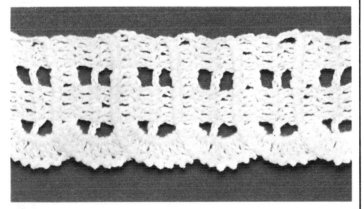

Sample 6

Using size E hook and a cotton yarn, make a length of chain with multiples of 10 + 9 stitches.

1st row Into 5th ch from hook work 1dc, *1ch, skip next ch, 1dc into next ch, rep from * to end. Turn.

2nd row 3ch to count as first dc, 1dc into first ch sp, 3ch, skip next ch sp, *2dc into next ch sp, 3ch, skip next ch sp, rep from * ending with 1dc into last ch sp, 1dc into 4th of 5ch. Turn.

3rd row 4ch, 1dc into first ch sp, *1ch, 1dc into next ch sp, 1ch, 1dc into same ch sp, rep from * to last ch sp, 1ch, 1dc into last ch sp, 1ch, 1dc into 3rd of 3ch. Turn.

4th row 1ch to count as first sc, 2sc into first ch sp, 8ch, *3sc into each of next 3 ch sp, 8ch, rep from * to last ch sp, 2sc into last ch sp, 1sc into 3rd of 4ch. Turn.

5th row Sl st into each sc worked and into each 8ch loop work 2sc, 2hdc, 9dc, 2hdc and 2sc. Fasten off.

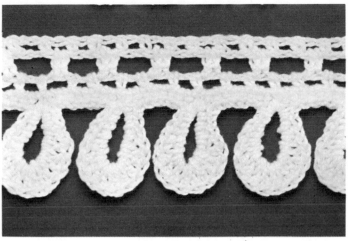

Sample 7

Using size E hook and a cotton yarn, make a length of chain with multiples of 8 stitches.

1st row Into 6th ch from hook work 1dc, *1ch, skip next ch, 1dc into next ch, rep from * to end. Turn.

2nd row 4ch, 1dc into first sp, 1ch, 1dc into next sp, *6ch, skip next sp, 1dc into next sp, 1ch, 1dc into next sp, 1ch, 1dc into next sp, rep from * to end. Turn.

3rd row Sl st into each of next sp, dc and foll sp, * into 6ch sp work 2sc, 2hdc, 5dc, 2hdc and 2sc, sl st into each of next 3 sts, rep from * to end. Turn.

4th row *3ch, 1dc into first dc of 5dc gr, 3ch, 1tr into center dc of gr, 3ch, 1tr into same dc, 3ch, 1dc into last dc of gr, 3ch, 1dc into center sl st, rep from * to end. Turn.

5th row *3sc into each of next 2 sp, into next sp work 3sc, 4ch, sl st into first ch worked so forming a picot and 3sc, 3sc into each of next 2 sp, rep from * to end. Fasten off. This forms a trim with one straight edge, although the crochet design may be worked on the other side of the foundation chain to produce a double sided trim as in our illustration.

EDGINGS FOR SOFT FURNISHINGS

Trimmings for soft furnishings

In the last chapter we showed samples of edgings and double sided braids suitable for trim on household articles. Here we extend the theme to include more decorative and elaborate trimmings, such as deep shaped edgings and crochet braids with long tassels and pompons. This work is ideal for trim on lampshades, both hanging from the ceiling and table lamps, window shades, curtains and valances.

Our samples have been worked in white cotton yarns, although certain other colors and types of yarn are quite suitable for most of the designs. One word of caution in this work is to choose a yarn that will not fray since tassels and pompons have cut edges that might easily shred with the use of the wrong yarn.

Sample 1

Using size E hook and a cotton yarn, make a length of chain with multiples of 2 stitches.

1st row Into 3rd ch from hook work 1sc, 1sc into each ch to end. Turn.

2nd row 1ch to count as first sc, skip 1sc, 1sc into each sc to end. Turn.

3rd row 4ch to count as first dc and sp, skip first 2sc, 1dc into next sc, *1ch, skip next sc, 1dc into next sc, rep from * to end. Turn.

4th row 3ch to count as first dc, *(yo and insert hook into next ch sp, yo and draw through a loop) 4 times, yo and draw through all loops on hook, 1ch, rep from * omitting 1ch at end of last rep and ending with 1dc into 3rd of 4ch. Turn.

5th row 4ch to count as first dc and sp, *skip next bobble, 1dc into next ch, 1ch, rep from * omitting 1ch at end of last rep and ending with last dc into 3rd of 3ch. Fasten off.

Fringe Cut 5 lengths of yarn each 5in long and fold in half lengthwise. Insert folded end through ch sp in the 5th row, then pull the cut ends through the loop. Pull up tightly. Repeat into each ch sp along the row. Trim ends to an equal length.

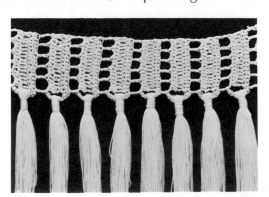

Sample 2

Using size E hook and a cotton yarn, make a length of chain with multiples of 4 +1 stitches.

1st–2nd rows As 1st–2nd rows of sample 1.

3rd row (crossed double trebles) Sl st into each of first 4 sts, 5ch to count as first dtr, yo 3 times, insert hook behind ch length into next st at right of ch just worked, yo and draw through a loop, (yo and draw through first 2 loops on hook) 4 times – called 1dtr –, work 1dtr into each of next 2 sts to the right of last dtr, *skip 3 sts to left of first dtr, 1dtr into next st, 1dtr into each of next 3 sts to the right of last dtr always placing hook behind the last st worked, rep from * to end. Turn.

4th row 1ch to count as first sc, 1sc into each st to end. Turn.

5th row As 4th.

6th row 6ch, skip first 2 sts, sl st into next st, *3ch, skip next st, sl st into next st, 6ch, skip next st, sl st into next st, rep from * to end. Fasten off.

Fringe Work as given for sample 1, and thread through each 6ch loop on 6th row.

Sample 3

Using size E hook and a cotton yarn, make 20ch.

1st row Into 8th ch from hook work 1dc, *2ch, skip 2ch, 1dc into next ch, rep from * to end. Turn.

2nd row 1ch to count as first sc, skip first st, 1sc into each st to last ch sp, 2sc into ch sp, 1sc into 5th of 7ch. Turn.

3rd row 3ch to count as first dc, skip first st, 1dc into each st to end of row. Turn.

4th row As 2nd row, working last sc into 3rd of 3ch, but do not turn, 5ch, sl st into base of first sc in 2nd row, 7ch, sl st into top of last sc worked. Turn.

5th row 5ch, skip first 3 sts, 1dc into next st, *2ch, skip next 2 sts, 1dc into next st, rep from * to end. Fasten off. The 2nd through 5th rows inclusive form the pattern and are repeated for the desired length.

Fringe Cut yarn into 12in lengths and using 34 of these lengths together place over a length of double chain. Tie very securely in place below the chain. Repeat into each length of double chain along the row, and then trim the ends.

Sample 4

Using size F hook and a thick cotton yarn, make a chain the desired length with multiples of 4+3 stitches.

1st row Into 3rd ch from hook work 1sc, 1sc into each ch to end. Turn.

2nd row (crossed double crochet) Sl st into each of first 2 sts, 3ch to count as first dc, placing the hook behind the length of chain work 1dc into next st to the right of the chain, * skip next stitch to left of first dc, 1dc into next st, placing the hook in front of the last dc worked, 1dc into next st to the right, skip next st, 1sc into next st, placing the hook behind the last dc worked, 1dc into next st to the right, rep from * to end. Turn.

3rd row 1ch to count as first sc, 1sc into each st to end. Turn.

4th row 6ch, skip first 4sts, 1sc into next st, * 5ch, skip 3 sts, 1sc into next st, rep from * to end. Fasten off.

Pompons Cut two circular pieces of cardboard both 2 inches in diameter and make a hole, 1 inch in diameter in the centers of each piece. Use the circles to make pompons in the usual manner, then work a length of chain for attaching them on to the 5ch loops of the 4th row.

Sample 5

This is a variation of the traditional filet crochet known as filet guipure. The techniques of working filet crochet are described in detail earlier. Here we give you a chart comprising blocks and spaces for you to follow. Our spaces are formed by one double crochet at either side of two chain, and blocks are spaces filled in with two trebles. Also in this design a double space has been worked in an unusual way by making three chain, then working one single crochet where the usual double crochet would be, three more chain and the next dc in its usual position. On the following row five chain will be worked above this particular group. This variation is shown on the chart below by the symbols on the diagram.

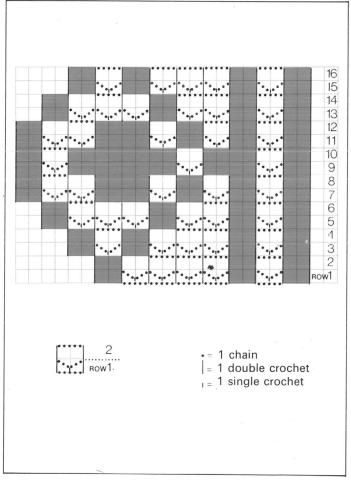

• = 1 chain
| = 1 double crochet
ı = 1 single crochet

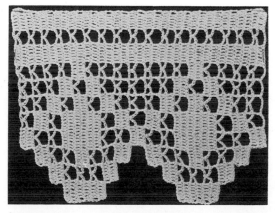

FRINGES

Continuing our chapters on trimmings and braids, we now give you instructions for making more of them, this time using fringes as the focal point. These are formed during the working of the crochet by the unusual technique of twisting the yarn to form the fringe. It is a method which requires some practice in order to master the work. Depending on the yarn chosen, the fringes are suitable for both household and dress trimmings.

Sample 1

Using size F hook and a rayon yarn, make a chain the desired length.

1st row Into 3rd ch from hook work 1hdc and 1hdc in each ch to end. Turn.

2nd row (loop row); 1ch to count as first st, skip first st, insert hook into next st, yo and draw through a loop, yo and draw through both loops on hook extending loop on hook for 6in, hold work over st with thumb and first finger of left hand, and with the hook in the extended loop, twist in a clockwise direction approx 24 times, halve the twisted yarn, placing the hook into the last st worked, the extended st will twist

firmly in an anti-clockwise direction, yo and draw through both loops on hook, rep from * to end of row. Fasten off. This completes the fringe.

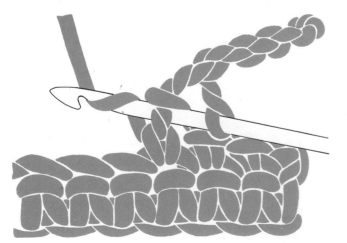

Note The depth of fringe will depend on the length of the extended stitch and the number of times that it is twisted. You must practice this stitch to obtain perfect results.

Sample 2

Using size F hook and a rayon yarn, make a chain the desired length.

1st row Into 4th ch from hook work 1hdc, 1dc into each ch to end. Turn.

2nd row Work loop row as for sample 1. Fasten off. Velvet ribbon, ½in wide, is drawn through between every other double crochet in the 1st row.

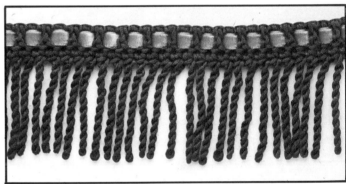

Sample 3

Using size F hook and a Knitting Worsted yarn, make a chain the desired length.

1st row Work a length of braid as for sample 1 of Chapter on "Intricate braids". Fasten off. Join in a different color of rayon yarn and work the loop row as foll:

2nd row Insert the hook into the loop at the top right hand edge of the braid and work a twisted loop as for sample 1, extending the loop for 5in, then insert the hook into the next loop, this time at the lower edge of the braid and make a twisted loop thus forming a stitch over the braid. Continue in this way, working a twisted loop into every other stitch along the top and bottom edges of the braid.
Fasten off.

Sample 4

Using a size F hook and Knitting Worsted, make a length of chain with multiples of 4+2 stitches.

1st row Into 3rd ch from hook work 1sc, 1sc into each st to end. Turn.

2nd row 1ch to count as first sc, skip first st, 1sc into next st, *1dtr into next st, 1sc into each of next 3 sts, rep from * to last 3 sts, 1dtr into next st, 1sc into each of next 2 sts. Turn.

3rd row 1ch to count as first sc, skip first st, 1sc into each st to end. Fasten off.

Join in a different color of rayon yarn and work a loop row as foll:

4th row Work as for loop row of sample 1, placing hook first into (a) next st of last row, then (b) into next st of row below, then (c) into next st of row below that and rep in the order of (b), (a), (b), (c), (b) and (a) for the required length. Fasten off.

Sample 5

Using size F hook and a rayon yarn make a chain of the desired length.

1st row In 4th ch from hook work 1dc, 1dc into each ch to end. Turn.

2nd row 1ch to count as first sc, skip first st, work 1sc into each st to end placing hook from back to front into sp between the regular chain st and the horizontal loop below it, thus giving a raised chain effect on the right side of the work. Turn.

3rd row (loop row): This is slightly different from the loop row of sample 1. Work 4ch to count as first

dc and sp, skip first 2 sts, *yo and insert hook in next st, yo and draw through a loop, (yo and draw through first 2 loops on hook) twice, extend loop on hook, twisting it as before, insert hook into last st worked, yo and draw through both loops on hook, 1ch, skip next st, rep from * ending with last dc into turning chain. Fasten off. Velvet ribbon has been drawn through every other double crochet on the loop row.

Sample 6

Using size D hook and a cotton yarn, make a chain of the desired length.

1st row Into 4th ch from hook work 1dc, 1dc in each ch to end. Turn.

2nd row 1ch to count as first sc, 1sc into each st to end. Turn.

3rd row 1ch to count as first sc, 1sc into back loop only of each st to end. Turn.

4th row 2ch to count as first dc, 1dc into each single loop rem from last row—now to the back of the work—to end of row. Turn.

5th row (loop row): Work as given for loop row of sample 1. Fasten off.

6th row (loop row): Rejoin yarn to sts of row 3 on front of braid and work as for loop row of sample 1.

Velvet ribbon has been drawn through every other double crochet in the 1st row.

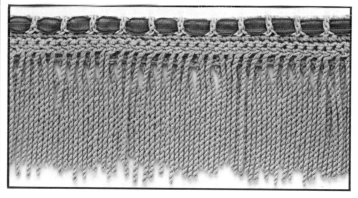

DECORATIVE FRINGES

Exciting fringes may be worked in many ways and in this chapter we cover a variety of very decorative ones which are most suitable for fashion garments. The fringes illustrated could be used on vests, long scarves, stoles and dresses. Master the techniques described here and when you feel competent, try experimenting with different yarns, beads and threads.

Sample 1

This has been worked in two yarns, a gold ribbon—A and a tubular rayon—B. Using size F hook and B, make 6ch.

1st row Place yarn A between the incoming yarn B and the hook, placing the cut end to the right hand side of the work, 1ch with B, *take yarn A from left to right, placing it between incoming yarn B and the hook, leaving a 3in folded loop, 1ch with B, take yarn A now on the right and place it between the incoming yarn B and the hook leaving no loop, 1ch with B, rep from * for the desired length of fringe, then work 12ch with B. Break off A and reverse work.

2nd row Fold the 12ch length just worked in half and hold in the left hand with the loops to the right, the incoming yarn should be under or behind the work and the hook on top or towards you, *place hook over single thickness of next loop, yo and draw through st on hook, place hook over next single thickness of same loop, yo and draw through st on hook, rep from * to end of loops, then work 12ch and reverse work.

3rd row Fold the 12ch length just worked in half and hold in the right hand with the loops to the left, rep from * of 2nd row to end.

The 2nd and 3rd rows are repeated to give the required proportion of heading to the looped fringe.

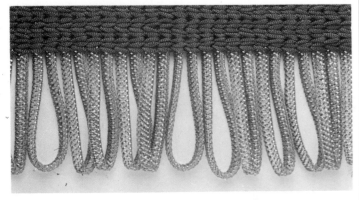

Sample 2

Two types of yarn have been used for this sample,

A for the working yarn and 4 thicknesses of B together for the fringe. Using size E hook and A, make 6ch.

1st row Place yarn B (all 4 thicknesses) between the incoming yarn A and the hook, placing the cut ends to the right hand side of the work, 1ch with A,* take yarn B from left to right placing it between incoming yarn A and the hook, leaving a 3in folded loop, 1ch with A, take yarn B now on the right and place it between the incoming yarn A and the hook leaving no loop, 1ch with A, rep from * for the desired length of fringe, then work 12ch with A. Break off B and reverse work.

2nd row Fold the 12ch length just worked in half and hold in the left hand with the loops to the right, the incoming yarn should be under or behind the work and the hook on top or toward you, * place hook over 4 thicknesses of next loop, yo and draw through st on hook, place hook over next 4 thicknesses of same loop, yo and draw through st on hook, rep from * to end of loops, then work 12ch and reverse work.

3rd row Fold the 12ch length just worked in half and hold in the right hand with the loops to the left, rep from * of 2nd row to end.

The 2nd and 3rd rows are repeated to give the required proportion of heading to the fringe. The loops can either be cut as in our sample or left uncut.

Sample 3

Here is an attractive method of making a beaded fringe. A lurex yarn has been used for the crochet while the beads have been threaded on to a separate length of yarn. The number of beads will of course depend on the amount of fringing required. Using size E hook and lurex yarn, make 6 ch.

1st row With cut end to the right, place yarn with beads between incoming yarn and the hook, 1ch with lurex yarn, *place yarn with beads from left to right, placing 21 beads on a loop plus 1 inch of free yarn, between incoming yarn and hook, 2ch with lurex yarn, place yarn with beads from right to left, leaving no loop between incoming yarn and hook, work 1ch with lurex yarn, rep from * to give desired length of fringe, then work 12ch with lurex yarn. Break off yarn with beads and reverse work.

2nd row Hold the work with the chain heading to the left and beaded loops to the right, work 1ch over next length of yarn with beads, having one bead on the left, *1ch, 1ch over next length of yarn with beads having one bead on the left, rep from * to end of fringe, work 12ch. Reverse work.

3rd row Hold the work with the chain heading to the right and beaded loops to the left, work as for 2nd row. Fasten off.

Note The yarn with beads will require tightening in order to give an all-beaded loop with no yarn showing between the beads.

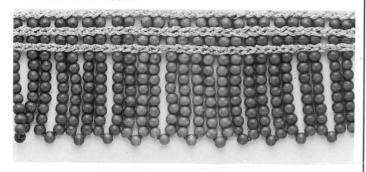

Sample 4

Using size F hook and Knitting Worsted, make 6ch.

1st row Into 3rd ch from hook work 1sc, 1sc into each ch to end. Turn. 4sts.

2nd row 1ch to count as first sc, skip first st, 1sc into each of next 3 sts. Turn.

3rd row As 2nd.

4th row As 2nd, but do not turn. Work 24ch. Turn.

5th row Into 4th ch from hook work 3dc, 4dc into each of the next 20ch, 1dc into each of next 4 sts. Turn. The 2nd through 5th rows inclusive are repeated for the length of trimming desired.

Sample 5

To work the braid: Using size F hook and Knitting Worsted make a chain with multiples of 4+2 stitches.

1st row Into 3rd ch from hook work 1sc, 1sc into each ch to end. Turn.

2nd row 1ch to count as first sc, skip first st, 1sc in each st to end. Turn.

3rd row 4ch to count as first dc and sp, skip first 2 sts, *(yo and insert hook into next st, yo and draw through a loop, yo and draw through first 2 loops on hook) 9 times, always inserting hook into same st, yo and draw through all 10 loops on hook, work 1ch very tightly to hold bobble, 1ch, skip next st, 1dc into next st, 1ch, skip next st, rep from * ending with 1dc into last st. Turn.

4th row 1ch to count as first sc, *1sc into next ch sp, 1sc in top of next bobble, 1sc into next ch sp, 1sc into next dc, rep from * to end. Turn.

5th row As 2nd. Fasten off.

To work the crochet balls: Using same yarn and hook, place the cut end of yarn in the palm of left hand and wrap yarn once around first finger, insert hook into loop around finger from underneath, yo and draw through a loop, slip loop off finger and hold between finger and thumb of left hand, *insert hook into ring, yo and draw through a loop, yo and draw through both loops on hook, rep from * 7 times more. Tighten ring by pulling the cut end of yarn. Mark beg of each round with a colored thread.

Next round Work 2sc into each of 8 sts. Do not join.

Next 2 rounds Work 1sc into each of 16 sts. Do not join. Place cotton batting into ball.

Next round (Work 2sc tog) 8 times. Do not join.

Next round Work 1sc into each of 8 sts. Draw sts tog by threading working st through each free st to make a neat end, do not break off yarn, 9ch, sl st to braid below bobble, sl st back along chain to ball, 9ch, skip next bobble on braid, sl st to braid below next bobble, sl st back along chain and fasten to ball. Continue in this way, first fastening each new ball below the bobble omitted in the previous joining, thus forming a cross-over design.

RUFFLES

Crochet ruffles are easy to work and make effective trimmings for a variety of garments. When working a ruffle, choose a yarn which is appropriate for the design and fabric of the main garment, such as a lurex yarn for evening wear or a fine cotton yarn for lingerie. Our samples in the photographs are worked with a size G crochet hook and Knitting Worsted.

Here we explain two methods of making ruffles. One way is to work more than one stitch into each stitch of the previous row, and this is illustrated in samples 1, 2, 4 and 5. Sample 3 demonstrates the method of gathering crochet to form a ruffle. This is simple to work and produces a very attractive trim. Crochet ruffles can be starched before being applied to the garment, if desired.

Sample 1

Make 31ch. This can be made longer by adding multiples of 4 stitches.

1st row Into 3rd ch from hook work 1sc, 1sc into each ch to end. Turn.

2nd row 5ch, skip first 4sc, sl st into next sc, *(5ch, skip 3sc, sl st into next sc), rep from * 5 times more. Turn. Seven 5ch sps.

3rd row 1ch to count as first sc, 7sc into first 5ch sp, 8sc into each 5ch sp to end.

Rep 2nd and 3rd rows now along the opposite side of the foundation chain. Turn.

4th row 4ch to count as first dc and ch, *1dc, 1ch into next sc, rep from * around both sides of foundation chain. Turn.

5th row Using a contrast color, join yarn into first 1ch sp, sl st into same sp, *3ch, sl st into next ch sp, rep from * to end. Fasten off.

This ruffle can be used to trim the center front of a long evening gown.

Sample 2

This ruffle is ideal for a decorative cuff. To work the fabric shown in our sample make 26ch.

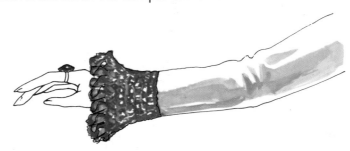

1st row Leaving the last loop of each st on hook, work 1dc into each of 4th and 5ch from hook, yo and draw through all 3 loops on hook, 1ch, then * leaving the last loop of each st on hook, work 1dc into each of next 2ch, yo and draw through all 3 loops on hook, 1ch, rep from * to last ch, 1dc into last ch. Turn.

2nd row 3ch to count as first dc, *leaving the last loop of each st on hook, work 2dc into next 1ch sp, yo and draw through all 3 loops on hook, 1ch, rep from * ending with 1dc into 3rd of the turning ch. Turn. The 2nd row is repeated throughout.

To work the ruffle:

1st row 5ch, sl st into top of first pair of dc, *5ch, sl st into top of next pair of dc, rep from * to end. Turn.

2nd row 3ch to count as first dc, 2dc into first sp, 3ch, 3dc into same sp, *2ch, sl st into next sp, 2ch, (3dc, 3ch, 3dc) into next sp, rep from * to end. Turn.

3rd row 1ch to count as first sc, 1sc into each st to end, working 5sc into each 3ch sp. Turn.

4th row 3ch to count as first dc, 1dc in each of next 4 sts, *2dc into each of next 3 sts, 1dc into each of next 13 sts, rep from * ending last rep with 1dc into each of next 3 sts, 1dc into the turning ch. Fasten off.

Sample 3

This sample would also be very effective as a cuff trimming. Using the first color, make a foundation chain to fit the desired measurement; we worked on 30 chain.

1st row Work 1dc by placing the hook under the complete ch so that the st will move freely over the chain when done, *3ch, work 1dc in the same way, rep from * 8 times more. Turn.

2nd row *3ch, sl st into next ch sp, rep from * to end. Turn.

3rd row *5ch, sl st into next ch sp, rep from * to end. Turn.

4th row *7ch, sl st into next ch sp, rep from * to end. Turn.

5th row *9ch, sl st into next ch sp, rep from * to end.

Turn.

6th row *11ch, sl st into next ch sp, rep from * to end. Turn.

7th row Into each 11ch sp work 12sc. Fasten off.

Next row Using second color, join yarn into right hand sp at base of first dc worked on the foundation ch, 6ch to count as first dc and 3ch, 1dc into next sp between dc working over foundation ch as before, *3ch, 1dc into next sp between dc, rep from * to end. Turn.

Next 4 rows Rep 2nd through 5th rows as given for first color.

Next row Into each 9ch sp work 11sc. Fasten off.

Note When using the second color, if the same side of the sc row is to appear on both ruffles then the yarn should be cut and rejoined between the 5th and 6th rows in order to work from the correct side. The double crochets are arranged along the foundation chain to give the desired amount of ruffling.

Sample 4

Worked in a fine yarn, this ruffle would look lovely on a nightgown, or in a thicker yarn, it could be added for trim to a circular hat, such as a beret. The basic fabric in our sample is worked in double crochet with a repeat of 5 stitches plus one. Work your design until the position for the ruffle is reached, then continue as follows:

Next row *5ch, skip next 4 sts, sl st into next st, rep from * to end. Turn.

Next row Into each ch sp work 1sc, 1hdc, 1dc, 3ch, 1dc, 1hdc, 1sc. Turn.

Continue in double crochet until the position for the next ruffle is reached.

Sample 5

This is a narrow ruffle which could be used for any type of trimming. Make a foundation chain the required length of the ruffle.

1st row Into 3rd ch from hook work 1sc, 1sc into each ch to end. Turn.

2nd row *5ch, skip next st, sl st into next st, rep from * to end. Turn.

3rd row Into each ch sp work 1sc, (3ch, 1sc) 5 times. Fasten off.

FINISHING TOUCHES
BUTTONS

Sample 1 *Sample 2* *Sample 3*

Covered buttons

So often it is difficult to purchase the right button for a garment that you are making. Sometimes the size is wrong and sometimes you are unable to match the color; there are also times when you would like an unusual button at a reasonable price to be used as an important trim on a simple garment. Crochet covered buttons can be very decorative and can add a great deal to a design.

The wooden or metal forms for covered buttons are available on most notions counters and they come in a variety of shapes and sizes. The method of work is simple, but before starting try a sample piece of crochet with the yarn and hook you are going to use. This sample should look right on the garment for which the buttons are being made, and the crochet fabric should be firm enough entirely to cover the form beneath it. We recommend a smaller size hook than usual in order to achieve a close stitch.

Sample 1

6 yards of Soutache braid is required to cover this large round button which is $1\frac{3}{4}$in in diameter.

1st round Form a ring with the braid in the left hand, using size D hook, work 8sc into the ring, draw the short end tight to close it. Join with a sl st into first sc.

2nd round 1ch to count as first sc, 1sc into st at base of ch, *2sc into next sc, rep from * to end. Join with a sl st into first sc.

3rd round 1ch, 1sc into st at base of ch, 1sc into next sc, *2sc into next sc, 1sc into next sc, rep from * to end. Join with a sl st into first sc.

4th round 1ch, 1sc into each sc to end. Join with a sl st into first sc.

5th round As 4th.

In this sample the back of the crochet work is the most effective, and we have placed it on the button mold as the right side. Lace the edge of the crochet circle now on to the wrong side of the mold and secure it very firmly in several places around the edges, then place the metal covering disc over the back, or neatly hem a circle of lining fabric to cover the edges. All the following methods of covering buttons should be finished in this way.

Sample 2

This is a more unusual method of working the crochet covering for a $1\frac{3}{4}$in button. Five shades of yarn and a size E crochet hook are used. Using A, make 7ch.

1st row In 3rd ch from hook work 1sc, 1sc into each ch to end. Turn.

2nd row 1ch to count as first sc, 1sc into st at base of ch, 2sc into each st, ending with 2sc into turning ch. Turn. 12sc.

3rd row 1ch, 1sc into st at base of ch, 1sc into next st, *2sc into next st, 1sc into next st, rep from * ending with 1sc into turning ch. Turn. 18sc.

4th row 1ch, 1sc into st at base of ch, 1sc into each of next 2 sts, *2sc into next st, 1sc into each of next 2 sts, rep from * ending with last sc into turning ch. Turn. Break off A.

5th row Using B, 1ch, skip first st, 1sc into each of next 8 sts, then using C, 1sc into same st as last sc, 1sc into each of next 4 sts, using D, 1sc into same st as last sc, 1sc into each of next 4 sts, using E, 1sc into same st as last sc, 1sc into each of next 7 sts. Turn.

Note When joining in new colors, follow the instructions given earlier.

6th row As 5th, dec one st at each end of row and omitting increased sts between colors.

7th row As 5th, dec one st at each end of row and inc between colors as before.

Dec one st at each end of every row now and, omitting increased sts, continue in this color sequence until there are no sts left. Fasten off.

Sample 3

Eight colors of cotton and a size D hook have been used here to give a subtly shaded look to another 1¾in diameter button. Using a new color for each round, follow the instructions given for 1st–3rd rounds of sample 1. Continue in rounds of sc, working 1 more sc between the increased stitches on each round.

Sample 4

This tiny, ½in diameter button has been delicately covered with a very fine Lurex embroidery thread. Using No. 12 steel hook, work as for sample 3.

Sample 5

Using a Lurex yarn and size D hook, work as for sample 3.

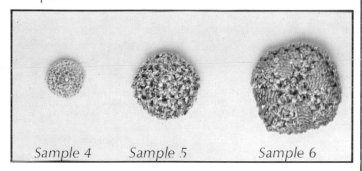

Sample 4   *Sample 5*   *Sample 6*

Sample 6

Lurex and cotton yarns are combined in this design to cover a 1in diameter button. Using size D hook and the Lurex yarn, work as given for 1st–3rd rounds of sample 1.

Break off yarn.

4th round Using cotton yarn, 2ch, *1sc into next st, 1sc into next st inserting hook into 2nd round, 2sc into next st on 1st round, 1sc into next st on 2nd round, 1sc into next st, 1ch, rep from *, omitting 1ch at end of last rep. Join with a sl st into first ch.

5th round 1ch to count as first sc, 1sc into each st to end. Join with a sl st into first ch. Fasten off.

Sample 7

Seven colors of a cotton yarn have been used to cover this square button with varying widths of diagonal stripes. You can change the colors in any way you desire. Using Size D hook make 3ch.

1st row Into 3rd ch from hook work 1sc. Turn.

2nd row 1ch to count as first sc, 1sc into st at base of ch, 2sc into next st. Turn.

3rd row 1ch, 1sc into st at base of ch, 1sc into each st to turning ch, 2sc into turning ch. Turn.

Continue to inc one st at each end of every row in this way until the crochet is the required diagonal width for the button mold, then dec one st at each end of every row until there are no sts left. Fasten off.

Sample 8

This button cover consists of 2 triangular shapes joined together, then decorated with chain stitch. Three colors of cotton yarn, A, B and C and a size D crochet hook are required. Using A, make 15ch.

1st row Into 3rd ch from hook work 1sc, 1sc into each of next 5sts, join in B, 1sc into each of next 7 sts. Turn.

2nd row Using B, 1ch to count as first sc, 1sc into each of next 6 sts, using A, 1sc into each of next 7 sts. Turn.

Working in colors as above, dec one st at each end of every row until there are no sts left. Make another triangle in the same way, then crochet the shapes together and, using C, work a chain st over the color join.

Sample 9

Work in the same way as sample 8, using 3 colors for each triangle and begin by working 7sc in A, 3sc in B and 4sc in C. When 2 triangles have been completed, place the alternate color sequence side by side and crochet together.

Sample 7   *Sample 8*   *Sample 9*

FASTENINGS

Crochet fastenings

This chapter illustrates some decorative fastenings achieved by various crochet techniques. These fastenings are useful when working with fabrics where it is difficult to use the more traditional types of fastening, such as fabric or machine-made button-holes.

The crochet stitches which have been used are all simple, and have been explained in previous chapters. The important thing to bear in mind when making your fastening for the type of garment you are trimming is just how decorative you want the fastening to be.

Sample 1

This toggle fastening is most suitable for a casual garment. Using string make two lengths of cord, one 7in and the other 12in long, as described in sample 10.

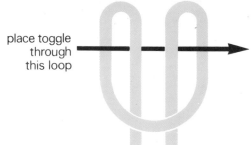

place toggle through this loop

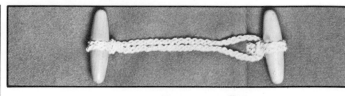

The longer piece of cord is fastened into a circle and looped over a traditional wooden toggle. The cord and toggle are then sewn on to the right hand side of a garment, leaving a loop extension over the outer edge. The shorter piece of cord is not joined into a circle, but is looped over another toggle which is then sewn in position on the left hand side of the garment.

Sample 2

The finished effect of these loops and buttons can be very decorative, this depending on the buttons and yarn you choose to use. To make the loops in our sample you will need a Lurex yarn, a string of medium thickness and a size D crochet hook. Hold the string in the left hand with the cut end to the right and the incoming string to the left. Holding the yarn in the usual way, place the hook under the string, and catch the yarn to form a loop on the hook, place the hook over the string, yo and draw yarn through loop on hook, *place cut end of string in the right hand and continuing to hold incoming yarn in the left hand, place the hook under the string, yo, place the hook

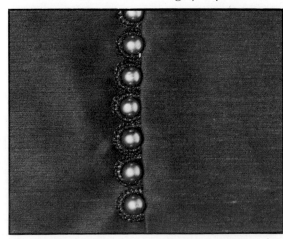

over the string, yo and draw through both loops on hook, rep from * for the required length. (Our sample took approx 2½in of string for each loop.) Position the loops one below another so that the chain extends over the outer edge, on the right side of the fabric, and making all loops an even size, tack them firmly in place as shown in the diagram. With right sides of the fabric together, now tack the facing over the cording and machine stitch it firmly along the stitching line. Line up the extended loop with the left hand side of the garment and attach buttons.

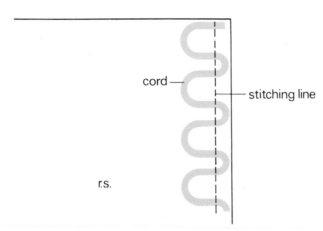

cord —
— stitching line

r.s.

Sample 3

This single frog fastening is still more decorative and could probably be used on its own as trim on an evening cape. Using size D hook and Lurex yarn, work

over piping cord, 15 inches to 20 inches long as explained in sample 2. Then work the second row by turning the work so that you crochet back along the first row, *(yo, insert hook into next st, yo and draw through a loop) 3 times into same st, yo and draw through all loops on hook, sl st into each of next 2 sts, rep from * to end of cord.

Form the cord into the required shape for four loops on the right hand side of the garment, with one loop extending over the outer edge, and sew it firmly in place. Line up the extended loop with the left hand side of the garment and attach button.

Sample 4

For the cord here you will require two lengths of piping cord, one approx 20 inches long and the other approx 17 inches long, a size E crochet hook and a chenille yarn.

Make 4ch. Join with a sl st in first ch to form a ring. Thread piping cord through the ring. Tie an overhand knot about 6 inches from the end of the cord and place the knot behind the ring so that the free-cord is coming towards you.

To work the crochet Insert the hook into the back loop of the first ch, yo and draw through the loop and the st on hook—one sl st has been worked—, *insert the hook into the back or lower single loop of the next st and work one sl st. rep from * working around the cord until the required length has been covered.

Position the longer piece of cord on the right hand side of the garment, forming the desired size of loops, with one loop extending over the outer edge. Sew in place. Line up the extended loop with the left hand side of the garment and position the shorter length of cord to make three loops equal in size to those at the opposite side. A covered button has been sewn on to the join of the loops on both the right and left hand side.

To cover the button shape You will need a 1 inch ball button, some chenille yarn and a size E crochet hook. Form a ring with the yarn in the left hand, work 8sc into the ring, draw the cut end of yarn tightly to close the ring and sl st into the first sc worked.

2nd round 1ch to count as first sc, 1sc into st at base of ch, *2sc into next st, rep from * to end. Join with a sl st to first ch.

3rd round 1ch, 1sc into st at base of ch, 1sc into next st, *2sc into next st, 1sc into next st, rep from * to end. Join with a sl st into first ch.

4th round 1 ch, 1sc into each st to end. Join with a sl st into first ch.

5th round As 4th.

6th round 1ch, work 2sc tog in next 2 sts, *1sc into next st, work 2sc tog in next 2 sts, rep from * to end. Join with a sl st into first ch.

7th round 1ch, *work 2sc tog in next 2 sts, rep from * to last st, 1sc into last st. Join with a sl st into first ch. Fasten off.

FLOWERS

Fluted crochet

Flowers for trim are very much a part of the fashion scene. They are used on day and evening dresses, and on hats and other accessories. Most commercial flowers are made of fabric, but here we illustrate how you can make your own by using the technique of fluted crochet.

The type of yarn you choose for making your flower will depend on the type of garment you want to trim, and might be a crisp cotton for a hatband or a glitter yarn for an evening outfit. A selection of centers for different flowers are shown.

1st flower

This flower consists of two circles.

1st circle Using size F hook and a 4 ply yarn, make 5ch. Join with a sl st into first ch to form a ring.

1st round 1ch to count as first sc, 15sc into ring. Join with a sl st into first ch.

2nd round *4ch, sl st into next sc, rep from * to end. 16ch loops.

3rd round Sl st into each of first 2ch of next loop, sl st into center of same loop, 5ch, *sl st into center of next ch loop, 5ch, rep from * to end. Join with sl st into sl st at center of first loop.

4th round Sl st into each of first 3ch of next loop, sl st into center of same loop, 6ch, *sl st into center of next ch loop, 6ch, rep from * to end. Join with a sl st into sl st at center of first loop.

5th round Sl st into each of first 3ch of next loop, sl st into center of same loop, 7ch, *sl st into center of next ch loop, 7ch, rep from * to end. Join with a sl st into sl st at center of first loop. Fasten off.

2nd circle Using size F hook and a 4 ply yarn make 5ch. Join with a sl st into first ch to form a ring.

1st round 1ch to count as first sc, 20sc into ring. Complete as given for 1st circle.

Finishing: Place the larger, more fluted circle over the first circle and sew the centers together. In our sample wooden beads in groups of three, five and seven on a loop have been used as additional decoration.

2nd flower

Using size F hook and a 4 ply yarn, make 6ch. Join with a sl st into first ch to form a ring.

1st round 1ch to count as first sc, 20sc into ring. Join with a sl st into first ch.

2nd round 3ch to count as first dc, 1dc into st at base of ch, *2dc into next sc, rep from * to end. Join with a sl st into 3rd of 3ch. 42 sts.

3rd round 3ch to count as first dc, 1dc into st at base of ch, *2dc into next dc, rep from * to end. Join with a sl st into 3rd of 3ch. 84 sts.

4th round As 3rd. 168 sts.

5th round 1ch to count as first sc, 1sc into each of next 9 sts, insert hook from front to back into next st, skip next 9 sts, insert hook from front to back into next st, yo and draw through first 2 loops on hook, yo and draw through both loops on hook, *1sc into each of next 10 sts, insert hook from front to back into next st, skip next 9 sts, insert hook from back to front into next st, yo and draw through first 2 loops on hook, yo and draw through both loops on hook, rep from * to end. Fasten off.

Finishing Make the tufted center by cutting 40 lengths of yarn, each 3 inches long, and firmly bind them together around the center with another piece of yarn. Fold the lengths in half and insert the bound section into the center of the flower.

3rd flower
Using size D hook and a Lurex yarn, make 6ch. Join with a sl st into first ch.

1st round 1ch to count as first sc, 17sc into ring.

2nd round 5ch, skip next 2sc, *1sc into next sc, 4ch, skip next 2sc, rep from * to end. Join with a sl st into 2nd of first 5ch. 6ch loops.

3rd round *Into next 4ch loop work 1sc, 1hdc, 5dc, 1hdc and 1sc, rep from * to end. Join with a sl st into first sc.

4th round *5ch, pass this ch length behind next gr of sts and work 1sc in next sc of 2nd round, inserting the hook from behind, rep from * to end.

5th round *Into next 5ch loop work 1sc, 1hdc, 10dc, 1hdc and 1sc, rep from * to end. Join with a sl st into first sc.

6th round *7ch, pass this ch length behind next gr of sts and work 1sc into next sc of 4th round, inserting the hook from behind, rep from * to end.

7th round *Into next 7ch loop work 1sc, 1hdc, 15dc, 1hdc and 1sc, rep from * to end. Join with a sl st into first sc.

8th round *8ch, pass this ch length behind next gr of sts and work 1sc into next sc of 6th round, inserting the hook from behind, rep from * to end.

9th round *Into next 8ch loop work 1sc, 1hdc, 5dc, 10tr, 5dc, 1hdc and 1sc, rep from * to end. Join with a sl st into first ch. Fasten off.

A large pearl bead makes an attractive center to this silver flower.

4th flower
Here is an unusual method of working a chrysanthemum. Using size D hook and a cotton yarn, make 21ch. Skip first ch, sl st into each ch to end, turn.
Skip first st, sl st into each of next 2 sts, inserting hook into back loop only of each st, work 17ch, skip first ch, sl st into loop at back of each ch to end, turn. Rep from * to * until approximately 60 to 70 petals have been completed. Fasten off.

Finishing Beginning at one end of the work, twist the base of all the petals around, until they are placed as desired, then sew together.

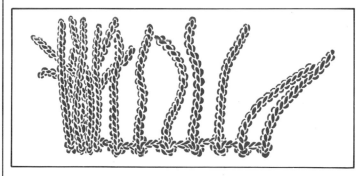

AFGHAN CROCHET
BASIC STEPS

Afghan stitch is a form of work which can look like either crochet or knitting. It is also known as Tunisian crochet. The special tool used for this craft is a single hooked afghan crochet hook. These hooks are extra long to accommodate the large number of stitches in use with this stitch and they come in a size range with the smallest starting at E and then grading up to F, G, H, I, J and K. The fabric produced with this method is very strong and firm and, depending on the stitch used, the finished appearance can resemble crochet or look deceptively like knitting. It is ideal for making fabrics for house furnishings and is also suitable for heavier outer garments where the intricacies of fine detail would be superfluous. Several basic points make this form of crochet different from ordinary crochet, and they should be referred to throughout all afghan stitch instructions.

a) When making an initial length of chain stitches to begin work, you will not require any extra chains for turning, i.e. a chain length of 20 will give you exactly 20 working stitches.

b) The work is not turned at the end of each row, and the right side of the work faces you throughout.

c) afghan stitch is worked in pairs of rows, with the first row worked from right to left and then another row worked from left to right to complete the stitches.

d) Apart from a very small number of exceptions, no turning chains are required at the beginning of each new row.

To work the basic afghan stitch:
Using size G afghan hook and Knitting Worsted, make a length of chain.

1st row Working from right to left, skip first ch, insert hook into 2nd ch from hook, yo and draw through a loop, *insert hook into next ch, yo and draw through a loop, rep from * to end of ch, keeping all loops on hook.

2nd row Working from left to right, yo and draw through first 2 loops on hook, *yo and draw through next 2 loops on hook, rep from * to end until one loop remains on hook.

3rd row Working from right to left, skip first vertical bar on the front of the fabric, insert hook from right to left into next vertical bar, yo and draw through a loop, rep from * to end, keeping all loops on hook.

4th row As 2nd.
The 3rd and 4th rows are repeated throughout.

Note Care should be taken to check the number of stitches at the end of each row as it is very easy to miss the last stitch when working the 3rd row.

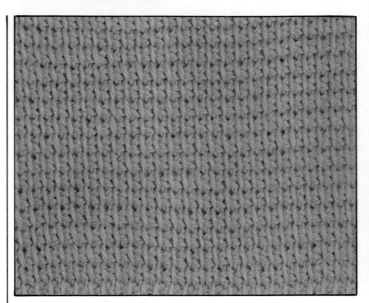

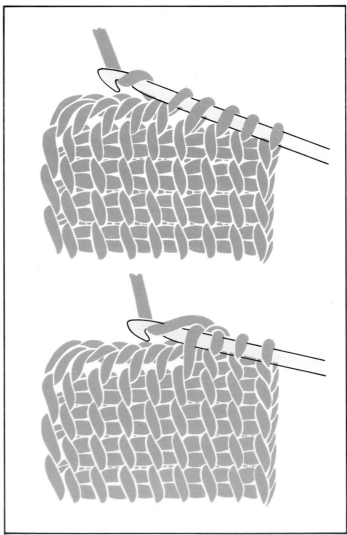

Shaping an afghan stitch

When it is necessary to increase or decrease, this is usually done on the first of the pair of rows you are working.

To increase on the sides of your work fabric: The increased stitch is worked by inserting the hook into the single horizontal loop between two vertical bars.

To increase one stitch at the beginning of a row: This is usually done between the first and second vertical bars.

To increase one stitch at the end of the row: This is usually between the last and next to last vertical bars.

To increase more than one stitch at the beginning or end of a row: Remembering that increases are made on the first row of the required pair, to increase several stitches at the beginning of a row, work the extra chain stitches required and go back along these extra chains picking up the working stitches. To increase several stitches at the end of a row complete the row then take a spare length of matching yarn and join this into the last stitch. Work the extra chain stitches required with spare yarn, then continue working into this extra chain length with main yarn.

To decrease on the sides of your work: One stitch is decreased just inside the beginning of a row by inserting the hook into the 2nd and 3rd vertical bars at one time, and then working the stitch in the usual way. At the end of a row the last two stitches before the end stitch are worked together in the same way.

To increase in the middle of a row: One stitch is increased in the middle of a row by inserting the hook into the single horizontal loop between the vertical bars at the point where the increased stitch is required.

To decrease in the middle of a row: At the required position, decrease one stitch as above.

To decrease more than one stitch at the beginning or end of a row: At the beginning of a row slip stitch over the required number of stitches to be decreased and at the end of a row work until only the required number of stitches to be decreased remains, then work the second of the pair of rows required.

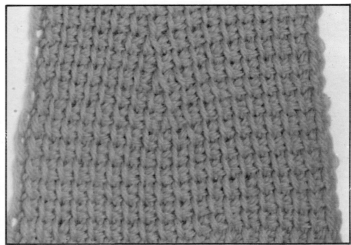

FABRIC STITCHES

An introduction to afghan stitch was made in our last chapter. The stitches may be worked in a variety of ways to give very different patterned effects and textures. These are achieved by different positions of the hook insertion on the first row of the pair necessary for the afghan stitch. For all our samples, it is only the first row which varies, and the second one remains the same throughout.

3rd row *Insert hook into space between vertical bars from front to back, yo and draw through a loop, rep from * to end.

4th row As 2nd.

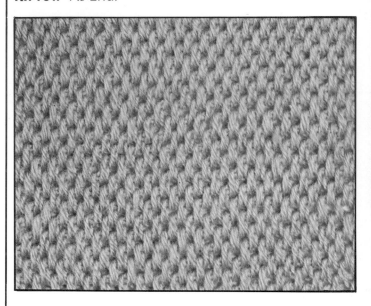

5th row Skip space between first two vertical bars, * insert hook into space between next two vertical bars from front to back, yo and draw through a loop, rep from * to end, inserting hook into last vertical bar.

6th row As 2nd.

The 3rd through 6th rows are repeated throughout.

Sample 2

Using size G afghan hook and Knitting Worsted, make a length of chain.

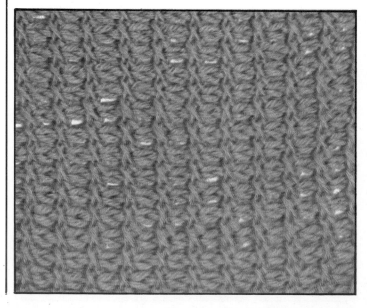

Sample 1

Using size G afghan hook and Knitting Worsted, make a length of chain.

1st row Insert hook into second ch from hook, yo and draw through a loop, * insert hook into next ch, yo and draw through a loop, rep from * to end.

2nd row Yo and draw through first 2 loops on hook, *yo and draw through next 2 loops on hook, rep from * to end leaving one loop on hook.

1st-2nd rows As 1st-2nd rows of sample 1.
3rd row Skip first vertical bar, * skip next vertical bar, insert hook from right to left through next vertical bar, yo and draw through a loop, insert hook from right to left through the skipped vertical bar, yo and draw through a loop, rep from * to end, inserting hook in last vertical bar.
4th row As 2nd.
The 3rd and 4th rows are repeated throughout.

Sample 3
Using size G afghan hook and Knitting Worsted, make a length of chain with multiples of 3+2 stitches.
1st-2nd rows As 1st-2nd rows of sample 1.

3rd row Skip first vertical loop, * yarn over hook from front to back, (insert hook into next vertical loop, yo and draw through a loop) 3 times, pass 4th loop from hook from right to left over last 3 loops on the hook, rep from * to end, insert hook into last vertical loop, yo and draw through a loop.
4th row As 2nd.
The 3rd and 4th rows are repeated throughout.

Sample 4
Using size G afghan hook and Knitting Worsted, make a length of chain.
1st-2nd rows As 1st-2nd rows of sample 1.

3rd row Skip first vertical bar, * insert hook directly through center of next vertical bar from front to back

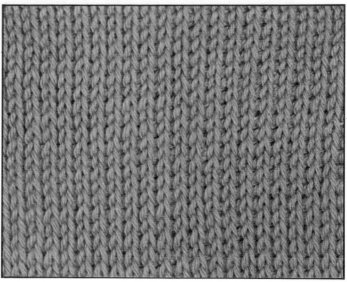

of work, yo and draw through a loop, rep from * to end.
4th row As 2nd.
The 3rd and 4th rows are repeated throughout.

Sample 5
Using size G afghan hook and Knitting Worsted, make a length of chain with multiples of 3+2 stitches.
1st-2nd rows As 1st-2nd rows of sample 1.

3rd row Skip first vertical bar, * insert hook under next three vertical bars, yo and draw through a loop, insert hook under middle loop only of this group of three, yo and draw through a loop, insert hook under first loop only of this group of three, yo and draw through a loop, rep from * to end, then insert hook into last vertical bar, yo and draw through a loop.
4th row As 2nd.
The 3rd and 4th rows are repeated throughout.

DECORATIVE STITCHES

There are so many different patterns to be achieved when working in afghan stitch that we would like to give the instructions for making several more of them for you to practice.

The tension of your work can be gauged in the same way as for other crochet work. Any tendency for the fabric to curl and twist can be overcome by working the stitches more loosely. Always pull the yarn around the hook adequately through the stitch and, when working back along a row from left to right, never pull the first stitch through so tightly that the height of the row is flattened.

Sample 1

This is a variation of the basic afghan stitch. Using size G afghan hook and Knitting Worsted, make a length of chain with multiples of 2 stitches.

1st row Insert hook into second ch from hook, yo and draw through a loop, *insert hook into next ch, yo and draw through a loop, rep from * to end.

2nd row Yo and draw through first 2 loops on hook, *yo and draw through next 2 loops on hook, rep from * to end leaving one loop on hook.

3rd row Skip first vertical bar, *insert hook from right to left through next 2 vertical bars on right side of work, yo and draw through a loop, insert hook from right to left into first of these bars, yo and draw through a loop, rep from * to end, insert hook into last vertical bar, yo and draw through a loop.

4th row As 2nd.

5th row Skip first vertical bar, insert hook into next vertical bar, yo and draw through a loop, *insert hook from right to left through next 2 vertical bars on right side of work, yo and draw through a loop, insert hook from right to left into first of these bars, yo and draw through a loop, rep from * to end.

6th row As 2nd.

The 3rd through 6th rows are repeated throughout.

Sample 2

Here crossed stitches within the pattern give a vertical ribbed effect. Using size G afghan hook and Knitting

Worsted, make a chain with multiples of 2 stitches.

1st-2nd rows As 1st-2nd rows of sample 1.

3rd row 1ch, skip first 2 vertical bars, insert hook from right to left through next vertical bar on right side of work, yo and draw through a loop, insert hook into skipped vertical loop to the right of the one just worked, yo and draw through a loop, and cont in this way, working in groups of 2 and crossing the threads, ending by inserting the hook into the last vertical bar, yo and draw through a loop.

4th row As 2nd.

The 3rd and 4th rows are repeated throughout.

Note If you are using this pattern for a shaped garment where you are increasing and decreasing, take care to see that the crossed stitches come immediately above those on the previous row so that the ribbed effect will not be broken.

Sample 3

Here bobbles are made on a basic afghan background by working extra lengths of 4ch before continuing with the next stitch. Using size G afghan hook and Knitting Worsted, make a length of chain with multiples of 6 | 1 stitches.

1st-2nd rows As 1st-2nd rows of sample 1.

3rd row 1ch, skip first vertical bar on front of fabric, 1 vertical stitch into next vertical bar, *insert hook into next vertical bar on front of fabric, yo and draw through a loop, 4ch, Insert hook into horizontal loop at base of ch on WS of work, yo and draw through 2 loops on hook—called B1—, work 1 vertical stitch into each of next 2 vertical bars, rep from * to last 2 bars, Bl into next vertical bar, 1 vertical stitch into last vertical bar.

4th-6th rows Work in basic afghan stitch.

7th row 1ch, skip first vertical bar, *B1 in next vertical bar, 1 vertical stitch into each of next 2 vertical bars, rep from * to end of row.

8th row As 2nd.

The 3rd through 8th rows are repeated throughout.

Sample 4

An eyelet stitch gives this sample a simple openwork pattern. Using size G afghan hook and Knitting Worsted, make a chain with multiples of 2+1 stitches.

1st row Yo twice, insert hook into 3rd ch from hook, yo and draw through a loop, yo and draw through first 2 loops on hook, *skip next ch, yo twice, insert hook into next ch, yo and draw through a loop, yo and draw through first 2 loops on hook, rep from * to end.

2nd and 4th rows As 2nd row of sample 1.

3rd row 2ch, *yo twice, insert hook into both next vertical bar and slightly sloping vertical bar to right of it made on the previous row, yo and draw through a loop, yo and draw through first 2 loops on hook, rep from * to end.

The 3rd and 4th rows are repeated throughout.

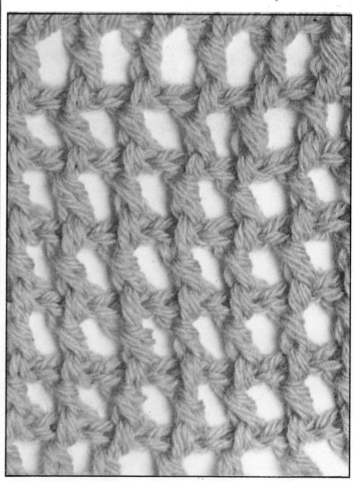

ADVANCED AFGHAN STITCHES

More advanced designs for afghan stitch

Five more interesting afghan stitch patterns are illustrated in this chapter, including two which show the technique of using different colors within the work. As all the samples are worked in a bulky knitting yarn they would be ideal for use in making pillows, rugs and blankets. Reference should be made to the first of these chapters on afghan stitch and checks should always be made during the working of these samples to keep the number of stitches correct.

Sample 1

Using size H hook and bulky yarn, make a length of chain with multiples of 2 stitches.

1st row Insert hook into 2nd ch from hook, yo and draw through a loop, *insert hook into next ch, yo and draw through a loop, rep from * to end.

2nd row *Yo and draw through two loops, rep from * to end, leaving one loop on hook.

3rd row Skip first vertical bar, *yo from front to back, insert hook under next 2 vertical bars, yo and draw through a loop, rep from * to last vertical bar, insert hook into last vertical bar, yo and draw through a loop.

4th row As 2nd.

The 3rd and 4th rows are repeated throughout.

Sample 2

Using size H afghan hook and bulky yarn, make a length of chain with multiples of 2 stitches.

1st-2nd rows As 1st-2nd rows of sample 1.

3rd row Skip first vertical bar, *insert hook into hole under chain st to right of next vertical bar, yo and draw through a loop, insert hook under vertical bar to left of last loop made, yo and draw through a loop, drawing it through one loop on hook, rep from * to last vertical bar, insert hook into last vertical bar, yo and draw through a loop.

4th row As 2nd.

The 3rd and 4th rows are repeated throughout.

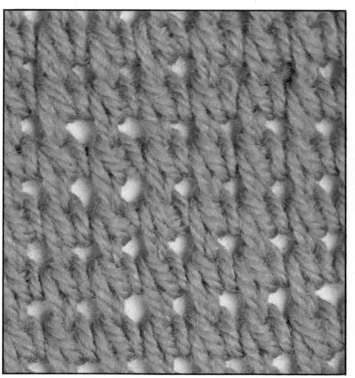

Sample 3

Using size H afghan hook and bulky yarn, make a length of chain with multiples of 2+1 stitches.

1st row (Yo and insert hook into 3rd ch from hook, yo and draw through a loop) twice, yo and draw through 2 loops on hook, yo and draw through 3 loops on hook, *skip next ch, (yo and insert into next ch, yo and draw through a loop) twice, yo and draw through 2 loops on hook, yo and draw through 3 loops on hook, rep from * to end.

2nd row Yo and draw through one loop, *1ch, yo and draw through 2 loops, rep from * to end. One loop remains on hook.

3rd row 2ch, *yo from front to back, insert hook from

front to back into space on right of next st, yo and draw through a loop, yo from front to back and insert into space on left of same st, yo and draw through a loop, yo and draw through 2 loops on hook, yo and draw through 3 loops on hook, rep from * ending with last st worked completely into last space.

4th row As 2nd.

The 3rd and 4th rows are repeated throughout.

Sample 4

For this sample you will need two colors of bulky yarn, coded as A and B. Using size H afghan hook and A, make a length of chain.

1st-2nd rows As 1st-2nd rows of sample 1.

3rd-6th rows Work 4 rows of basic afghan stitch. Do not break off yarn. Join in B.

7th row Using B, 2ch, *yo, insert hook from front to back through work under next horizontal st, yo and draw through a loop extending it to length of 2ch, rep from * ending with last st worked into last horizontal space.

8th row Yo and draw through 2 loops on hook, *yo and draw through 3 loops on hook, rep from * to end.

9th row Draw A through loop on hook, *yo and insert into horizontal loop at back of long st, rep from * to end.

10th-12th rows Work 3 rows basic afghan stitch. Repeat 7th through 12th rows throughout.

Sample 5

Here we have used two colors of Knitting Worsted coded as A and B. Using size F afghan hook and A, make a length of chain with any multiple of 4+7 stitches.

1st-6th rows As 1st-6th rows of sample 4.

7th row Skip first vertical bar, insert hook into next vertical bar, yo and draw through a loop—called one basic tricot st —, one basic tricot st into next bar,

*then using B, (yo and insert in 3rd vertical bar below next st, yo and draw through a loop extending it to meet the working st) 4 times, yo and draw through all loops in B on hook, insert hook in next vertical bar behind bobble, yo and draw through a loop, drawing it through one loop in B on hook—one bobble has been worked—, using A, work one basic tricot st into each of next 3 loops, rep from * to end.

8th-14th rows Using A, work 7 rows of basic afghan stitch.

15th row Skip first vertical bar, *using B, work one bobble into 3rd vertical bar below next st, using A, work one basic tricot st into each of next 3 bars, rep from * to last 2 bars, one bobble in next bar, one basic tricot st into last bar.

16th row Work in basic afghan stitch. Continue in this way, working 7 rows of basic afghan stitch between each bobble row for the required depth of pattern.

Clutch bag with woven threads

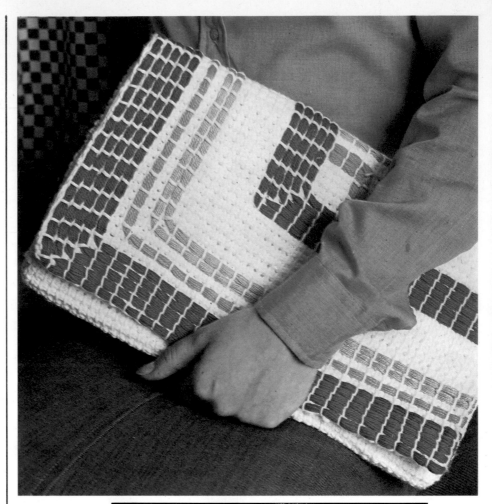

Size
Width, 14in
Depth, 9in

Gauge
14sts and 14 rows to 4in in basic afghan stitch worked on size J afghan hook.

Materials
3 hanks Lily Sugar 'n Cream yarn
Odds and ends of contrasting color for trim
One size J crochet hook
Lining material, heavy-weight interlining
Velcro for fastening

Bag
Using size J afghan hook make 50ch. Work in basic afghan stitch until piece measures approx 26 inches from beg. Fasten off.

Gusset (make 2)
Using size J afghan hook make 14ch. Work 8 double rows. Dec one st at each end of next and every 4th set of double rows until 6 working sts remain. Work 4 more double rows. Fasten off.

To finish
Cut a piece of interlining the same size as the main part of the bag. Sew the crochet neatly on to the interlining to hold its shape, and steam block. The gussets are not interlined. Cut out lining material to fit the main part and gussets, allowing $\frac{1}{2}$in for hemming on all sides. Using the same yarn and a tapestry needle sew the gussets to the main part as shown in the illustration, using an overcast st. Finish the lining as given for the bag, sewing in the gussets. Sew the lining on to the crochet. Sew the two pieces of Velcro fastening in position, one to the underside of the flap and one on the corresponding bag section. Follow the diagram and work any desired crochet design on the bag flap.

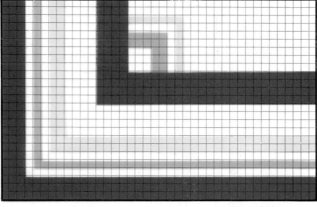

Working the design
You will notice that horizontal and vertical lines of loops are produced on the right side of the crochet fabric. A contrasting colored or textured yarn is then woven over and under these loops or stitches in straight rows. To achieve a good line, it is necessary to use several thicknesses of the yarn for decoration, and an afghan hook in a size smaller than the hook used for the background to draw the threads through the work.

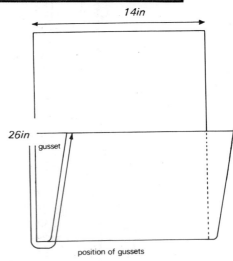

14in

26in

gusset

position of gussets